HALICHOS
BAS YISRAEL

A Woman's Guide to Jewish Observance

Rav Yitzchak Yaacov Fuchs

HALICHOS BAS YISRAEL

*A Woman's Guide to
Jewish Observance*

the English edition of
הליכות בת ישראל

prepared by
RAV MOSHE DOMBEY
in collaboration with the author

II
*From the Hebrew edition,
Chapters 14–25*

TARGUM PRESS
Southfield, Michigan

FELDHEIM
Jerusalem/New York

First Published 1987
ISBN 0-87306-431-3

Typesetting by Yael Kaplan, Jerusalem

Published by:
Targum Press, Inc.
22700 W 11 Mile Rd.
Southfield, Michigan 48034

Distributed by:
Philipp Feldheim Inc.
200 Airport Executive Park
Spring Valley, NY 10977

Feldheim Publishers Ltd.
POB 6525 / Jerusalem, Israel

Printed in Israel

הסכמות רבותינו הגאונים שליט"א

יצחק יעקב וייס
רב ואב"ד
לכל מקהלות האשכנזים פעיה"ק ירושלם תובב"א
מח"ס שו"ת מנחת יצחק
ירושלים, רחוב ישעיהו 20

בס"ד, ירושלים פעיהקת"ו

הן כבר איתמחי גברא רבא ויקירא מוכתר בנימוסין הרה"ג ירא ושלם
חו"ב מורה"ר יצחק יעקב פוקס מפעיהקת"ו בספרו החשוב והנכבד
התפלה בצבור שנתקבל באהבה אצל לומדי התורה, וכבר יצא טיבו
ותהילתו בספר הנ"ל.

ועתה עלה במחשבתו והעלה על הכתב ספר חשוב ומאד יקר אשר
בשם "הליכות בת ישראל" יכונה, והוא ע"ד המעשה אשר יעשון בנות
ישראל חיוביהן ופטוריהן, ושאר דינים ומנהגים המיועדים להן, ואסף
כעמיר גורנה מדברי רבותינו הפוסקים וסידרן בסידור יפה דבר דיבור על
אופניו בטוב טעם ודעת, וגם הוסיף הערות והארות בהשכל ובדעת
והעלה תמצית הדינים שבירר בידיעתו וביגיעתו בתוה"ק, וכאשר מבואר
בדברי ידי"נ הגאון המפורסם שלשלת היוחסין כש"ת רבי משה
הלברשטאם שליט"א מגדולי וחשובי מורי ההוראה בפעיה"ק, אשר האריך
הרחיב בשבח הספר והתועלת המרובה אשר יפיקו רצון ויאותו לאורו הני
רבנן ותלמידייהון וידעו את המעשה אשר יעשון והדרך אשר ילכו בה.

לכן ראוי המחבר ההי"ג שליט"א להחזיק לו טובה שזיכה את בנות
ישראל בספרו יקר ונעלה זה, ואמינא לפעלא טבא איישר, וידי תיכון עמו
להוציאו לאור לזכות את הרבים, וכל המזכה את הרבים זכותו גדולה
מאד שיזכה לברך על המוגמר בס"ד ויבואו רבים ויביאו ברכה בביתם.

וכבימים ההם יראנו הקב"ה ניסים ונפלאות בבנין בית מקדשנו
ותפארתנו בב"א

הכו"ח לכבוד התורה ומצוותי' זאת חנוכה תדש"ם.

יצחק יעקב וייס רב ואב"ד פעה"ק ת"ו.

שמואל הלוי ואזנר

רב אב״ד ור״מ

זכרון מאיר, בני ברק

ב״ה יום א וישלח תשד״מ לפ״ק

הנה כבוד ההה״ג המושלם הרבה זוכה ומזכה הרבים הרב יצחק יעקב פוקס שליט״א, יושב באהלה של תורה בירושלים תוב״ב — כבר זכה משולחן גבוה בספרו היקר התפילה בצבור שנתקבל באהבת תורה היות כי המחבר שואף אל מטרת האמת, ועתה הוסיף לחבר ספר יקר ״הליכות בת ישראל״ והמה הלכות כמסמרות נטועות הנוגעים להנהגת בת ישראל נשואה ופנויה — יום יום שבת ויו״ט — הלכות צניעות הנחוצות, וגם הרבה דברים חדשים אשר לקט המחבר החשוב מבין גן שושנים של גדולים אחרונים — והיות כי ספרים כאלה המה קרובים מאד לזכות הרבים וגם נתחבר לשם שמים וביגיעות הרבה, הרני מסכים להעלותו על מכבש הדפוס ויפוצו מעיינותיו חוצה.

ע״ז בעה״ח מצפה לרחמי ה׳

שמואל הלוי ואזנר

ראב״ד ור״מ זכרון מאיר בני ברק

בס"ד

הן הובא לפני עלים לתרופה מספר נעלה יקר וחשוב עד מאד — "הליכות בת ישראל", שיסדו וטיפחו משך שנים מרובות ביגיעה עצומה הי נידהו הרה"ג ירא ושלם מחבר חיבורים יקרים מורה"ר יצחק יעקב פוקס שליט"א מגדולי הלומדים באהלה של תורה פעיקת"ו, ומטרת הספר לדעת הני נשי במאי קא זכיין במצות ד' ברה, ובמאי פטרוה חז"ל והמסתעף, והרב המופלג הנ"ל נחית לעומקא דדינא דדינא הדין בבירור אחר בירור בעיון מרובה ובכובד המשקל הראוי לצורבא מרבנן.

עברתי על רובו ככולו של הספר, ונהניתי לראות ולהווכח שדבר טוב ומועיל פעל תעושה עמנו להוציא מעשיא דבר זה לאור עולם ולזכות בזה את הרבים. ומעלה יתירה בספר זה ששם דגש מיוחד על חילוקי הדינים והמנהגים בין העדות השונות שלדידן הוה מומא ולדידהו לא הוה מומא, וכן להיפך, כמו"כ דן בהרחבה בשאלות מעשיות לבעלי תשובה אשר ב"ה לשמחתנו רבו מאד באחרונה, כן ירבו. גם מצאתי שאלות רבות שנתחדשו בימינו, ובעיקר בנושא הצניעות של בנות ישראל הכשרות אשר רבות וכן טובות נכשלות שלא בכונה וגבהו בנות ציון ותלכנה הלוך וטפוף וכדרשתם ז"ל, ובטוחני כי רבים יברכוהו על המעשה הטוב אשר זכה להציל בנות ישראל הצנועות מכל סיג ופגם בהליכתן ובתלבושתן ואשר כל רואיהן יעידון ויגידון כי הם זרע ברך ד', ובזכות נשים צדקניות נגאלו אבותינו ממצרים, ובזכותן נגאל במהרה בימינו בביאת גואלנו צדק, אמן כי"ר.

וח"ש בפרוס יומא דחנוכה, שנת גדולה האורה של ימי חנוכה לפ"ק פעיה"ק והמקדש שיבב"א

משה הלברשטאם

בע"ה

אודה ה' בכל לבב על כי ספרי "הליכות בת ישראל" במהדורתו בלשון הקודש, נתקבל בברכה, ונדפס מאז הופעתו בס"ד פעמים רבות.

לבקשת רבים וטובים, אשר השפה האנגלית שגורה יותר בפיהם, נתתי ליבי לתור ולמצוא שלוחים נאמנים אשר יטו שכם לעסוק במלאכת התרגום והעריכה — משימה לא קלה כשהמדובר בספר הלכה הכולל אלפי פרטים בעניינים שונים ומגוונים.

והנה הקרה ה' לפני, אנשים חכמים וידועים, העוסקים בעבודת הקודש — חינוך בנות ישראל לתורה וליראה, ידידי היקרים, הרבנים החשובים: ר' יעקב מרדכי רפפורט, ר' משה דמבי ור' טוביה קרביץ שליט"א, אשר קיבלו על עצמם עבודת התרגום וחברי הוצאת "תרגום" בארה"ב שנטלו על עצמם כל הקשור בהוצאת הספר ובהפצתו בשפה האנגלית, ולא חסכו עמל וטורח להוציא מתחת ידם דבר נאה ומתקבל.

תודה מיוחדת לכב' ידידי הרב ישראל בערל שליט"א, אשר היה לנו לעיניים והואיל לעבור על הספר ולהעיר הערותיו המועילות. וכן לכב' הרב משה דמבי שליט"א על השעות והימים הארוכים בהם בררנו וליבננו גופי ההלכות לפרטי פרטיהן להתאימם לענות על מציאות הבעיות ההילכתיות השכיחות במדינות ארה"ב ואירופה.

בירכתי ותיקותי, כי בס"ד נזכה לראות ברכה בעמלינו, וזכות זיכוי הרבים תעמוד להם ולכל בני ביתם ויזכו להגדיל תורה ולהאדירה.

יצחק יעקב פוקס

ערב ראש השנה ה'תשמ"ו
פעיה"ק ירושלים ת"ו

Rabbi CHAIM P. SCHEINBERG

KIRYAT MATTERSDORF
PANIM MEIROT 2
JERUSALEM, ISRAEL

הרב חיים פנחס שיינברג
ראש ישיבת "תורה אור"
ומורה הוראה דקרית מטרסדורף
ירושלים טל.531652

I have seen the valuable book *Halichos Bas Yisrael*, which was excellently compiled by the young Torah scholar, HaRav HaGaon Rabbi Yitzchak Yaacov Fuchs, whom I have known for many years in our neighborhood, Kiryat Mattersdorf, and who spent many hours discussing many of the topics therein with me.

The purpose of this work is to educate and inspire the public to perform all of the complex details of the commandments incumbent on the "House of Jacob — these are the women". It excels in its clear presentation, concise language, and efficient organization, especially in its description of the laws of modesty, a basic area in which it is very necessary for women to be knowledgeable, proficient and cautious, and whose importance requires daily re-emphasis. Praised is the share of the author whom Providence has merited with the rare opportunity to successfully disseminate this important information. He has been doubly blessed with the opportunity to have his work presented in English, thus allowing a much wider audience to benefit from it. The English edition in no way deviates from the standard of excellence found in the Hebrew edition.

Since this book is a compilation of delicate halakhic opinion and conclusions drawn from a wide variety of differing authorities, I must be hesitant about expressing my absolute agreement with all of its contents; this would require a scrupulous and meticulous analysis of every sensitive detail. In no way, however, does this detract from the compendium's value as a medium for the aforementioned goals.

Many Torah giants have already praised the author's previous work, *HaTefillah B'Tzibur*, and my hand joins his present endeavor as well. I praise his strength in spreading, strengthening, and glorifying Torah, and may the Almighty grant him the stamina for many other worthwhile projects.

I sign with respect for the Torah and Her students, here in the Holy City of Jerusalem, on the 20th day of Cheshvan, 5746.

Rabbi Chaim P. Scheinberg

Acknowledgments

The publishers wish to express their sincere appreciation to all who gave so much time and effort to prepare *Halichos Bas Yisrael,* Volume 2.

Rav Moshe Dombey, who translated the original Hebrew work and saw the manuscript through its many stages to completion.

Rav Yaakov Rapoport, who reviewed the entire translation and offered many suggestions which were incorporated in the final version.

Reb Tuvia Krevit, who was deeply involved in shaping and .editing the manuscript at every stage of its preparation.

Katriel Blum for his valuable editorial help.

Debra Applebaum for preparing the index and glossary.

A special word of thanks is due to Rav Yitzchak Yaacov Fuchs, who so generously gave of his time to add new material to Volume 2 of the English edition for the particular needs of Jews living outside *Eretz Yisrael.* We deeply appreciate his warm encouragement and guidance.

Table of Contents

Contents

Chapter 20: Sukkoth

Chapter 21: Chanukah

Contents

HALICHOS
BAS YISRAEL

*A Woman's Guide to
Jewish Observance*

CHAPTER 14
Miscellaneous Mitzvoth and Blessings

Tzedakah

1.Both men and women are required to fulfill the *mitzvah* of *Tzedakah* (donating to charity). Every adult Jew is required to contribute each year, at a minimum, an amount equal to the value of ten grams of pure silver.[1] A woman who

---

1. *Shulchan Arukh, Yoreh De'ah* 248:1, and 249:1–2; *Rambam, Hilkhoth Matanoth Ani'yim* 7:5; *Sefer HaChinukh* 479. The *mitzvah* of *Tzedakah* is not time-bound. Moreover, whoever fails to donate to charity transgresses two negative commandments; men and women are equally obligated in all negative commandments of the Torah.

The *Rambam* and the *Shulchan Arukh* emphasize that the minimum amount applies to a destitute person who receives charity herself. Others should give according to their means. Ideally, twenty percent of one's earnings should be allocated for *Tzedakah*, but the average person is only expected to allocate ten percent—the *mitzvah* of *Ma'aser Kesafim*, which is discussed in paragraph 2. An allocation of less than ten percent is considered ungenerous.

The *Rambam* warns that a person who has fulfilled the obligation of *Tzedakah* is still forbidden to send a poor person away empty-

cannot afford more than the minimum should give her whole donation at one time.[2]

2. A woman should allocate ten percent of her earnings to *Tzedakah*. This is known as *Ma'aser Kesafim*.[3] It is customary for her husband to designate the recipients for her.[4]

3. A husband must honor all charitable vows made by his wife before their marriage.[5] Charitable vows made by a woman after marriage are only valid with her husband's consent. The only exception is when a woman makes a vow to atone for a sin; such vows may not be nullified by her husband.[6]

Many authorities rule that a husband may not nullify his wife's charitable vows if she manages the household finances.[7]

---

handed. This is based on the verse, "Do not turn away the destitute in disgrace" (*Tehillim* 74:21).

2. *Orchoth Chayim* of the *Rosh*, Chapter 4.

3. Rav Y. Blau writes in *Sefer Tzedakah U'Mishpat*, Chapter 5, note 35, "A working woman who needs to hire a housekeeper or babysitter may deduct the costs from income before calculating earnings for *Ma'aser Kesafim*. If their work enables the woman to reduce other expenses, for example the cost of laundry that would otherwise have been sent to a laundromat, the savings on these expenses must be added to the income from which *Ma'aser* is taken.

4. Many Rabbinical *responsa* have been written on the subject of separating *Ma'aser* from a woman's dowry and from the property she brings to a marriage. See, for example, *She'ilath Ya'avetz*, Vol. 1, No. 6.

5. *Maharam Mintz*, No. 17. See also the *Maharsham*, Vol. 1, No. 32.

6. *Chatham Sofer*, *Yoreh De'ah*, No. 155; *Rav Pe'alim*, Vol. 3, No. 4. Such a vow is viewed as an obligation. This expenditure is categorized as a "necessary household expense", and her husband's consent is not required. A similar ruling is found in the *Remah*, *Evven HaEzer* 91:4: A husband is held accountable if his wife transgresses a community ordinance, the penalty for which is the donation of a specific sum of money to *tzedakah*.

7. *Sefer Tzedakah U'Mishpat* 4:33–34. Some authorities rule that a

4. A *tzedakah* collector may accept a large donation from a married woman only if her husband is present. If she claims to have her husband's permission to make a large donation, she is believed and the donation accepted.[8] A small donation may always be accepted from a married woman[9] unless the collector is aware of specific objections on her husband's part, in which case he may not accept anything.[10]

---

husband's right to nullify his wife's charitable vows is forfeited only if she is the *primary* source of family income.

8. *Orukh HaShulchan, Yoreh De'ah* 248:13; *Nodah BeYehudah, Kama, Yoreh De'ah,* No. 72.

9. *Shulchan Arukh, Yoreh De'ah* 248:4; *Shulchan Arukh HaRav, Hilkhoth Metzi'ah U'Pikadon* 5; *Kitzur Shulchan Arukh* 182:14; *Chokhmath Adam* 147:17. *Chelkath Yaacov,* Vol. 2, No. 167, discusses this question in relation to monies collected at women's charity gatherings.

10. See the sources cited in note 9. "Nevertheless," adds the *Chokhmath Adam,* "if a woman of means wishes to give a generous gift to relatives, her husband may not object."

Sefer Chassidim 1047 comments that if a husband is fined by the community or if he steals money, his wife will be blessed if she makes the appropriate compensation, even if he objects.

Minchath Yitzchak, Vol. 5, No. 132, rules that if a woman makes a charitable donation from assets unknown to her husband, her gift is valid. (See the *Shulchan Arukh, Evven HaEzer* 90:11.) Moreover, if the woman transfers assets unknown to her husband to a third party with instructions on how to apportion them after her death, that party becomes a legal executor, and her husband has no claim on the assets. See also *Rav Pe'alim,* Vol. 4, *Choshen Mishpat,* No. 6.

In any case, it is preferable that a woman inform her husband of all of her assets and receive his consent to their donation.

Sefer Tzedakah U'Mishpat 1:20 cites authorities who go even further than *Minchath Yitzchak.* They assert that even when a woman gives assets known to her husband to charity, the donation is valid, even if her husband objects.

Be'er Moshe, Vol. 1, No. 53, and *Divrey Malki'eil,* Vol. 4, No. 79, cite cases where a husband is not permitted to object. Included in this category are donations made during times of crisis or sickness. At such times it is morally inappropriate for a husband to object to

5. According to many authorities, a large donation may be accepted from a married woman who manages the household finances even if her husband is unaware of it.[11] Similarly, some authorities maintain that a woman who provides financial support for her husband may make a large donation without his consent.[12] In neither case may a donation be accepted in the face of a husband's explicit objection.

6. A woman may not increase her husband's charitable donations on the grounds that he does not give an amount commensurate with his means. Anyone who accepts money

---

his wife's donating a large amount of her assets to charity. According to the letter of the law, he may even object in these situations.

The *Nodah BeYehudah, Tinyana, Yoreh De'ah*, No. 158, discusses whether a pregnant woman may donate a large sum of money to charity to increase her merit and assure herself a healthy childbirth. He concludes that her husband is allowed to object, unless it is customary in the woman's family to make such donations.

11. *Shakh, Choshen Mishpat* 96:9, and *Nodah BeYehudah, Tinyana, Yoreh De'ah*, No. 72. The Lubavitcher Rebbe writes in *Teshuvoth U'Biurim*, 5743, No. 173, "It is very common, especially in the United States, for a husband to give his wife free rein in the distribution of both small and large amounts of charity." In the final analysis, much depends on the preference of the couple. See also *Levushey Mordekhai*, Vol. 1, *Yoreh De'ah*, No. 172.

12. *Yam Shel Shlomo, Bava Kama*, Chapter 10, No. 59, explains that a man whose wife is supporting him will certainly not object to her donation, since she might refuse to continue the support. The *Orukh HaShulchan, Yoreh De'ah* 248:12, cites the view of the *Rashba* and the *Maharit*, which dismisses the application of the principle that a woman's income belongs to her husband when a woman runs her own business or is otherwise self-employed. The *Orukh HaShulchan* concludes that although their view is not generally accepted, it may be relied on in the area of *tzedakah*.

from a woman when her husband disapproves is guilty of theft.[13]

7. Although women may go out to collect charity, they should avoid places where men normally gather, such as the men's sections of synagogues or wedding halls.[14]

8. A girl is not required to separate ten percent from an allowance she receives from her parents for daily living and educational expenses.[15] Even if she wishes to separate *Ma'aser Kesafim* from what remains after expenses, she must first obtain her parents' permission.[16]

9. A poor woman's need for clothing or funds for a

---

13. *Nodah BeYehudah, Tinyana, Yoreh De'ah*, No. 158, cited in the *Pithchey Teshuvah, Yoreh De'ah* 248:3.

   The *Orukh HaShulchan* limits this ruling to communities which have the means to coerce their members to fulfill obligations. Since the Rabbinical Court of the city has the authority to force the husband to fulfill his obligations, his wife has no right to do so on her own. But if the community has no means of coercion, she may consult a local Rabbi to determine the amount of money her husband should donate and she may contribute that amount without his knowledge.

14. *BeTzeyl HaChokhmah*, Vol. 2, No. 36; *Mishneh Halakhoth*, Vol. 4, No. 124. *BeTzeyl HaChokhmah*, Vol. 2, No. 86, criticizes the practice of holding frivolous, mixed gatherings for a charitable cause. In the author's opinion, the end does not justify such means.

   HaGaon Rav Shlomo Zalman Auerbach discourages sending young children out to collect *tzedakah*; it may induce them to collect money from strangers for selfish purposes.

15. *Iggeroth Moshe, Yoreh De'ah*, Vol. 2, No. 112.

16. Since the money was intended for her personal use, HaGaon Rav Shlomo Zalman Auerbach argues that she may not spend it for other purposes without permission, even charitable ones.

wedding take precedence over a poor man's needs in the same areas.[17]

10. There are no words more appropriate with which to conclude this section than those of the *Mateh Moshe* in *Ma'alath HaTzedakah*, Chapter 7: "The charitable acts of women are more pleasing in the eyes of God than those of men... A Jew should give his wife free rein in giving *Tzedakah*... His reward for doing so will be great, since [her ability to give] depends on him. He will also prevent people from receiving stolen money, which would be the consequence [of his wife giving without his consent]."

It is stated in *Iggereth HaTeshuvah* of Rabbenu Yona: "When a woman gives charity, she should pray that her children will be God-fearing and successful in the study of Torah and performance of *mitzvoth*. Prayers are particularly potent at the time of performing a *mitzvah*."

Honoring Parents

11. Women are obligated in the *mitzvah* of *Kibbud Av V'Eim* (Honoring Parents). The observance of *Kibbud Av V'Eim* entails serving parents food and drink and attending to their personal needs.[18] Due to her marital responsibilities,

---

17. *Shulchan Arukh, Yoreh De'ah* 151:8; *Chokhmath Adam* 145:2.

   Imrey Yosher, Vol. 2, No. 98, states that the cost of a woman's first wedding takes precedence over those of a second wedding. An orphan's needs take precedence over the needs of others. It appears from the *Rambam, Hilkhoth De'oth*, Chapter 6, that a person is considered an orphan as long as he or she is not financially independent.

   The *Orukh HaShulchan* disagrees with this ordering of priorities and takes the position that when there are insufficient funds, a man's wedding expenses take precedence over a woman's since men, unlike women, are commanded to procreate.

18. *Shulchan Arukh, Yoreh De'ah* 240:17.

a married woman cannot always fulfill this *mitzvah* properly. When *Kibbud Av V'Eim* conflicts with marital responsibilities, she is exempt from the *mitzvah*,[19] but a considerate husband will encourage his wife to honor her parents.[20]

The *mitzvah* of *Yir'ath Av V'Eim* (Reverence for Parents) *can* be fulfilled just as fully after marriage as before. It entails standing when a parent enters a room, not sitting in their chairs, and not contradicting their words.[21]

12. Parents should avoid requesting assistance from a married daughter when it will conflict with her household duties.[22]

13. Cursing or striking a parent is an extremely serious transgression, whether a woman lives at home, by herself, or with her family.[23]

14. When a woman's parents do not observe *mitzvoth*, and she is unable to influence them in a respectful way to recite blessings, she may still serve them food. By acting with politeness and consideration, she may eventually influence them to observe the Torah's requirements.[24]

---

19. *Shulchan Arukh, Yoreh De'ah* 240:4.
20. *Shakh, Yoreh De'ah* 240:19. The *Sefer HaChinukh* 33 states, "This *mitzvah* is practiced at all times and in all places, by men and by women whenever possible, i.e., whenever their husbands' needs do not prevent them from doing so." See also the *Torah Temimah, VaYikra* 19:4; *Mishneh Halakhoth*, Vol. 7, No. 153; *Sefer Chassidim* 335.
21. *Shulchan Arukh, Yoreh De'ah* 240:2.
22. *Sefer Chassidim, Ibid.*
23. *Shulchan Arukh, Yoreh De'ah* 248:4; *Remah, Yoreh De'ah* 241:1; *Kitzur Shulchan Arukh* 34:2. Also see *Tzitz Eliezer*, Vol. 13, No. 78.
24. The *Shulchan Arukh, Orach Chayim* 169:2, states, "A person should only serve food to someone who recites the appropriate blessing."

15. A woman is not required to abide by a parent's choice of a husband.[25]

The *Remah* adds, "Some authorities are lenient with food which is given as charity to the poor." The *Mishnah Berurah* explains that the *mitzvah* of *Tzedakah* takes precedence over the *possibility* that the recipient will not recite a blessing. The *Mishnah Berurah* cautions, "If the donor is *certain* that the recipient will not recite the blessing, it is forbidden to give him food, even as charity."

Nevertheless, HaGaon Rav Shlomo Zalman Auerbach rules that food may be served to someone who will take offense at being asked to recite a blessing, and then be insulted if he is not served. This would further alienate him from Torah observance. HaGaon Rav Auerbach explains that the purpose of the prohibition against serving a person who refuses to recite a blessing is to avoid being an accessory to a transgression. To increase someone's alienation is more serious than being an accessory. These guidelines apply to serving parents, other family members, and guests.

25. *Remah, Yoreh De'ah* 240:25; *Givath Pinchus*, No. 3; *Nodah BeYehudah, Tinyana, Evven HaEzer*, No. 124. This ruling is derived from the *Maharik, Shoresh* 166, who explains that there is no obligation to concede to a parent's request when the parent will derive no benefit from it, or when the offspring will suffer physical pain.

A daughter should bear in mind that her parents' wishes stem from sincere concern for her welfare. She should be sensitive and carefully explain the reasons for her actions. She should not insult her parents in any way, and she should do everything in her power to help them understand the reasons for her decision.

An instructive incident concerning how great individuals go above and beyond the requirements of the law is cited in Rav Chayim Zeitchik's work, *Me'oroth HaGedolim*, p. 273: "The widowed mother of R. Yisrael Meir HaCohen, the *Chafetz Chayim*, married a distinguished citizen of Radin and took up residence in that town. Her husband had a grown daughter whom he was very anxious to marry off to R. Yisrael Meir, then seventeen years old. R. Yisrael Meir's mother and her family were unfavorably disposed to the match. At the same time, various wealthy families in the community made offers for him to wed their daughters; one family even offered a dowry of one thousand rubles.

Honoring a Husband and His Family

16. The foundation of a peaceful and successful marriage is the mutual respect and consideration that spouses show one another.[26]

17. Husband and wife are required to show in-laws as much respect as possible[27] even if the in-laws do not

---

"Realizing that his refusal to marry his stepfather's daughter would adversely affect his mother's relationship with his stepfather, R. Yisrael Meir agreed to the match and calmly and skillfully persuaded his mother and other relatives to accede to it. Throughout his life, the *Chafetz Chayim* pointed to the success of the match. His wife, a righteous and upright woman, was satisfied with minimal physical comfort. In her merit, the *Chafetz Chayim* was able to follow the path he had chosen for himself — uninterrupted Torah study."

26. *Rambam, Hilkhoth Ishuth* 15:19–20: "Our Sages command a man to honor his wife more than himself, and to love her as he loves himself. He should spend as much money as possible on her behalf, not impose unnecessary fear on her, and speak to her gently without sadness or anger. Our Sages command women to honor and revere their husbands as much as possible. A woman should seek her husband's counsel in all areas, and he should be in her eyes as a prince or king, who can do whatever he wishes. She should refrain from things which displease him. This is the ideal basis for tranquil family life, the hallmark of daughters and sons of Israel."

See also Tractate *Bava Metzia* 59a; *Menorath HaMaor, Ner* 3, *Klal* 6, Vol. 4, Chapter 2; *Pele Yo'etz, Erekh Ahavath Ish V'Ishah*.

Although the *Rambam* requires a woman to show reverence for her husband, the *Sefer HaMakneh*, commenting on Tractate *Kiddushin* 30b, points out that the specific prohibitions which apply to parents, i.e., not sitting in their chairs, rising when they enter a room, and not contradicting their words, do not apply to a husband.

27. *Shulchan Arukh, Yoreh De'ah* 240:24; *Birkey Yosef, Yoreh De'ah* 240:22; *Ben Ish Chai, Shanah Sh'niah, Parshath Shoftim* 30. The source for this ruling is *Shmuel* I, 24:11, where David addresses his father-in-law, King Saul, with the words, "See my father, surely see."

reciprocate.[28]

Honoring an Older Sister

18. A man should respect his older sister. Some authorities do not view this as an actual obligation, but a guideline for proper behavior.[29]

Mezuzah

19. Women are obligated to have *mezuzoth* on their doorposts.[30] They may affix *mezuzoth* and recite the blessing *Likvo'ah mezuzah* even if a man is present.[31]

Some authorities rule it is preferable for a man to affix *mezuzoth* on doorposts, but if a woman has already done so, there is no need to remove the *mezuzah* and replace it.[32]

---

28. *Kerem Shlomo,Hilkhoth Kibbud Av V'Eim,* derives this from the verse cited in note 27, where David addresses Saul with respect in spite of the fact that Saul is pursuing him with the intention to kill him. The *Birkey Yosef,* in *Shiur'ey Brakhah* 240:16, cites the *Tana D'vey Eliyahu* which derives from the juxtaposition of the prohibition against adultery with the *mitzvah* of honoring parents in the Ten Commandments that a man who marries a woman and fails to respect her parents is living in a relationship similar to adultery.

29. *Birkey Yosef, Yoreh De'ah* 240:17; *Pithchey Teshuvah, Yoreh De'ah* 240:19, citing *Shevuth Yaacov.*

30. *Shulchan Arukh, Yoreh De'ah* 291:3; *Keseth HaSofer,* No. 1:2–3; *Shakh, Yoreh De'ah* 291:4. There are two reasons why women are obligated in this *mitzvah*: It is not time-bound, and the Torah promises long life for its fulfillment. See Tractate *Berakhoth* 20b and Tractate *Yoma* 11a. In his glosses to *Yoma* 11b, Rabbi Akiva Eiger explains why both reasons are necessary.

31. *Sha'arey Shlomoh,* commentary on the *Kitzur Shulchan Arukh* 11:69; *Yabia Omer,* Vol. 3, *Yoreh De'ah,* No. 18.

32. *Be'er Moshe,* Vol. 2, No. 100, cites authorities who extend the

20. Women may not write *mezuzoth*.[33]

Circumcision and Redemption of the First-Born Son

21. Women are not commanded to circumcise their sons.[34] In an emergency, when a *mohel* is not available, a competent woman may perform a *brith milah*.[35]

---

disqualification of women from writing *mezuzoth* (See paragraph 20.) to their affixing them to doorposts. The author concludes that this view should be followed, but if a woman has already affixed a *mezuzah* to a doorpost, opposing authorities may be relied on; there is no need to remove it.

33. *Mishnah Berurah* 39:1. Tractate *Gittin* 45b disqualifies women from writing *tefillin*, based on the verse, "And you shall bind them [the *tefillin*] for a sign on your hand...and you will write them..." (*Devarim* 6:8–9). This implies that only those required to wear *tefillin* are qualified to write them. The *Mishnah Berurah* notes that many later authorities extend this disqualification to writing *Sifrey Torah* and *mezuzoth*. The *Biur Halakhah* adds that a woman should not even correct an improperly written letter. When her correction makes the *tefillin* valid, it is as if she wrote it.

34. *Remah, Yoreh De'ah* 261:1 and 265:11. Tractate *Kiddushin* 29a infers that women are exempt from the obligation to circumcise their sons from the verse, "And Abraham circumcised Isaac...as God commanded *him*" (*Bereshith* 21:4). See *Tzitz Eliezer*, Vol. 6, No. 28, for a thorough analysis of this subject.

35. Tractate *Avodah Zarah* 27a recounts a dispute between Rav and R. Yochanan, in which Rav maintains that women are not only exempt from the obligation to circumcise their sons, but they are actually disqualified from doing so. R. Yochanan counters that the exemption does not disqualify them from performing the *mitzvah*, on their own or other people's sons.

The *Shulchan Arukh, Yoreh De'ah* 264:1, cites the view of the *Rambam, Hilkhoth Milah* 2:1, which favors R. Yochanan's qualification of women as *mohaloth*.

The *Remah* cites the opposing views of the *Smak* and *Hagahoth Mordekhai*. They rule in favor of Rav. The *Remah* concludes that

22. A woman may not serve as *sandek* (the person who holds the baby during the *brith milah*).[36] If her husband is the *sandek*, she may assist by carrying the baby to the *brith* and handing him to her husband. A woman who is a *niddah* may not hand the baby to her husband. For the same reason, the mother may not carry her baby into the room and hand him to her husband.[37]

23. Women are not commanded to redeem their first-born sons.[38]

---

their view should be considered and the services of a male *mohel* obtained. The *Orukh HaShulchan* explains that the *Remah* would insist on importing a male *mohel* from another town rather than permitting a local woman to perform the *brith milah*. A woman may only perform a *brith milah* when the only other option would be to postpone it beyond the eighth day.

The *Shulchan Arukh, Yoreh De'ah* 265:6, notes that a *minyan* should be present at a *brith milah* whenever possible. *Koreith HaBrith* maintains that women may be counted for this *minyan* if ten men are not available; its only purpose is to publicize the event. See Chapter 22, note 14.

36. The *Remah, Yoreh De'ah* 265:11, considers it immodest for a woman to perform this function.

The *Orukh HaShulchan, Yoreh De'ah* 265:35, comments, "Today, it is no longer customary for a woman to assist the *sandek*. Rather, a woman is given the honor of bringing the baby into the room on a pillow or cushion. She then hands him to her husband or some unmarried man, who brings him to Eliyahu's chair. This is known as *kvaterin*."

37. The restriction against a woman who is a *niddah* assisting the *sandek* also applies to her serving as *kvaterin*. The term *kvaterin*, explains the *Orukh HaShulchan*, comes from the Hebrew word *k'toreth* (incense). Tractate *Kerithoth* 6b compares the *mitzvah* of *Brith Milah* to offering the incense in the *Beith HaMikdash*. The person who brings a baby to his *brith* is bringing in the incense.

38. "All your first-born sons you shall redeem" (*Shemoth* 34:20). This

Tzitzith and Tefillin

24. Women are exempt from the *mitzvah* to wear *tzitzith* (fringes) on four-cornered garments.[39] Unlike men, who are

---

mitzvah is fulfilled by a father giving a *cohen* five pieces of silver (or an object of equal value) on or after the thirtieth day from the birth of his first-born son. "First-born" means a first-born of the mother even if the father has other children. Only a normally delivered first born is redeemed; a son delivered by Caesarean section is exempt, as are sons born to a woman who has miscarried. The first-born sons of *cohanim* and *levi'im* and those of their daughters are not redeemed.

Tractate *Kiddushin* 29a deduces from the above verse that just as girls are not required to be redeemed, so mothers are not required to redeem their sons. See the *Shulchan Arukh, Yoreh De'ah* 305:2.

The *Pithchey Teshuvah* 305:3 notes that if a woman makes unauthorized use of her husband's money to redeem her first-born son, the *mitzvah* has not been properly fulfilled. The father should redeem his son again without reciting the blessing.

The *Chatham Sofer, Yoreh De'ah*, No. 301, discusses the case of a father who cannot find a *cohen* from whom to redeem his son. He rules that the father may give the redemption money to the daughter of a *cohen* without reciting the blessing. The father should stipulate that he is only fulfilling the *mitzvah* in this way because he cannot find a male *cohen*, and that if he finds one later he will redeem his son again. If he does redeem his son from a male *cohen* later, he should recite the blessing. The money originally given to the woman becomes a gift.

39. *Shulchan Arukh, Orach Chayim* 17:2. *Chazal* explain that the verse, "And you shall see them [the *tzitzith*]" (*BaMidbar* 15:39), indicates that the *mitzvah* of *Tzitzith* is not practiced at night. The *Rambam* and the *Rosh* disagree over the meaning of this exclusion. The *Rambam, Hilkhoth Tzitzith* 3:7, maintains it is linked to time: One is required to attach *tzitzith* to a four-cornered garment when it is worn during the day, but not when it is worn at night. The *Rosh* understands the exclusion to be linked to the kind of garment: A garment which is normally worn during the day requires *tzitzith*, even when it is worn at night; conversely, a garment which is normally worn at night is exempt, even when it is worn during the day. Both opinions consider *Tzitzith* time-bound and women are thus exempt. See note 46.

commanded to attach *tzitzith* to their four-cornered garments, women may wear such garments without *tzitzith*.[40]

25. Although from a strictly technical viewpoint women may fulfill the *mitzvah* of *Tzitzith* — Ashkenazic women may even recite the blessing[41] — such behavior is considered arrogant.[42]

Some authorities actually prohibit women from wearing *tzitzith* on the grounds that they are men's garments.[43]

26. The *mitzvah* of *Tzitzith* applies to four-cornered garments owned by two people.[44] In cases where one of the owners is a woman, many authorities require the man to

---

40. *Shulchan Arukh HaRav* 17:1; *Ben Ish Chai, Shanah Rishonah, Parshath Lekh L'kha* 13.
41. *Remah, Orach Chayim* 17:2, based on the view of Rabbenu Tam, cited in *Tosafoth*, Tractate *Eruvin* 96a, that women may recite blessings when they voluntarily fulfill time-bound *mitzvoth*. Sephardic custom follows the view of the *Rambam, Hilkhoth Tzitzith* 3:9, and the *Shulchan Arukh, Orach Chayim* 589:6, which prohibits women from reciting blessings under these circumstances.
42. *Remah, Ibid.*, based on the *Rambam, Hilkhoth Tzitzith* 3:9. The *Agur*, No. 27, cites the *Maharil*, and warns that it is foolish and arrogant for women to don *tzitzith*. The *Kaf HaChayim* 17:5 cites the *Ari*, in *Sha'ar HaKavanoth*, who states that women have no connection with this *mitzvah* at all.
43. *Targum Yonathan Ben Uziel* renders the verse, "A man's garment shall not be [worn] by a woman" (*Devarim* 22:5), into Aramaic as, "The garments of *tzitzith* and *tefillin*, which are men's garments, should not be worn by women." See also the *Ben Ish Chai, Ibid.*

   Iggeroth Moshe, Orach Chayim, Vol. 4, No. 49, castigates women who insist on fulfilling the *mitzvah* of *Tzitzith* in the name of "equality": "Their motivation is fundamentally a complaint against God and His Torah. Because their intention is not a truthful desire to serve God, their actions do not constitute a *mitzvah*. Their disrespect for Torah and *Chazal* amounts to nothing less than blasphemy."
44. *Shulchan Arukh, Orach Chayim* 14:5.

attach *tzitzith* to the garment before he wears it, but he does not recite the blessing before he puts it on.[45]

27. A man should attach *tzitzith* to a four-cornered garment which he owns before wearing it, even if the garment is normally worn by his wife. In such a case, he does not recite the blessing before putting it on.[46]

28. A woman may spin and twist the threads for *tzitzith*. Before she begins, she must say aloud that she is spinning and twisting them *l'shem mitzvath Tzitzith* (for the sake of the *mitzvah* of *Tzitzith*).[47] It is preferable for a man to attach the

---

45. *Mishnah Berurah* 14:17, based on *Artzoth HaChayim*, contrary to *Damesek Eliezer*, Tractate *Chullin*, p. 424.

46. *Yeshuoth Yaacov* 10:2. The *Pri Megadim, Eshel Avraham* 18:3, cites *Chemed Moshe*, which explains that this ruling depends on the two views cited in note 39. A garment normally worn by a woman is analogous to a garment normally worn at night. According to the *Rambam*, who obligates men to attach *tzitzith* to all four-cornered garments worn during the day, the fact that a garment is normally worn by a woman does not exempt a man from his obligation. But according to the *Rosh*, for the same reason that a nighttime garment is exempt from *tzitzith* even when worn during the day, a "woman's garment" is also exempt from *tzitzith*, even when worn by a man. Since the obligation to perform the *mitzvah* is questionable, the blessing should be omitted.

It should be noted that although the garment in queston is normally worn by a woman, it was not specifically manufactured for women. Had it been manufactured for women, men would be forbidden to wear it, in keeping with the prohibition against wearing a woman's garment. (See Chapter 7, paragraph 1.)

A man who borrows a four-cornered garment from either a woman or a man is not obligated to attach *tzitzith* to it. See the *Shulchan Arukh, Orach Chayim* 14:3.

47. *Shulchan Arukh, Orach Chayim* 11:1 and the *Mishnah Berurah* 14:3. Spinning and twisting the threads *lishmah* (for the sake of the *mitzvah*) is essential to the *mitzvah*. If they were spun and twisted

threads to the garment,[48] but if a woman did so, the *tzitzith* are valid, and the appropriate blessing may be recited when the garment is put on.[49]

29. A woman's word is to be believed when she says that she produced threads *lishmah* (for the sake of the *mitzvah*).[50]

30. A minor may not spin or twist the threads or attach them to a garment.[51]

---

without the proper intention, the *tzitzith* are invalid. See *Mishkanoth Yaacov*, No. 21.

The *Nodah BeYehudah, Kama, Yoreh De'ah*, No. 95, writes in passing, "Please accept[with this letter] *tzitzith*...that were made for the sake of the *mitzvah* by a trustworthy woman..."

48. *Remah, Orach Chayim* 14:1, and *Mishnah Berurah*. Although most authorities permit women to attach *tzitzith* to a garment, the *Remah* takes into account the view of Rabbenu Tam, which disqualifies them from doing so. The *Mishnah Berurah* explains that Rabbenu Tam interprets the verse, "Speak to *b'ney Yisrael*, and they shall make for themselves *tzitzith*" (*BaMidbar* 15:38), as emphasizing that only *b'ney Yisrael* (the *sons* of Israel) may make *tzitzith*. Since the threads are "made" into *tzitzith* when they are attached to the garment, Rabbenu Tam disqualifies women from attaching them to the garment. The *Biur Halakhah* cites a second explanation of Rabbenu Tam's view, which is cited in Chapter 20, note 6.

49. *Remah, Ibid*. Once a woman has already attached the threads onto the garment, the *Remah* concedes that we may rely on the majority view, which permits women to attach them. This is also the ruling of the *Shulchan Arukh, Orach Chayim* 11:1.

Most authorities rule that the threads of the *tzitzith* must be attached to the garment *lishmah*. Threads which were attached to a garment without the proper intention should be removed and re-attached properly. If this is not possible, for example, when the time is very close to the onset of *Shabbath*, the *tzitzith* may be worn without the blessing. See the *Shulchan Arukh* 11:2 and the *Mishnah Berurah*.

50. See the *Mishnah Berurah* 11:7 and 14:5.

51. In *halakhah*, minors are deemed incapable of performing an action

31. Women are forbidden to perform the *mitzvah* o *Tefillin.*[52]

32. *Tefillin* parchments written by a woman are invalid.[53] Women are also prohibited from participating in the differen stages of the production of *tefillin* — making the *batim* (the containers which house the parchments), smoothing them sewing them, squaring them and making the *shin* on the

---

lishmah. The *Biur Halakhah* 11, beginning *Tav'an*, concludes that a minor should not spin, twist, or attach the threads even if an adult stands over him and constantly reminds him to do it *lishmah*. See also the *Mishnah Berurah* 14:4 and the *Biur Halakhah*, beginning *V'tov la'asoth.*

The *Biur Halakhah* rules that a girl of *bath mitzvah* age whose physical maturity has not been firmly established (See Chapter 11, note 1.) may spin and twist the threads if an adult stands over her and reminds her to maintain the proper intention.

52. *Shulchan Arukh, Orach Chayim* 38:3. The *mitzvah* of *Tefillin*, which is not practiced on *Shabbath* and *Yom Tov,* is time-bound. The *Remah* cites the *Kol Bo*'s report that the *Maharam* of Rothenberg prohibited women from wearing them. The *Mishnah Berurah* 38:3 explains that *tefillin* should not be worn on a voluntary basis because the person who wears them must maintain a pure mind and pure body. He may not forget that he is wearing them and he may not sleep or pass wind while he is wearing them. If men were not *obligated* to wear *tefillin*, they also would not risk doing so. In fact, men no longer observe the tradition of wearing *tefillin* the entire day. The *Eliyahu Rabbah* 38:2 emphasizes that this prohibition applies to all women, even those who claim they can maintain a pure mind and body.

The *Shiltey HaGiborim*, Tractate *Rosh HaShanah*, Chapter 4, adds, "A woman who wears *tefillin* disregards the words of the Sages." The *Maharam Shick, Orach Chayim*, No. 15, notes that *tefillin* are a "man's garment". See note 43. Also see the *Levush, Orach Chayim* 17:2; *Kaf HaChayim* 38:9; *Maharam Shick, Yoreh De'ah*, No. 173; *Iggeroth Moshe, Orach Chayim*, Vol. 2, No. 2.
53. *Shulchan Arukh, Orach Chayim* 39:1.

tefillin shel rosh (*tefillin* for the head).[54] They may, however, process hides for the parchment[55] and paint the *retzuoth* (straps) black.[56]

33. A woman may wrap *tefillin* on a man. For example, if her father or husband is sick and unable to wrap his *tefillin*, she may assist him. The man recites the blessing.[57]

Writing a Sefer Torah

34. Most authorities exempt women from the *mitzvah* to write one's own *Sefer Torah*.[58] Nevertheless, a woman who

---

54. *Shulchan Arukh, Orach Chayim* 39:2, and *Mishnah Berurah.* See also the *Mishnah Berurah* 39:23, citing the *Pri Megadim.*
55. *Mishnah Berurah* 39:10.
56. *Mishnah Berurah, Ibid.,* and 33:23. The processing of the hides and the painting of the *retzuoth* must be done *lishmah.* A woman may perform these functions, which are not performed on the *tefillin* themselves.
57. *Kaf HaChayim* 27:8, and *Da'ath Torah* 39:2. See also the novellae of the *Chatham Sofer* on Tractate *Chullin* 87a; *Maharam Shick, Orach Chayim*, No. 25; *Machaneh Chayim, Orach Chayim*, No. 6.

   A woman whose husband is sick may help him wrap *tefillin* even when she is a *niddah*, in which case she must be careful not to touch him. See *Sugah BaShoshanim*, Chapter 36:25. No matter how weak he is, she may not recite the blessing for him — a person who is not obligated in a *mitzvah* cannot *motzie* someone who is obligated in that *mitzvah.*

   The *Shulchan Arukh, Orach Chayim* 2:4, teaches that the left arm is given precedence in all acts of tieing because a person ties *tefillin* on his left arm. For this reason, a person puts on the right shoe first, to show respect to the strong arm, but ties the left shoe first. *Rivevoth Ephrayim*, Vol.1, No. 5, adds that women should observe the custom of tieing the left shoe first even though they are exempt from *Tefillin.* A left-handed person wraps *tefillin* on his right arm and ties the right shoe first.
58. "Now write this song for yourselves, and teach it to the children of

contributes to the cost of writing a community *Sefer Torah* receives great reward. Her donation enables the community to fulfill the *mitzvah* of *Kri'ath HaTorah.*[59]

35. A woman may not sew the columns of a *Sefer Torah* together.[60] If she has already done so, they should be taken apart and resewn by a man. If this was not done, some authorities permit the *Sefer Torah* to be used by the congregation, while others do not.[61]

Israel" (*Devarim* 31:19). This is the final *mitzvah* of the Torah. It obligates every Jew to write a *Sefer Torah* for himself, or have one written for him. Many people fulfill this *mitzvah* by contributing to the cost of a public *Sefer Torah*. Others rely on the view of the *Rosh*, that the purpose of the *mitzvah* is to have a *Sefer Torah* to study, and a person can also fulfill it by purchasing holy books.

The *Sefer HaChinukh* 613 exempts women from this *mitzvah* because they are exempt from *Talmud Torah*: "This *mitzvah* is practiced in every place and at all times by males, for they are obligated to study Torah and therefore to write one, but not by females." At the end of *Sefer HaMitzvoth*, the *Rambam* also includes this *mitzvah* among the eighteen positive *mitzvoth* from which women are exempt. See also *Mishnath Avraham*, No. 1:36, and *Da'ath Kedoshim, Yoreh De'ah* 270:2.

After a lengthy analysis, the *Sha'agath Aryeh*, Nos. 35–36, comes to the conclusion that women should be obligated in this non-time-bound *mitzvah*.

59. *Teshuvoth HaRashba*, No. 324. Donations toward a poor orphan's wedding costs take precedence over donations for writing a *Sefer Torah*. This can be inferred from a ruling in the *Shulchan Arukh, Evven HaEzer* 1, that a *Sefer Torah* can be sold in order to raise funds for an orphan's wedding. In a community which lacks even one *Sefer Torah*, purchasing a *Sefer Torah* takes precedence.

60. *Maharam MiLublin*, No. 68, cited in the *Biur Halakhah* 39, beginning *B'kol.*

61. *Biur Halakhah, Ibid.*, citing *Magen HaElef.* In some communities, women are given the honor of sewing the last few columns of a new *Sefer Torah* together during the celebration honoring its completion. Where this is the custom, the scribe should sew the top, bottom, and

36. Women may not make corrections in a *Sefer Torah*.[62]

37. Authorities disagree as to whether women may write a *Megillath Esther*.[63]

Terumoth and Ma'asroth

38. Men and women are forbidden to eat produce grown by a Jew in *Eretz Yisrael* unless *terumoth* and *ma'asroth* have been separated.[64] A person who spends any time in Israel

---

middle stitch of each column. The custom, however, is best abolished.

62. *Ibid.* The *Biur Halakhah* distinguishes between a correction which involves the separation of two letters which are stuck together, and a correction which involves the separation of two parts of the same letter which have blurred into each other. In the first case, the woman does not actually form the letter, and the *Sefer Torah* may still be used. (If possible, a man should trace over her correction.) In the second case, the woman forms the letter itself. If a man does not erase the letter and rewrite it, the *Sefer Torah* may not be used. To avoid making corrections which might invalidate the *Sefer Torah*, it is best that women refrain from making any corrections.

63. *Pri Megadim, Mishbetzoth Zahav* 691:2; *Birkey Yosef* 691:6. Those who permit women to write a *Megillah* argue from the fact that they are obligated to hear it on *Purim*. Moreover, Tractate *Megillah* 19a deduces many of the laws of writing a *Megillah* from the verse, "And Queen Esther wrote" (*Esther* 9:29). More stringent authorities counter with the observation that women may not write a *mezuzah* even though they are obligated in that *mitzvah*. The verse in *Esther*, they argue, means that Queen Esther instructed others to write the *Megillah*. See *Mikra'ey Kodesh, Purim*, No. 33.

64. Produce grown by a Jew in *Eretz Yisrael* may not be eaten until four separations have been made:
1. *Terumah Gedolah*. In the days of the *Beith HaMikdash*, only *cohanim* and their families were allowed to eat it. Both the *terumah gedolah* and the person eating it had to be *tahor* (ritually pure).

must become acquainted with these laws.[65]

Today, when it is no longer possible to be *tahor* (See Chapter 13, note 18.), the *terumah gedolah* is thrown away.

The *terumah* given to *cohanim* consisted of a minimum of one-sixtieth of a person's crops. Today, separation of even the smallest amount is sufficient.

2. *Ma'aser Rishon.* This consists of a separation of one-tenth of what remains after *terumah gedolah.* It may be eaten by anyone.

3. *Terumath Ma'aser.* This consists of a separation of one-tenth of the *ma'aser rishon*; it is therefore equivalent to one percent of the entire crop after *terumah gedolah.* Like *terumah gedolah*, it may only be eaten by a *cohen* who is *tahor.* Therefore, it is also thrown away today.

4. *Ma'aser Ani* and *Ma'aser Sheni.* These consist of a separation of one-tenth of what remains of the original produce after *terumah gedolah* and *ma'aser rishon* have been separated. *Ma'aser ani* is separated in the third and sixth years of the seven-year *Shmittah* cycle and given to the poor. It may be eaten by anyone. *Ma'aser sheni* is separated in the first, second, fourth, and fifth years of the *Shmittah* cycle. In the days of the *Beith HaMikdash*, *ma'aser sheni* was only eaten within the walls of Jerusalem. Today, the *ma'aser sheni*'s sanctity is transferred to a coin. Only then may the produce be eaten. The coin may not be used for any other purpose.

See note 65 for the actual procedure of separating *terumoth* and *ma'asroth.*

65. *Shulchan Arukh, Yoreh De'ah* 331:40–41; *Chazon Ish, Hilkhoth Ma'asroth*, No. 7:15. *Terumoth* and *ma'asroth* must also be separated from store-bought produce of *Eretz Yisrael* unless a reliable rabbinical supervisor has certified that they have already been separated. Before carrying out the separation, a coin must be designated for the redemption of *ma'aser sheni.* It should be set aside in a special place so it will not be spent. Its monetary value must be equal, at a minimum, to the value of .025 grams of pure silver, one *prutah.* The number of times a coin may be used as a repository for *ma'aser sheni* is equal to the number of *prutoth* it is worth. The size of the coin, which must be local currency, must be adjusted according to fluctuations in the market price of silver in relation to the local currency. When there is a doubt as to the number of *prutoth* in a particular coin, a competent halakhic authority should be consulted.

39. When visiting a family which is not particular about separating *terumoth* and *ma'asroth*, a woman must separate them herself from all the food she eats. This also applies when she visits a hotel, or guesthouse, or the like. If she wishes to separate *terumoth* and *ma'asroth* from all the host's

---

The procedure for separating *terumoth* and *ma'asroth* is as follows:

1. Separate slightly more than one percent of each kind of produce, and recite the following declaration of separation:

"The excess of one percent on the south side of (each kind of) the separated produce shall be *terumah gedolah* (for each kind of food respectively).

"The separated one percent (of each kind of food), together with a further nine-percent on the south side of (each kind of) the unseparated produce, shall be *ma'aser rishon* (for each kind of food respectively).

"The separated one percent (of each kind of food) which I have made *ma'aser rishon* shall be *terumath ma'aser* (for each kind of food respectively).

"*Ma'aser ani* shall be on the north side of (each kind of) the produce (for each kind of food respectively).

"If *ma'aser sheni* need be taken, it shall be on the north side of (each kind of) the food (for each kind of food respectively).

"The *ma'aser sheni* shall be redeemed, if necessary, with an additional *chomesh* (fifth), on a *prutah*, and if it is worth less than a *prutah*, it shall be redeemed on its value, on the coin I have set aside for this purpose.

"If there is *r'vai* in the produce, it shall be redeemed, if necessary, with an additional *chomesh*, on a *prutah*, and if it is worth less than a *prutah*, on its own value, in the above-mentioned coin." (*R'vai* refers to fruit which grows on a tree in the fourth year after planting. Fruit of the first three years is called *orlah* and may not be eaten at all. The fruit of the fourth year has a legal status identical to *ma'aser sheni*.)

2. Wrap the separated food in plastic or paper and throw it away.

The following points regarding the separation of *terumoth* and *ma'asroth* should be borne in mind:

a) When the separation is made from one kind of produce, there is no need to add the words in parentheses in the declaration of separation.

produce, she must first ask his permission. Once the food is

---

b) The declaration may also be used for liquids. One should be careful not to move the liquids while it is being recited.

c) Some people are particular to moisten the separated food before beginning the declaration. This ensures that the *terumah* will be *tam'ey* and that there will be no questions about throwing it away. (See Chapter 13, note 18.)

d) If the *ma'aser sheni*'s value is less than a *prutah*, it must be redeemed with a coin which was previously used for the redemption of *ma'aser sheni* worth at least a *prutah*. The special status of this coin, known as a *prutah chamurah*, cannot be established with store-bought produce because *ma'aser sheni* may have been separated from such produce before it was marketed. A visitor to *Eretz Yisrael* who wishes to obtain a *prutah chamurah* should consult a local Rabbi.

e) *Ma'aser sheni* coins which have been used the maximum number of times must be cleared before being used again. Take a small coin, worth at least a *prutah*, and say, "The *prutah chamurah* in the coins I have set aside for the redemption of *ma'aser sheni* and *r'vai* shall remain in the coins. The remainder of *ma'aser sheni* and *r'vai* in these coins shall be transferred, if necessary with their *chomesh*, to this other coin."

After reciting this formula, the *ma'aser sheni* coins may be used again. When their quota is complete, they must be cleared again. After each clearing, the small coin should be destroyed.

f) A woman who does not have the declaration of separation at hand may say, "All separations of *terumah* and *ma'aser* and all transfers of *kedushah* (sanctity) shall take effect in accordance with Jewish Law and the wording specified in *Halichos Bas Yisrael*." She may use this abbreviated version of the declaration only if she understands the basic content of the full text and has a coin designated for the redemption of *ma'aser sheni*. (See the *Chazon Ish*, *Demai*, No. 15.)

g) Today, Israeli produce is widely exported. People must be on guard not to eat such produce until *terumoth* and *ma'asroth* have been separated unless it is marketed under strict rabbinical supervision.

h) Questions regarding *terumoth* and *ma'asroth* should be addressed to a competent halakhic authority.

served to her, she may separate *terumoth* and *ma'asroth* without asking permission.[66]

40. *Terumoth* and *ma'asroth* may not be separated on *Shabbath* or *Yom Tov*.[67] Separations from produce to be served on *Shabbath* or *Yom Tov* should, therefore, be made in advance. A guest at a home which is not particular about separating *terumoth* and *ma'asroth* may recite the declaration of separation in advance of *Shabbath* or *Yom Tov*. Once the declaration has been made, the physical separation may be carried out on *Shabbath* or *Yom Tov*.[68]

---

66. This is based on a ruling of HaGaon Rav Shlomo Zalman Auerbach. When it involves expense, one may not perform a *mitzvah* on behalf of another without his knowledge. Since part of the food that is separated must be thrown away, the *mitzvah* involves expense. Once food has been served to her, she is separating from produce that belongs to her.

67. *Shulchan Arukh, Orach Chayim* 339:4.

68. This is based on the *Mishnah, Demai* 7:1, and on the *Chazon Ish, Demai* 9:13. The declaration made on *Erev Shabbath* or *Erev Yom Tov* is the same as the normal declaration (See note 65.) with one change — "The excess of one percent on the south side of the food *which will be separated tomorrow...*" For a more detailed explanation, see *Shemirath Shabbath KeHilkhethah* 11:20.

   The advance declaration should only be made when necessary. It is always better to obtain the host's permission and separate *terumoth* and *ma'asroth* from all the produce in the house before *Shabbath* or *Yom Tov*.

   The advance declaration is only effective for store-bought produce when it is probable that the separations were made before the produce was marketed. If *terumoth* and *ma'asroth* have definitely or even probably not been separated, for instance, from vegetables carried into the house from the host's garden just before *Shabbath*, the advance declaration may not be used. In most Israeli cities, *terumoth* and *ma'asroth* are usually separated before marketing. In small outlying areas, the local rabbinical authority should be consulted.

Shmittah

41. Every Jew living in Israel must master the laws governing the purchase of fruits and vegetables during *Shmittah* (the Sabbatical year) before it begins. A person who is unversed in the rules and regulations of *Shmittah* will find it virtually impossible to avoid transgressing the prohibitions concerning buying, selling, and eating its produce. The laws relating to gardening and plant care must also be mastered.[69]

Lashon Ha'ra

42. Men and women are cautioned to observe all the prohibitions against *lashon ha'ra* (derogatory speech) and *rekhiluth* (gossip).[70] No exceptions are made to these laws for a daughter's speech to her parents or a wife's to her husband.[71] It is extremely beneficial for a woman to set a

---

HaGaon Rav Shlomo Zalman Auerbach adds that a person who separates *terumoth* and *ma'asroth* on *Shabbath* should say, "All the separations should take effect in accordance with the declaration I made yesterday." See *Shemirath Shabbath KeHilkhethah* 11, notes 76 and 96; *HaHalakhah BaMishpachah* 20.

69. *Sdeh Chemed*, Vol. 5, *Ma'arekheth Mem*, No. 137. The prohibition against marketing and purchasing *Shmittah* produce is derived from the verse, "And the produce of the *Shabbath* year shall be for you *for food*" (*VaYikra* 25:6), and not for merchandise. The *Chatham Sofer, Orach Chayim*, No. 103, explains that although the prohibition against marketing *Shmittah* produce is derived from a positive, time-bound commandment, women are included. All negative commandments, including those derived from positive ones, are incumbent on women.

70. *Chafetz Chayim, Hilkhoth Lashon HaRa* 8:1, and *Hilkhoth Rekhiluth* 7:1. Also see *Iggereth HaGra*.

71. Listening to *lashon ha'ra* also comes under the prohibition. When one spouse speaks *lashon ha'ra*, the other spouse may not listen. It goes without saying that it is forbidden to accept *lashon hara* as true.

fixed time to study *Shemirath HaLashon* and *Chafetz Chayim*, the two definitive works on the subject.[72]

Blessing Over a Tree in Bloom

43. The blessing recited on seeing a tree in bloom during the month of *Nissan*[73] may be said by men and women.[74]

Husbands and wives should reprimand one another when these laws are disregarded between them.

The prohibition against *lashon ha'ra* does not apply when information is being transmitted for the benefit or the safety of the listener. Although the listener may take appropriate action to protect herself from the *possibility* that the information is true, she should not completely believe it. See *Hilkhoth Rekhiluth* 6:7 and 7:5. At the end of Chapter 9 of *Hilkhoth Rekhiluth*, the *Chafetz Chayim* discusses the laws of *lashon ha'ra* in the context of acquiring information necessary when considering a marriage possibility or a business transaction.

72. A condensed adaptation of this work, *Guard Your Tongue*, by R. Zelig Pliskin, is available in English.

73. Tractate *Rosh HaShanah* 11a: "Rav Yehudah said that a person who goes out in the days of *Nissan* and sees trees in bloom should recite the blessing, *Barukh...she'lo chaseir b'olamo klum u'varah vo beriyoth tovoth v'ilanoth tovoth l'hithanoth ba'hem b'ney adam* (Blessed...Who lacks nothing in His world and created in it good creatures and good trees for the benefit of man). The laws concerning this blessing may be found in the *Shulchan Arukh* 226.

74. *Har Tzvi, Orach Chayim*, No. 118. Although *Halakhoth Ketanoth*, Vol. 2, No. 28, rules that the blessing may only be recited during the month of *Nissan*, it is not considered time-bound because the time limits imposed on its recitation are a function of an empirical event — the blooming of trees. This is similar to the *Turey Evven's* explanation of why women are obligated in the *mitzvah* of *Bikkurim* (bringing first fruits to the *Beith HaMikdash*) although it can only be fulfilled between *Shavuoth* and *Chanukah*. There, too, the time factor is a function of the growing season and not intrinsic to the *mitzvah.* See the Introduction, note 7, Chapter 17, note 7, and *Tzitz Eliezer*, Vol. 12, No. 20:5.

Blessing Over the Sun

44. Most halakhic authorities consider the blessing over the sun (*Birkath HaChamah*) to be a time-bound *mitzvah* from which women are exempt.[75] In practice, many authorities permit women to recite it.[76] Some do not.[77] The latter advise women to recite the blessing without *shem* and *malkhuth* or to listen to a man recite it.[78]

Birkath HaGomel

45. A special blessing, which thanks God for His help, is

---

75. *Birkath HaChamah* is a blessing said over the sun when it returns to its original position in the heavens at the time of its creation. This happens when the sun appears on the morning following the vernal equinox which has occurred at 6:00 PM on Tuesday evening, an event which occurs once every twenty-eight years. The blessing, *Barukh...o'seh ma'aseh bereshith* (Blessed...Who performs works of creation), was last recited on April 8, 1981. For a detailed analysis of the scientific and philosophical background of this *mitzvah*, see the ArtScroll Mesorah Series, *Birkath HaChamah*.

76. The *Chatham Sofer, Orach Chayim*, No. 56, does not understand why women refrain from reciting this blessing. See also *Kethav Sofer, Orach Chayim*, No. 34. *Birur Halakhah* 229 cites *Maharil Diskin*, who maintains that *Birkath HaChamah* is not a time-bound *mitzvah*, and that women are obligated to recite it.

   The argument against classifying *Birkath HaChamah* as a time-bound *mitzvah* is similar to the argument concerning the blessing over a tree in bloom discussed in note 74. The time factor — the event's occurrence once in twenty-eight years — is irrelevant.

   The Lubavitcher Rebbe writes in *Teshuvoth U'Biurim* (5743), "It is our practice for women to recite this blessing with the rest of the congregation. Of course, men and women should stand separately during its recitation."

77. *Kaf HaChayim* 229:8.

78. *Ibid.*; *Ben Ish Chai, Shanah Rishonah, Parshath Ekev* 19. The *Ben Ish Chai* reports that in the year 5657 (1897), he personally recited the blessing on behalf of the assembled women of his community.

recited when a person escapes danger.[79] Many authorities report that it is not customary for women to recite it because it is normally recited in the presence of ten men.[80] If possible, it is appropriate for a woman to recite it in the women's section of the synagogue at a time when ten men can hear her from the men's section, or invite ten men to her home to hear it.[81] If neither possibility is practical, she may recite the blessing in the presence of nine other women and one man.[82] If this is also impractical, she may recite the blessing by herself without *shem* and *malkhuth*.[83]

46. A father may not recite *Birkath HaGomel* over his daughter's deliverance from danger.[84] It is questionable whether a husband may recite it over a wife's deliverance.[85] If

---

79. *Barukh...ha'gomel l'chayavim tovoth sheg'malani kol tov* (Blessed... Who rewards the undeserving with goodness and Who has rewarded me with all manner of good). A person recites this blessing after recovering from an illness, crossing the sea or a desert, or being freed from captivity. Details regarding its recitation may be found in the *Shulchan Arukh* 219.

80. *Mishnah Berurah* 219:3, citing the *Halakhoth Ketanoth*, Vol. 2, No. 161. The *Magen Avraham* adds that *Birkath HaGomel* is voluntary.

81. The *Kaf HaChayim* 219:3 urges women to take this blessing seriously and arrange to recite it in the presence of ten men. See also the *Kitzur Shulchan Arukh* 65:2 and *Siddur Ya'avetz*, p. 274.

82. *Mishnah Berurah, Ibid.*, citing the *K'neseth HaGedolah*. The *K'neseth HaGedolah* maintains that reciting the blessing in the presence of ten people publicizes that person's deliverance from danger. Thus, there is no need for a formal *minyan* of ten men. It is unclear why the *K'neseth HaGedolah* requires that one of the ten be a man. See also the *Chaye Adam* 65:16.

To the contrary, the *Kaf HaChayim* infers that those authorities who require ten Jews for *Birkath HaGomel* would insist that they qualify for a *minyan*, i.e., that they be males. For this reason, the *Kaf HaChayim* prefers the solution cited in note 81.

83. *Ben Ish Chai, Shanah Rishonah, Parshath Ekev* 5.

84. This is based on a ruling of HaGaon Rav Ben Zion Abba Shaul.

85. The *Remah* 219:4 permits a person to recite *Birkath HaGomel* over

the man's wife is present, some authorities permit him to say, *Barukh...sheg'maleikh kol tov* (Who has rewarded *you* with all manner of good). His wife should answer *amein* to his blessing. If she is not present, the same authorities suggest that he conclude the blessing with the words *she'gamal l'ishti kol tov* (Who has rewarded my wife with all manner of good).[86]

Blessings After Childbirth

47. Women are required to recite *Birkath HaGomel* after recuperating from childbirth.[87] At least seven days should

---

the deliverance of a friend from danger. The *Biur Halakhah*, beginning *V'ein zeh*, cites the *Eliyahu Rabbah* and the *Magen Avraham*, who question this ruling and limit its application to a son or a student who may recite the blessing when a father or teacher is delivered from danger. The *Biur Halakhah* then cites another ruling of the *Eliyahu Rabbah* — just as a son may recite the blessing over his father's deliverance, a husband may recite it over his wife's deliverance. But the *Biur Halakhah* questions the analogy and remains undecided.

86. The *Mishnah Berurah* 219:6 reports this custom in the name of the *Magen Avraham*. It is based on the view of the *Eliyahu Rabbah* cited in note 85. As noted there, the *Biur Halakhah* questions the *Eliyahu Rabbah*'s ruling. He prefers that women recite the blessing themselves.

87. *Beith Yosef* 219, citing the *K'neseth HaGedolah*. Other authorities put forward arguments exempting women from *Birkath HaGomel* after childbirth. One such authority points to the word "undeserving" in the blessing, contending that a woman who has weakened herself to fulfill the great *mitzvah* of bringing new life into the world cannot refer to herself as "undeserving"! See *Mateh Levi*, Vol. 2, No. 18.

Har Tzvi, Orach Chayim, No. 163, adds that since the woman's "sickness" stems from a natural occurrence, not from disease, the blessing may be inappropriate.

Ye'chaveh Da'ath, Vol. 4, No.14–15, refutes all these arguments and concludes, "It is proper to adopt the view of the *K'neseth HaGedolah* and recite the blessing." This is also the conclusion of

pass before the blessing is recited.[88]

In Jerusalem, it is customary to hold Saturday night services in the new mother's home so that she may recite the blessing.[89]

48. When a woman is informed that she has given birth to a boy, she recites the blessing *Barukh...ha'tov v'ha'mei'tiv* (Who is good and does good for others) with *shem* and *malkhuth*, even if she has not seen her new son yet and she has given birth to other boys. This blessing is also recited by the father. If she did not recite the blessing shortly after the birth, she may recite it later.[90]

The blessing *Hatov v'ha'mei'tiv* is not recited over the birth of a girl. When a father first sees his new daughter, he recites *She'he'che'yanu*. No blessing is recited by the mother.[91]

---

the *Chidda*, in *Birkey Yosef*, and the *Ben Ish Chai, Shanah Rishonah, Parshath Ekev* 5.

88. *Kaf HaChayim* 219:7. This is also the view of HaGaon Rav Yosef Chayim Sonnenfeld in *Salmath Chayim*, No. 51. The *Shulchan Arukh* 219:6 and *Mishnah Berurah* 219:19 explain that although the blessing should be said as soon as possible, it may also be said any time later.

89. *Ke'tzoth HaShulchan*, Vol. 2, No. 65:2; *Salmath Chayim*, No. 51.

The *Eliyahu Rabbah* describes a different custom. The first time a woman attends the synagogue after giving birth, her husband is called to the Torah. When he says *Barukh HaShem ha'mvo'rakh*, she answers *amein* intending to give thanks to God for the birth of their child. This intention substitutes for *Birkath HaGomel*. A hint of this custom may found in the verse, *Hodu LaShem — barkhu Sh'mo* (Give thanks to God [by] blessing his Name). This suggestion is also offered by *Torath Chayim*, Tractate *Sanhedrin* 94a.

90. *Shulchan Arukh* 223:1, and *Mishnah Berurah*. See also the *Sha'ar HaTziyun* 223:3.

91. *Mishnah Berurah* 223:2. The *Kaf HaChayim* 223:6 and the *Ben Ish Chai, Shanah Rishonah, Parshath Ekev* 8, mention authorities who rule it is no longer customary to recite blessings on these occasions. The *Remah* 223:1 also writes, "It has become customary to be lenient with regard to these blessings because they are not obligatory."

49. If food or drink is brought to a woman immediately after she gives birth, she should wash her hands, or at least clean them, before reciting the appropriate blessing.[92]

Naming a Daughter

50. There are various customs regarding the proper time to name a daughter. These include naming her on the first *Shabbath* after her birth, waiting at least five days after her birth, and naming her at the first Torah reading after her birth.[93]

Blessing Over a Miracle

51. A person who experienced a miracle recites a blessing on returning to the place where the miracle occurred. A woman does not recite the blessing where a miracle happened to her husband, nor does a man recite the blessing where a miracle happened to his wife.

---

92. HaGaon Rav Yosef Sholom Eliashiv explains that there is nothing wrong with a mother reciting a blessing in the delivery room as long as the lower part of her body is covered, and the room is clean. Even if she cannot clean her hands or recite the blessing, if she needs to drink, she should.

93. *Minchath Yitzchak*, Vol. 4, No. 107, concluding, "Each community should follow its established custom."

Ta'amey HaMinhagim, Kuntres Acharon, Inyaney Milah, notes, "When a daughter is named, it is a *mitzvah* to make a festive meal; a person's soul comes down from the higher worlds when the name is given."

See *Iggeroth Moshe, Orach Chayim* Vol. 4, No. 67, for the exact language of the *mi she'beirakh* that is said when naming a girl.

The custom of Lubavitch is to add the words, "May she grow for Torah, *chupah*, and good deeds," just as for a boy. (See *Teshuvoth U'Biurim* (5743), No. 49.) Although not commanded to study Torah, Tractate *Berakhoth* 17a explains that women receive a reward equal

Children and grandchildren do recite the blessing where a miracle happened to a mother or grandmother.[94]

Reciting One Hundred Blessings Every Day

52. A man is obligated to recite one hundred blessings every day.[95] Since many of the daily blessings that typically make up this number are not applicable to women, it appears that they are not obligated to do so.[96]

---

to their husbands' and children's for encouraging them to study.
94. *Biur Halakhah* 218, beginning *V'kol.*
95. *Shulchan Arukh, Orach Chayim* 46:3.
96. *Shevet HaLevi*, Vol. 5, No. 23.

נ׳

CHAPTER 15
Shabbath

Preparing for Shabbath

1. Even those authorities who maintain that the *mitzvoth* of *Kavod* and *Oneg Shabbath* (Honoring and Enjoying *Shabbath*) are Rabbinic in origin[1] stress that they must be observed meticulously. Conscientious observance of these *mitzvoth* merits great reward.[2]

---

1. *Rambam, Hilkhoth Shabbath* 30:1: "There are two [*mitzvoth*] of the Scribes that have been explained by the Prophets...*Kavod* and *Oneg*." The *Rambam*'s view runs counter to those who maintain that *Kavod* and *Oneg* can be traced to Biblical sources. See *Sefer HaChinukh* 297, *Beith Yosef* 487, and the *Ramban*'s commentary on *VaYikra* 23:3.

2. *Mishnah Berurah* 242:1, and *Sha'ar HaTziyun.* As the *Shulchan Arukh HaRav* 242:1 points out, "The *mitzvoth* of the Scribes are more stringent than those of the Torah, and their reward is guaranteed by the Prophets. As it states, 'Then you shall delight in the Lord, and I will cause you to ride on the high places of the earth and feed you with the heritage of Yaacov, your father' (*Yesha'yahu* 58:14). Our Sages have said that a person who delights in *Shabbath* is rewarded with a limitless inheritance, saved from the oppression of

A woman who has many maids and servants should still personally prepare something in honor of *Shabbath*.[3]

2. It is best to purchase and prepare food for *Shabbath* on Friday morning.[4] If time does not permit, food may be purchased and prepared in advance.[5]

---

the Exile, and merits wealth." Rabbenu Yona, in *Sha'arey Teshuvah, Sha'ar Shlishi*, explains how the words of the Scribes are more stringent than the words of the Torah.

3. *Shulchan Arukh* 250:1. Tractate *Shabbath* 117a and *Kiddushin* 41a report that many great Sages involved themselves in *Shabbath* preparations. Rav Chisda would chop vegetables, Rabba and Rav Yosef would chop wood, Rav Zera would kindle the fire, and Rav Nachman would clean the house and prepare the dishes to be eaten on *Shabbath*. The *Shulchan Arukh* 250:1 advises, "Everyone should learn from them and not say, 'How can I degrade myself?' Whoever honors *Shabbath* is truly honored."

The *Mishnah Berurah*, citing the *Magen Avraham*, adds, "Especially on short [winter] Fridays, when *Shabbath* is near, all members of the family must lend a helping hand. I have seen men of great deeds and Torah giants sweep the floors on short Friday afternoons to avoid desecrating *Shabbath*. This is an actual obligation for everyone."

4. *Shulchan Arukh* 250:1: "A person should arise early [on Friday] to begin *Shabbath* preparations." Tractate *Shabbath* 117b traces this to the verse, "And God said to Moshe, 'Behold I will rain down for you bread from the heavens. And it shall be on Friday and they shall prepared what they will bring" (*Shemoth* 16:4–5). The *Netziv*, in his commentary *Ha'amek Davar*, and the *Malbim* understand the verse as emphasizing that *Shabbath* preparations should be carried out on Friday. The verse continues, "And they gathered it [the manna] each and every *morning*", indicating that the gathering on Friday, in preparation for *Shabbath*, was carried out in the morning.

The *Mishnah Berurah* 250:4 adds that shopping for *Shabbath* is permitted before Friday morning prayers if it will be difficult to shop afterwards. Although men and women are forbidden to attend to personal matters before praying (*Shulchan Arukh* 89), the needs of *Shabbath* are not considered to be personal. If shopping must be done early, *Shema* and the morning blessings should be recited first.

5. *Mishnah Berurah* 250:2. Some dishes must be prepared in advance,

When purchasing and preparing food for *Shabbath*, it is a good practice to state, "This is *le'kavod Shabbath* (in honor of *Shabbath*)."[6]

3. Ezra enacted that laundry should be done on Thursday.[7] This enactment can be assumed to apply today, in spite of the use of washing machines and driers.[8]

---

especially during the winter when Fridays are very short.

Tractate *Betzah* 16a notes the practices of *Shamai HaZaken* and *Hillel HaZaken*. Whenever *Shamai* came upon a choice food, he would set it aside for *Shabbath*. Later in the week, if he found something better, he would set that food aside for *Shabbath* and eat the first food. *Hillel*, however, would not set aside any food in advance. He had perfect trust that God would help him find something choice on Friday. Because their level of trust in God is not as perfect as *Hillel*'s, *Shamai*'s practice is recommended for most people.

The *Mishnah Berurah* 250:2 explains that *Shamai*'s practice should only be applied to food items that may not be found later in the week. Readily available items should be purchased as close to *Shabbath* as possible, preferably on Friday.

6. The *Mishnah Berurah*, *Ibid.*, citing the *Magen Avraham*, points out that verbalizations help to sanctify objects.

7. *Shulchan Arukh* 242. This is one of Ezra's Ten Enactments, cited in Tractate *Bava Kama* 82a. The *Magen Avraham* explains that Ezra wanted to ensure that people would have enough time on Friday to prepare for *Shabbath*. The *Mishnah Berurah* 242:5 cites the *Eliyahu Rabbah* and others, who argue that the purpose of the enactment was simply to ensure that people would have clean clothes for *Shabbath*. Although *Shabbath* preparations should be done on Friday, Ezra *permitted* laundering on Thursday so people would have time on Friday for other preparations. According to the *Magen Avraham*, laundry should not be done on Friday. According to the *Eliyahu Rabbah*, laundry should actually be done on Friday, but it may also be done earlier in the week, as close to *Shabbath* as possible.

8. Even today time must be devoted to washing, folding, and ironing.

The Law does not require taking laundry in from the line before *Shabbath*. Hanging clothes on the line during *Shabbath* is forbidden

4. Some authorities rule that a husband may fulfill his obligation to prepare for *Shabbath* through his wife,[9] but there is greater reward in performing a *mitzvah* oneself than performing it through an agent.[10]

Time may be taken from Torah study to participate in *Shabbath* preparations.[11]

5. No effort should be spared in preparing for *Shabbath*. It is said that perspiration from the exertion of preparing for *Shabbath* can wipe away one's sins as much as tears of repentance.[12]

---

because onlookers might suspect that laundry is being done on *Shabbath*. Laundry that was hanging on the line before *Shabbath* would not be looked at with the same suspicion.

Clothes that were damp at the beginning of *Shabbath*, but not actually wet, may be taken in off the line after they are dry, if they are needed. See *Shemirath Shabbath KeHilkhethah* 15:9.

Imrey Yosher reports that the *Chazon Ish* was not pleased with the practice of leaving laundry on the line on *Shabbath*. In our lax generation people may draw the wrong conclusion, and hang laundry out on *Shabbath*.

9. *Orukh HaShulchan* 250:4: "Our wives do all the *Shabbath* preparations themselves and a man's wife is as himself."

10. *Shulchan Arukh* 250:1: "Even one who has many servants should make an effort to prepare something in honor of *Shabbath*." Although the *Mishnah Berurah* 250:3 expresses this in terms of a preference, in the *Biur Halakhah* he cites the *Rambam*, who describes it as an obligation.

11. The *Sha'ar HaTziyun* 250:9 explains that since *Kavod Shabbath* entails personal involvement, time may be taken from Torah study to fulfill it because it is a *mitzvah* that cannot be performed by others. Although the *Ketzoth HaShulchan*, citing the *Shulchan Arukh HaRav*, states that a man should only take off minimal time for *Shabbath* preparations, for example, time enough to prepare one dish, the *Sha'ar HaTziyun* indicates that he should become fully involved, even at the expense of Torah study.

12. Cited in *Sha'arey Teshuvah* 250:2. The same is also said of perspiration caused by the exertion of baking *matzoth* for *Pessach*.

Even if preparations were completed in advance, it is proper to prepare some small item just before *Shabbath*.[13]

6. It is proper for women to bake loaves of bread on Friday[14] and fulfill the *mitzvah* of separating *Challah*.[15] (See Chapter 13 for a discussion of this *mitzvah*.)

7. Tasting the dishes that have been prepared for *Shabbath* on Friday is a *mitzvah*.[16] After tasting a meat dish without swallowing any of it, it is not necessary to wait before dairy.[17]

---

13. *Magen Avraham*, cited in the *Mishnah Berurah* 250:2. This final preparation is hinted at in the verse, *Ve'hayah mishneh* (It [the portion of manna] shall be double [on Friday]), which can also be read, "It shall be a second time," meaning they should prepare again.

14. *Remah* 242, based on the *Yerushalmi*, *Megillah*, Chapter 2. The *Biur Halakhah*, beginning *V'hu mi'kavod Shabbath*, expands: "A hint of this is found in the verse, 'And it shall be on the sixth day and they shall prepare what they shall bring; that which you [need to] bake you shall bake...'(*Shemoth* 16:23), indicating that one should bake on Friday for *Shabbath*. In Talmudic times this was an established custom... But due to the multitude of our sins, today many women have stopped this practice, and they buy from the baker. This is not proper, for by doing so they diminish the honor of *Shabbath*."

15. *Mishnah Berurah* 242:6. The *mitzvah* of separating *Challah* is primarily a woman's *mitzvah*, because it serves to rectify Eve's sin, which took place on *Erev Shabbath*.

16. *Mishnah Berurah* 250:2. If one intends to swallow any amount of food, a blessing should be recited first. The ruling of the *Shulchan Arukh* 210:2, exempting one who tastes up to a *kezayith* of solid food or up to a *revi'ith* of liquids from reciting a blessing, only applies when someone is cooking, and the tasting is only to determine if enough spice has been added, not for pleasure. When a person intends to derive pleasure from tasting food, a blessing is required for any amount which is to be swallowed. Indeed, it is preferable to intend to take pleasure from tasting food (and recite a blessing), even when the main purpose is to determine the amount of spice to add.

17. *Kaf HaChayim*, *Yoreh De'ah* 89:4, based on the *Shulchan Arukh*;

When the fast of the Tenth of *Teveth* falls on Friday, *Shabbath* food may be tasted without swallowing.[18]

It is certainly a *mitzvah* to taste all the dishes served on *Shabbath* itself.[19]

Washing and Shampooing for Shabbath

8. Bathing on Friday in honor of *Shabbath* is a *mitzvah*.[20] During the winter, when Fridays are short, a woman may bathe on Thursday,[21] but she should still wash her hands and face with hot water on Friday afternoon.[22]

A person is cautioned to leave enough time for bathing to avoid any possible transgression of the laws of *Shabbath*.[23]

Darkey Teshuvah 89:10. This only applies when the food is not chewed. The mouth should be washed out before eating dairy.

18. See the *Mishnah Berurah* 567:6.

19. *Mishnah Berurah* 250:2. Some find a hint of this practice in the phrase from the *Mussaf* prayer, *to'ame'ha chayim zakhu* (those who taste [from] it merit to life).

20. *Mishnah Berurah* 260:2.

21. *Mishnah Berurah* 260:5. Citing the *Maharshal, Eliyahu Rabbah* and others, the *Mishnah Berurah* explains that bathing on Thursday does not fully express the honor of *Shabbath* if it can just as easily be done on Friday.

22. *Mishnah Berurah* 260:2. Although the *Shulchan Arukh* 260:1 includes washing the feet, this does not apply in modern times when people no longer walk barefoot. See the *Biur Halakhah*, beginning *B'chamin*, for a discussion of whether lukewarm water is sufficient for *kavod Shabbath*. Washing with cold water definitely does not fulfill the *mitzvah*.

23. The *Mishnah Berurah* 260:1 explains, "A person must be on guard not to desecrate *Shabbath* when bathing. In our multitude of sins, many people stumble during the short winter days when they bathe just before *Shabbath* begins. Even if a bath is completed on time, it is still possible to transgress by combing the hair on *Shabbath*, which is prohibited by the Torah, or by wringing out a wet towel, which is considered laundering on *Shabbath* [and also prohibited by the

9. It is preferable, time permitting, to get hair cut on Friday. Shampooing the hair and cutting the fingernails on Friday is a *mitzvah*.[24]

Torah]...It is fitting for all those whose hearts have been imbued with fear of Heaven to stop people from acting in this manner...The saying of our Sages, 'Anyone who is capable of objecting and does not is held responsible for the transgression', is well known."

24. *Shulchan Arukh* 260:1. The *Biur Halakhah*, beginning *LaChof*, notes that authorities do not explicitly state that shampooing must be done with hot water.

The *Remah* 260:1, and the *Mishnah Berurah* 260:6, cite a number of laws and customs concerning cutting fingernails:

Fingernails and toenails should not be cut on the same day. Toenails should preferably be cut on Thursday, fingernails on Friday.

The fingernails should be cut in the following order: On the right hand, the nail of the second, and then the nails of the fourth, first, third and fifth fingers. On the left hand, the nail of the fourth, and then the nails of the second, fifth, third, and first fingers.

Some authorities discourage cutting fingernails on Thursday because they will begin to grow on *Shabbath*, which is inconsistent with the honor of *Shabbath*. The *Taz* recommends for this reason that a person refrain from getting the hair cut on Thursday. To the contrary, the *Pri Megadim*, in *Mishbetzoth Zahav*, cites the *Tosafoth Shabbath*, par. 3, who maintains that hair begins to grow immediately after it is cut. Moreover, it is explicitly stated in the *Mishnah*, *Ta'anith* 2:7, that hair may be cut on Thursday. It is known that the *Ari* was not particular about cutting hair or fingernails on Thursday.

Tractate *Niddah* 17a states that a person who burns fingernail cuttings is a *chasid* (pious person), while one who buries them is a *tzaddik* (righteous person). One who throws them where people may walk over them is a *rasha* (wicked person). The *Ba'er Heytev* explains, "Before his sin, *Adam HaRishon*'s entire body was clothed in nail. When he sinned, he shed this 'garment', and the nail remained only on his fingertips. It is feared that a woman who walks over fingernail cuttings might arouse Heavenly wrath and be punished. If she is pregnant, she may, God Forbid, abort."

The Talmud explains that fingernail cuttings only cause harm in the place where they were thrown. After they have been swept away

Special Preparations

10. Among the preparations that must be completed before *Shabbath* are:

a) In *Eretz Yisrael*, separating *terumoth* and *ma'asroth* from all produce to be eaten on *Shabbath*.[25]

b) Separating *Challah* from all breads and cakes that require separation.

c) Opening all cans, food bags, and ring bottle caps.[26]

d) Preparing all foods whose preparation is forbidden on *Shabbath*, for example, jello or techinah.[27]

e) Unscrewing bulbs which turn on when the refrigerator door is opened.[28]

f) Covering the flame on the stove.[29]

11. The table should be set and the house arranged before the men return from the synagogue.[30] Some authorities

---

or moved to another place, there is no longer reason to fear.
The hands should be washed after cutting the fingernails or hair.

25. *Terumoth* and *ma'asroth* may not be separated on *Shabbath*. Regarding the separation of *terumoth* and *ma'asaroth* during twilight, the rule is the same as for *Challah*. See Chapter 13, paragraphs 20 and 21, and note 30.

26. For details, see *Shemirath Shabbath KeHilkhethah*, Chapter 9.

27. This is based on the prohibition against kneading on *Shabbath*. It is forbidden to form a thick batter (the first dilution of the techinah mix), even if it will be thinned with more water later. The prohibition applies to the preparation of all powdered mixes that thicken when water is added. For further details, see *Shemirath Shabbath KeHilkhethah*, Chapter 8.

28. See *Shemirath Shabbath Kehilkhethah*, Chapter 1.

29. *Ibid.*

30. *Shulchan Arukh* 262:1. The source is cited in the *Mishnah Berurah* 262:3: "*Chazal* relate that two angels accompany a man home from the synagogue on Friday night, a good angel and a bad one. When he arrives home and finds the candles lit, the table set, and the beds made, the good angel proclaims, 'May it be God's Will that [the

maintain that the *mitzvah* of setting the *Shabbath* table should be performed by the woman of the house.[31] It is proper to cover all the tables in the house in honor of *Shabbath.* Tables in the dining room should certainly be covered.[32]

12. It is debatable whether women are obligated in the *mitzvah* of *Tosafoth Shabbath*[33] (Bringing *Shabbath* in early).[34]

13. Women are exempt from the *mitzvah* to review the Portion of the Week, which consists of reading the text twice and the *Targum* (Aramaic translation of Onkelos) once.[35]

---

house should be so arranged] next week.'"

31. *Kaf HaChayim* 262:1. See Chapter 23, note 41, concerning setting the table for the *Pessach Seder.*

Citing the *Ben Ish Chai,* the *Kaf HaChayim* comments, "After covering the *challoth,* she should place both hands on the table and recite the verse, 'And he spoke to me [saying], this is the table that is before God.' This will cause the *Shekhinah* (Divine Presence) to rest on the table."

32. *Shulchan Arukh* 262:1, and *Biur Halakhah.* The *Mishnah Berurah* 262:4 notes that some people cover the table with two tablecloths; if one is removed, or falls off, the table will still be covered.

33. *Pri Megadim, Mishbetzoth Zahav* 291:6. Also see the *Kaf HaChayim* 261:16. The *Mishnah Berurah* 261:22 explains that this *mitzvah* is fulfilled by accepting *Shabbath* at least ten minutes before sunset.

34. *Kethav Sofer, Orach Chayim,* Nos. 56 and 104; *Sefath Emeth* on Tractate *Rosh HaShanah* 9a; *Minchath Chinukh* 317; *Orchoth Chayim* (Sphinka) 261:4; *Az Nid'biru,* Vol. 1, No. 2. The debate stems from *Tosafoth, Kethuboth* 47a. It is based in the question of whether the *mitzvah* of *Tosafoth Shabbath* is an integral part of the *mitzvoth* of *Shabbath.* If it is, women are obligated to fulfill it, as with all the *mitzvoth* of *Shabbath.* If it is a discrete *mitzvah,* women are exempt because it is time-bound.

35. *Mishneh Halakhoth,* Vol. 6, No. 60, cites authorities who link this *mitzvah* to the *mitzvah* of Torah study. See Chapter 9.

Candle-Lighting

14. Lighting candles on late Friday afternoon, which will burn into Friday evening, is a *mitzvah*.[36] Although both men and women are obligated to light candles,[37] the woman of the house lights on behalf of the family. Because their principle work is in the home, and they are primarily responsible for its care, women were chosen to perform this *mitzvah*.[38] They

---

36. *Shulchan Arukh* 263:2, and *Mishnah Berurah*. Three reasons are given for the *mitzvah* of Candle-lighting: Light maintains family harmony by helping people to avoid accidents in the dark; lighting candles in the dining room honors *Shabbath*; and, dining by the light of the candles increases the diner's enjoyment of the food, fulfilling *Oneg Shabbath*.

That the *mitzvah* of Candle-lighting is connected to both *Kavod* and *Oneg Shabbath* can seen from the *Rambam*'s discussion of these *mitzvoth*. In *Hilkhoth Shabbath* 5:1, he states, "Men and women are obligated to have a candle burning in their homes on *Shabbath*...This is included in the *mitzvah* to enjoy *Shabbath* (*Oneg Shabbath*)." In *Hilkhoth Shabbath* 30:2–5, he discusses the *mitzvah* of *Kavod Shabbath*: "How is the *mitzvah* of honoring *Shabbath*[fulfilled]? The Sages have said that it is a *mitzvah* for a person to bathe...in hot water on Friday in honor of *Shabbath*...The table should be set, *candles lit*, and the beds made... All these things express the honor of *Shabbath*."

It is evident from the *Rambam*'s words that two *mitzvoth* are fulfilled through the *Shabbath* candles: Lighting candles before *Shabbath* is part of *Kavod Shabbath*, while having them burn on *Shabbath* is part of *Oneg Shabbath*. In general, *Oneg Shabbath* is fulfilled by enjoying *Shabbath* on *Shabbath* and *Kavod Shabbath* is fulfilled through actions done in anticipation of *Shabbath*. See the *Beith HaLevi*, Vol. 1, No. 11, and the novellae of HaGaon Rav Chayim of Brisk (stensil) in the name of HaGaon Rav Yitzchak Ze'ev Soloveitchik.

According to those authorities who maintain that the *mitzvoth* of *Kavod* and *Oneg* are prescribed by Torah Law, candle-lighting is part of both Torah obligations. See the *Sha'ar HaTziyun* 242:1 and the *Eliyahu Rabbah* 671:2.

37. *Shulchan Arukh* 263:2.

38. *Shulchan Arukh* 263:3.

were also chosen because lighting candles rectifies Eve's sin, which caused "the light of the world" to be extinguished.[39] Husbands participate in the *mitzvah* by preparing the wicks and singeing them.[40]

15. If necessary, a person must go to extremes, even to the point of begging door-to-door, or selling personal clothing, to obtain money to purchase at least one candle for *Shabbath*.[41] Purchasing a *Shabbath* candle takes precedence over all other household needs, except buying bread for the first two *Shabbath* meals, because bread is used to fulfill two

---

39. *Mishnah Berurah* 263:12. This refers to the tradition that death came to the world as a result of Adam's sin. Adam is referred to as the "light of the world"; by bringing him to sin, Eve caused this "light" to be extinguished. By fulfilling the *mitzvah* of lighting *Shabbath* candles, a woman helps to rectify this sin.

40. *Ibid.* The *Mishnah Berurah* 264:28 explains that singeing the wicks ensures the candles will light quickly. In Tractate *Shabbath* 29a, *Tosafoth* states that it is customary for men to prepare the wicks. The *Shulchan Arukh HaRav* 264:14, however, finds evidence from the *Tur*, and the *Rosh* on Tractate *Shabbath* 2:18, that women should singe the wicks.

Some commentators find evidence that the husband prepares the wicks in the *Mishnah, Shabbath* 2:7: "Friday afternoon, towards evening, a husband must say three things to his household — 'Have you separated *ma'asroth*? Have you set up the *eiruv*? Kindle the [*Shabbath*] lights.'" The seemingly unnecessary request to kindle the lights may signify that the husband is telling his wife, "I have finished preparing the wicks, and you may now kindle them." See the commentary of Rabbi Akiva Eiger on the *Mishnah*.

Imrey Yosher, citing the halakhic decisions of the *Chazon Ish*, par. 14, mentions that since the candles we use today burn efficiently, there is no need to singe them. According to the *Chazon Ish*, a husband participates in the *mitzvah* by placing the candles in the candlesticks. The *Mishnah Berurah* 264:28 indicates, to the contrary, that our candles should also be singed.

41. *Shulchan Arukh* 263:3, *Mishnah Berurah* and *Biur Halakhah*.

mitzvoth, Kiddush and *Oneg Shabbath.*[42]

16. Although lights should be lit in any dark room that might be used on Friday night,[43] the primary *mitzvah* is fulfilled with candles lit in the dining room.[44]

17. Since it is the woman's right to perform the *mitzvah* on behalf of the family,[45] she may, if necessary, appoint an agent to light for her, which is considered as if she herself lit.[46]

A husband who wishes to participate in the *mitzvah* may light extra candles in the dining room or in another room, but he may not recite the blessing.[47]

---

42. *Shulchan Arukh* 263:2-3, and *Mishnah Berurah.*

43. *Mishnah Berurah* 263:2. One purpose of the *mitzvah* of Candle-lighting is to preserve family harmony. (See note 36.) Lights should therefore be lit in any room in which a person might stumble. A hall or bathroom light that beams into a room so that people can find their way in the dark performs the same function.

44. *Remah* 263:10, and *Mishnah Berurah.*

45. *Mishnah Berurah* 263:11. A woman's performance of the *mitzvah* takes precedence even if her husband wishes to light. The rest of the family fulfills its obligations through her. If both parents are away from home, one of the girls should light, even if there are boys at home. If the mother is away, the father should light even if his daughters beyond *bath mitzvah* age are at home. See the journal *Ohr Torah*, p. 486. If only boys are at home, one of them is required to light. Concerning a blind woman, see *Kitzur Shulchan Arukh* 75:13.

It is worthwhile to bring to mind the cautionary words of the *Mishnah Berurah* 262:11: "When a husband sees that the time is late, it is a great *mitzvah* for him to light candles even if his wife strongly objects. It is better to sit in the dark than desecrate *Shabbath*, God Forbid."

46. *HaElef LeKhah Shlomoh, Orach Chayim*, No. 110.

47. *Shulchan Arukh* 263:6; *Mishnah Berurah* 263:11 and 31; *Shulchan Arukh HaRav* 263:5. *Az Nid'biru*, Vol. 3, No. 3, advises this husband to listen to his wife's blessing and then light in other rooms. Even if he does not listen to her blessing, he may not recite a blessing when he lights. See also *Ye'chaveh Da'ath*, Vol. 2, No. 32.

A Woman Away from Home

18. A man whose wife is away lights *Shabbath* candles at home.[48] It is customary for her to light wherever she is. She should have intention not to fulfill the *mitzvah* through anyone's lighting but her own.[49]

19. A woman who is a *niddah* lights candles and recites the blessing. Some authorities report that a husband should light on the first *Shabbath* after his wife has given birth.[50] Some Sephardic authorities rule that if his wife is home on that *Shabbath* she should light,[51] and this appears to be the custom among many Ashkenazic women as well.[52]

---

48. This applies even when there are grown daughters at home. See note 45.
49. *Tehillah LeDavid* 263:7. For this reason, it is customary for a guest to light her own candles. Since she could fulfill the *mitzvah* through her hostess (See the *Shulchan Arukh HaRav* 263:15 and *Kuntres Acharon.*), she should specifically have in mind to fulfill it only with her own lighting. See paragraph 23.
50. *Mishnah Berurah* 263:11, citing the *She'lah*. The *Mishnah Berurah* indicates that she does not light even if she is home for the first *Shabbath*. *Mateh Ephrayim* 599:9 reports this also to be the custom when *Yom Tov* occurs in the first week after a woman has given birth. But the *Ba'er Heytev* 599:3 cites the opinion of the *K'neseth HaGedolah* that a candle should be brought to her bedside so she can light it and recite the blessing.

    The custom of the *She'lah* may be based on the concept referred to in paragraph 13 — women perform the *mitzvah* of Candle-lighting to rectify Eve's sin, which "extinguished the light of the world". By giving birth to a baby, she has "kindled" a new light, the soul of man.
51. *Kaf HaChayim* 263:23.
52. This has been pointed out by HaGaon Rav Shlomo Zalman Auerbach.

Single Girls

20. A single girl who lives at home fulfills the *mitzvah* through her mother.[53] In some families, it is customary for girls over the age of three to light one candle and recite the blessing.[54] Where this is the custom, they should light before their mothers.[55]

A girl under twelve years of age cannot light *Shabbath* or *Yom Tov* candles for her family.

21. A girl living in a dormitory should light *Shabbath* candles in her room, even if candles are lit in the dining room.[56] If a group of girls share a room, they may contribute

---

53. *Mishnah Berurah* 263:33; *Shulchan Arukh HaRav* 263:15.

54. A summary of the Lubavitcher Rebbe's talks, encouraging people to renew the traditional custom for young girls to light *Shabbath* candles from the age at which they begin to speak, is cited in *Likutey Sichoth, Parshath Chaye Sarah*, 5736. The *Orukh HaShulchan* 263:7 writes that even though the whole family fulfills the *mitzvah* through the mother, since it is particularly designed for women, it is customary for single girls to light and recite the blessing. He adds that it is preferable for each girl to light in a separate room. In the journal *Yagdil Torah*, No. 10, p. 72, many reasons for the Lubavitcher Rebbe's ruling that single girls light only one candle are cited. It also states there that no distinction is to be made between *Shabbath* and *Yom Tov*. See also *Teshuvoth U'Biurim*, 5743, No. 75.

55. *Orukh HaShulchan, Ibid.; Az Nid'biru*, Vol. 7, No. 68. If single girls, who could fulfill the *mitzvah* through their mothers, light after their mothers, they will have already fulfilled the *mitzvah*, pre-empting them from reciting the blessing. Also see the pamphlet *Chovereth Neiroth Shabbath*.

Ye'chaveh Da'ath, Vol. 2, No. 32, observes that the custom for single girls to light *Shabbath* candles at home is not prevalent in Sephardic families. The author rules that a single girl may not recite the blessing even if she lights in her room. She may listen to her mother's blessing, answer *amein*, and then light in her room without a blessing.

56. Although the girls all eat together in the dining room, since they

to the cost of candles and designate one girl to light for them. This is the preferred practice for Sephardic girls.[57]

Eating Out

22. When a family intends to eat out and return to sleep at home on Friday night, the mother should light candles before leaving. She should either remain at home until dark and then leave, or light long candles that will burn until the family returns home; it is a *mitzvah* to derive benefit from the light of the *Shabbath* candles on *Shabbath* itself.[58]

If the family must leave home early, and they will not return while the candles are burning, or if they intend to sleep away from home, they should light candles where they eat and/or sleep.

---

sleep in their own rooms, they must light there, with a blessing, so they will not stumble in the dark. See note 63. *Az Nid'biru*, Vol. 5, No. 1, points out that it is preferable for them to light in their rooms before candles are lit in the dining room. If a girl lights in the dining room, *Chovath HaDar*, p. 97, rules that her roomates should not recite the blessing when they light in their room.

57. See paragraph 23, note 59.
58. *Chovath HaDar*, p. 94; *Az Nid'biru*, Vol. 3, No. 3; *Mishneh Halakhoth*, Vol. 5, No. 41. *Chovath HaDar*, p. 88–90, rules that a woman who plans to sleep away should light where she sleeps. If her husband plans to return home and sleep there, he should light at home without a blessing.

 If she plans to return home alone, she should light candles at home with a blessing. Her husband fulfills the *mitzvah* when she lights, even if he does not plan to return with her. See the *Shulchan Arukh* 263:6, and the *Mishnah Berurah*.

When Families Dine Together

23. Some authorities rule that when two or more families dine together on Friday night, and all the women light candles in the same room and recite their own blessings, the blessings have been recited in vain.[59] They recommend that one woman recite the blessing on behalf of all of them, and the others listen and light without a blessing. This is the common practice among many Sephardic women.

The Ashkenazic custom accords with other authorities who permit each woman to recite the blessing, providing that they each light separately.[60] Anyone who cannot afford her own candelabra may share someone else's.[61]

All authorities permit each woman to recite her own blessing if they each light in a separate room. They may light in rooms which are not theirs and which they are not using, as long as some activity related to the meal is carried out by the light of their candles.[62]

24. The rules outlined in the previous paragraph only apply when the women do not eat at the same table or sleep in the same room. Families or single women who are guests and eat with their host are not required to light their own *Shabbath* candles.[63]

---

59. This view is cited in the *Shulchan Arukh* 263:8. Also see the *Mishnah Berurah* 263:35–36.
60. This custom follows the view of the *Remah* 263:8. The *Mishnah Berurah* 263:35 explains that the blessings are not said in vain because extra light adds to the joy and harmony of *Shabbath*. The *Kaf HaChayim* 263:56 reports that certain Sephardic communities follow the *Remah*'s ruling. See also *Eshel Avraham* (Butchach) 263:8.
61. *Mishnah Berurah* 263:37.
62. *Magen Avraham* 263:13 and 263:21; *Shulchan Arukh HaRav* 263:6, 14, and 15; *Mishnah Berurah* 263:29 and 263:38.
63. *Shulchan Arukh HaRav* 263:9. Guests who eat their host's food are considered part of his family. *Chovath HaDar* explains that they

Nevertheless, many women specifically keep in mind not to fulfill the *mitzvah* through their hostess, and they light their own candles. As noted above, many Sephardic women only recite the blessing when they light in separate rooms.

Although families who eat at a restaurant could fulfill the *mitzvah* through the proprietor, it is customary for the woman of each family to light her own candles.[64]

Accepting Shabbath Through Candle-Lighting

25. A woman accepts *Shabbath* when she lights candles[65] unless she stipulates otherwise. This stipulation may only be

---

fulfill their obligations through the hostess even when they eat in different rooms.

The *Shulchan Arukh HaRav* points out that a guest who sleeps alone in a room into which light does not shine is required to light there with a blessing. This is based on the need to avoid accidents. See note 36 and the *Mishnah Berurah* 263:28–30.

64. *Rivevoth Ephrayim*, Vol. 1, No. 183. *Be'er Moshe*, Vol. 1, No. 12, and *Chemdath Tzvi*, No. 19, strongly object to the practice of hotel guests lighting candles and reciting the blessing in the lobby, then eating in the dining room. Since they are not lighting in their rooms or where they eat, the blessing is recited in vain.

HaRav Moshe Sternbuch, writing in the journal *Olam HaTorah*, *Cheshvan*, 5733, rules that women should have in mind not to fulfill the *mitzvah* through the proprietor of the hotel, but light in the dining room instead. This follows the Ashkenazic practice cited in paragraph 23.

R. Dov Eisenberg, in *Guide for the Jewish Woman and Girl*, p. 50, reports the practice of HaGaon Rav Yaacov Kamenetzky when he would stay in a hotel for *Shabbath*. First, he would light the electric light in the bathroom. Then his wife would light candles in the dining room with the intention that her blessing include the electric light. R. Eisenberg further reports that when a guest would light in HaGaon Rav Kamenetzky's dining room, the Rav's wife would light candles in the kitchen.

65. The *Remah* 263:10 explains that Ashkenazic custom follows the view

made in "a time of need",[66] for example, when traveling to a late Friday afternoon wedding,[67] or concluding *mikvah* preparations.[68] Some authorities permit a woman who wishes to drive to the *Kothel HaMa'aravi* for Friday evening services to make a stipulation.[69]

---

of the *Halakhoth Gedoloth*, that women accept *Shabbath* when they light.

The *Biur Halakhah* 263, beginning *Asurim*, cites the *Pri Megadim*'s and *Derekh HaChayim*'s ruling that a woman who thought the hour was late and mistakenly lit candles before the prescribed time is forbidden to do *melakhah* after lighting.

The *Chatham Sofer, Orach Chayim*, No. 65, points out that actions which are permitted during twilight may be performed by a woman after candle-lighting. See, for example, note 78. But the *Shulchan Arukh HaRav* 261:3 rules to the contrary.

66. *Remah, Ibid.*, and *Mishnah Berurah* 263:44. *Har Tzvi*, Vol. 1, No. 139, adds that a woman who needs to do *melakhah* after candle-lighting should not limit her stipulation to that act alone, but intend not to accept *Shabbath* until later.

According to the *Shulchan Arukh HaRav* 263:11, if a woman does not accept *Shabbath* when she lights, her husband should. Otherwise, the blessing, which is not accompanied by an acceptance of *Shabbath*, is said in vain. (See paragraph 44.) Other authorities do not specify such a requirement.

67. *Siddur Derekh HaChayim*. In certain communities it was customary to celebrate the *chupah* late Friday afternoon.

68. For example, if she did not have time to complete preparations which involve *melakhah*. A woman who wishes to travel to the *mikvah* by car may also make a stipulation.

A *hefsek taharah* (See Chapter 12, note 32.) which needs to be carried out on Friday should be completed before candle-lighting. A woman who does not have time available before candle-lighting, and must therefore perform some *melakhah* to complete the *hefsek taharah*, may make a stipulation and complete the *hefsek taharah* after lighting. If completing the *hefsek taharah* does not entail *melakhah*, it may be done after candle-lighting without a stipulation, as long as the sun has not set.

69. *Tzitz Eliezer*, Vol. 10, No. 19, and Vol. 11, No. 21–22. See note 117.

A stipulation need not be verbalized.[70]

26. Once a community accepts *Shabbath*, even before the prescribed time, women are forbidden to perform *melakhah* (categories of work forbidden on *Shabbath*), including the lighting of candles.[71]

A woman's "community" is defined as the synagogue in which her husband normally prays.[72]

27. Although women accept *Shabbath* through candle-lighting, other members of the family are still permitted to do *melakhah*.[73] Similarly, a woman is not required to accept *Shabbath* at the time her husband lights.[74]

---

70. *Remah, Ibid.* The *Pri Megadim* disagrees, arguing that the stipulation should be verbalized. *Chiddushim U'Biurim, Orach Chayim*, Vol. 2, No. 6 states, "It appears from [the *Remah*] that as long as she has in mind the performance of any act that is forbidden on *Shabbath*, even the recitation of the weekday *Minchah Shemoneh Esrey*, she is considered to have made a stipulation."

71. *Iggeroth Moshe, Orach Chayim*, Vol. 3, No. 38, infers from the *Shulchan Arukh* 263:12 that the minority must abide by the majority's decision to begin *Shabbath* early. See also *Mahari Shteiff*, No. 42.

72. *Iggeroth Moshe, Ibid.*, cites the *Mishnah Berurah* 263:51, who rules that the inhabitants of a city in which there are many synagogues are not bound to adopt a uniform practice.

Iggeroth Moshe concludes that a woman is bound by an early acceptance of *Shabbath* in her husband's synagogue only if the early acceptance is to fulfill the *mitzvah* of *Tosafoth Shabbath* or to prevent people from starting *Shabbath* late. If the congregation decides to begin a particular *Shabbath* early for some special reason, it is not considered the "custom of the community", and she is not bound.

73. *Remah* 263:10. *HaElef LeKhah Shlomoh*, No. 110, adds that a woman who appoints an agent to light candles for her is not required to begin *Shabbath* when the agent lights.

74. *Iggeroth Moshe, Orach Chayim*, Vol. 3, No. 38. Even if a husband stipulates that his wife is forbidden to do *melakhah* after he lights,

When a man accepts *Shabbath*[75] earlier than the community does,[76] his wife is not bound to do so; she may light *Shabbath* candles at the normal time.[77]

28. A woman who has lit *Shabbath* candles and accepted *Shabbath* may ask someone who has not yet accepted *Shabbath* to do *melakhah* for her.[78]

29. Although it is not necessary for the whole family to be present when the candles are lit,[79] some authorities advise men not to leave home for the synagogue until their wives have lit candles.[80]

---

the stipulation is invalid, except, perhaps, for *melakhoth* done on his behalf.

A contrary opinion from HaGaon Rav Zalman Nechemyah Goldberg is cited in the journal *Yagdil Torah*, *Teveth* 5737: When a husband lights, his wife is assumed to accept *Shabbath*, unless she stipulates to the contrary. This is so in spite of the fact that he is *not* assumed to accept *Shabbath* when he lights.

75. See the *Shulchan Arukh* 263:10–12, and the *Mishnah Berurah*.

76. This refers to the synagogue he normally attends. See paragraph 26.

77. *Mahari Shteiff*, No. 42.

78. *Shulchan Arukh* 263:17. For example, she may ask members of her family to turn a light on or off.

The *Kaf HaChayim* 263:65 rules that a woman may wrap warm food in insulating material after lighting candles if she forgot to do so beforehand. Wrapping food to keep it warm, an act forbidden on *Shabbath* itself, is permitted during twilight. This is based on the view of the *Chatham Sofer* cited in note 65. The *Shulchan Arukh HaRav* rules to the contrary.

79. *Tzitz Eliezer*, Vol. 11, No. 21. The author reports that in certain communities it is customary for the whole family to stand near the mother when she lights. The concept underlying this custom is that the blessing over candle-lighting includes the *mitzvoth* of *Kavod* and *Oneg Shabbath*. Everyone stands near the mother while she recites the blessing with the intention that it include all aspects of these *mitzvoth*.

80. *Likutey Mahari'ach*.

The Number of Candles

30. Although the *mitzvah* of Candle-lighting can be fulfilled with one candle,[81] it is customary to light two, one commemorating *Zakhor* (Remember [the *Shabbath*]), the other commemorating *Shamor* (Guard [the *Shabbath*]).[82] There are also other customs — to light three, seven, or ten candles.[83] Many people light a candle for each member of the family.[84]

Some authorities maintain that a woman whose custom is to light many candles should separate two of them from the rest in order to express *Zakhor* and *Shamor*.[85]

---

81. *Mishnah Berurah* 263:22.
82. *Shulchan Arukh* 263:1. The *Mishnah Berurah* 263:5 quotes the Sages, "*Zakhor* and *Shamor* were uttered simultaneously by God," and adds, "Some people are accustomed to braid two wax candles and combine them as one...This is a beautiful custom." In the commentary *Elef LaMagen* on the *Mateh Ephrayim* 625:3, the author quotes the *Pri Megadim*, who maintains that at least two candles should also be lit on *Yom Tov*.
83. These customs are cited by the *Remah* 263:1, and the *Mishnah Berurah* 263:6 in the name of the *She'lah*. Seven candles commemorate the seven days of the week and the seven lights of the *menorah* in the *Beith HaMikdash*. Ten candles commemorate the Ten Commandments. *B'ney Yisaskhar* cites a custom of lighting thirty-six candles to commemorate the thirty-six hours during which the special Light of Creation illuminated the world before it was hidden away for the righteous. (See *Rashi*'s commentary on *Bereshith* 1:4.) *Ma'asey Rav*, par. 112, recounts that the Vilna Gaon would light many candles. *Ya'avetz* speaks in a similar vein: "One should add to the number of candles according to one's ability. One who adds to the *Shabbath* lights will merit illustrious descendants" (Laws of *Erev Shabbath*, par. 30).
84. This custom is cited by a number of later authorities. Each time a baby is born, an additional candle is added.
85. See *Ma'amar Mordekhai*, commenting on the *Shulchan Arukh* 263.

31. A person in financial straits should purchase one high-quality candle rather than two poor-quality ones.[86]

32. A woman should not light fewer candles than usual.[87] If, for some reason, she wishes to add candles for a particular *Shabbath*, she should stipulate that she does not wish to adopt this practice permanently.[88]

A woman who omits candle-lighting one *Shabbath* should light an additional candle from then on.[89] But if she lit *fewer*

---

86. *Mishnah Berurah* 263:3. *Levushey Mordekhai*, No. 49, states that a woman accustomed to light many candles and can no longer afford to do so may light two candles. Her original practice may be considered a vow, which she should annul.

87. *Pri Megadim, Eshel Avraham* 263:3.

88. For example, if a few candles remain in the package, or she expects many guests and adds extra candles in their honor, or she fears a power failure.

   Tzitz Eliezer, Vol. 13, No. 26, points out that a woman may not add to her usual number of candles over her husband's objection.

   A question is raised regarding lighting longer candles than usual: Is it necessary for a woman to stipulate that she does not wish to adopt this practice permanently? A possible answer may be inferred from the *Eliyahu Rabbah*'s discussion of a poor woman who omits candle-lighting one week. In view of her financial situation, she may light longer candles from then on. If she normally uses oil, she may increase the amount. It may be inferred from this ruling that lighting a longer candle is equivalent to adding an additional one. Indeed, HaGaon Rav Chaim Pinchus Sheinberg advises women who light longer candles than usual to stipulate that they do not intend to adopt this practice permanently. He adds that they need to make a stipulation only if regular sized candles were available, and they chose longer ones instead. If only the longer candles were available, or if a woman is away from home and her host only has long candles, a stipulation is not required.

89. *Remah* 263:1, and *Mishnah Berurah*. A person who normally lights with oil should add a wick and use the same amount of oil for it that she uses for each of the other wicks. She should not simply add another wick and divide the usual amount of oil among all the wicks.

candles than usual one *Shabbath*, she does not have to increase the number of candles she lights on subsequent *Shabbathoth.*[90]

See the *Kaf HaChayim* 263:11.

A woman who frequently forgets to light must add a candle each time she fails to perform the *mitzvah*. The *Mishnah Berurah* 263:7 rules that a poor woman may light a longer-burning candle rather than add a candle. (See note 88.) If she uses oil, she may add a small amount. The *Mishnah Berurah* further points out that if her failure to light was due to pressing circumstance, or a lack of funds, she is not required to add a candle. See also the *Kaf HaChayim* 263:10.

Rivevoth Ephrayim, Vol. 1, No. 184, discusses the case of a woman who intentionally neglected to light *Shabbath* candles and subsequently repented. The author cites the *Mishnah Berurah*, who explains that the purpose of the "fine" is to remind a woman who forgot to light of her mistake in order to prevent her from forgetting again. It is not intended to be a punishment for intentional neglect of the *mitzvah*, and therefore does not apply to one who was intentionally neglectful.

Iggeroth Moshe, *Orach Chayim*, Vol. 3, No. 14:6, rules that a married woman who spends *Shabbath* at her mother's home and forgets to light her own candles should add a candle on subsequent *Shabbathoth*.

Az Nid'biru, Vol. 3, No. 5, rules that a woman who adds a candle on *Shabbath* must also add one on *Yom Tov*. The converse is also true: A woman who omits to light *Yom Tov* candles must add a candle on future *Shabbathoth* and *Yamim Tovim*. *Kinyan Torah*, Vol. 1, No. 87, however, indicates that the "fine" of adding a candle does not apply to a woman who forgets to light candles on *Yom Tov*. It is unlikely that she will forget to light candles on *Yom Tov*, when she may even light after dark. Generally, fines are not imposed in unlikely situations. Since this case is subject to dispute, perhaps a woman may apply the *Mishnah Berurah*'s ruling for a poor person and light longer candles instead of an additional one.

Az Nid'biru, *Ibid.*, concludes that it is probable that a woman who forgets to light candles on the second night of *Yom Tov* need not light an additional candle in the future.

90. *Biur Halakhah* 263, beginning, *Ve'sha'chi'khah*, contrary to the *Pri Megadim*, *Eshel Avraham* 263:3.

33. A guest lights only two candles, even if her custom is to light more.[91]

Some authorities maintain a woman should light her usual number of candles when visiting her mother or mother-in-law.[92]

Types of Candles

34. Only candles or oil that give a clear, smooth-burning flame should be used.[93] Commonly-sold *Shabbath* candles are ideal for the *mitzvah*.[94] Nevertheless, olive oil fulfills the *mitzvah* in the most beautiful way.[95]

35. The candles should be long enough to burn until the end of the Friday night meal.[96] If the candles will burn out before dark, the blessing is said in vain.[97]

---

91. *Yesodey Yeshurun*, Vol. 3, No. 135. Since a guest usually lights only two candles, there is an assumed stipulation that a woman only intends to light extra candles at home.

92. This is based on a *responsum* of HaGaon Rav Moshe Stern, cited by R. Dov Eisenberg in *Guide for the Jewish Woman and Girl*. See also *Iggeroth Moshe*, cited in note 89.

93. *Shulchan Arukh* 264.

94. *Mishnah Berurah* 264:23. The *Mishnah Berurah* 275:4 explains that the Rabbinical prohibition against reading by the light of a lamp, "lest he tilt" the oil in it, does not apply to our candles because there is no need to tilt them, even during the week.

95. *Shulchan Arukh* 264:6. In *Ma'asey Rav*, par. 112, it is reported that the Vilna Gaon lit with olive oil. *Siddur Ha'Ari Zal* and *Shulchan HaTahor*, No. 263, also recommend kindling at least two lights with olive oil. Many people who are particular in the fulfillment of *mitzvoth* have adopted this practice.

96. *Remah* 263:10; *Mishnah Berurah* 263:45; *Kitzur Shulchan Arukh* 75:12; *Chaye Adam* 5:13.

97. *Shulchan Arukh* 263:9. The *Mishnah Berurah* 263:40 points out that

36. Candles which are not lit in the dining room must burn long enough for their light to be used later that night.[98]

37. Many authorities rule that the *mitzvah* of Candle-lighting may be fulfilled with a gas lamp.[99] Some authorities permit the use of a kerosene lamp,[100] but forbid reading by its light.[101]

38. Many authorities rule that the *mitzvah* may be fulfilled with an electric light that has been switched on in honor of *Shabbath*. They even permit reciting the blessing over electric lights.[102] Some of them limit this to incandescent bulbs, excluding fluorescent ones.[103] It is best to take into account

---

when the *Shabbath* meal is eaten near burning candles before dark, the blessing has not been said in vain, because candles add to the *Shabbath* atmosphere even during daylight. Kindling long-burning candles that will burn into the night is a greater *mitzvah*.

98. *Shulchan Arukh, Ibid.* The *Mishnah Berurah* 263:41 explains that preparing the meal by the light of candles which are burning in the house satisfies the *mitzvah* when the meal is eaten outside.

   Mishneh Halakhoth, Vol. 5, No. 41, paragraph 37, offers another suggestion. Citing authorities who maintain that the *mitzvah* can be fulfilled with electric lights (See paragraph 38.), the author recommends turning on an electric light before lighting candles indoors, with the intention that the blessing include the electric light. Even if the family comes inside after the candles have burnt out, they will still derive benefit from the electric light. This suggestion may also be utilized by a family that eats the Friday night meal away from home. (See paragraph 22.)

99. The blessing may be recited over this lamp. See *Beith Yitzchak*, Vol. 1, No. 120; *Me'lamed LeHo'il*, No. 46; *Meishiv Halakhah*, Vol. 1, No. 220; *Pekudath Elazar*, No. 23.

100. *Biur Halakhah* 264, beginning *BeItran.*

101. *Orchoth Chayim*, commenting on the *Shulchan Arukh* 264:3.

102. *Beith Yitzchak*, Vol. 1, No. 120, and Vol. 2, No. 31; *Tzitz Eliezer*, Vol. 1, No. 20:11; *Yabiah Omer*, Vol. 3, No. 17; *Az Nid'biru*, Vol. 3, No. 1, and Vol. 7, No. 5.

103. See *Sefer HaChashmal L'Ohr HaHalakhah*, No. 3:6. Incandescent

other authorities, who rule that the *mitzvah* should be fulfilled with a light that is distinguishable as a *Shabbath* light.[104] A person who wishes to fulfill the *mitzvah* with electric lights should, therefore, light at least one candle, reciting the blessing over it.[105]

39. The *Shabbath* candles should belong to the person who lights them.[106]

---

bulbs may be used because they contain a filament which "burns". Fluorescent lights do not contain a filament which "burns" continually.

104. *Az Nid'biru*, Vol. 3, No. 1.

105. *Az Nid'biru, Ibid.* In *Brith Olam*, par. 12, and *Az Nid'biru*, Vol. 5, No. 3, HaRav Binyamin Zilber outlines the procedure to be followed if one lights electric lights and candles. First the electric lights should be turned on in honor of *Shabbath*. Then, without speaking, the candles should be kindled and the blessing recited with the intention that it include the electric lights. Alternatively, the wife may kindle the *Shabbath* candles, after which her husband turns on the electric lights. In this case also, the wife should intend that the blessing include the electric lights.

106. *Shulchan Arukh HaRav* 263:10. This is also indicated in the *Ran's* commentary on Tractate *Pesachim* 7a, regarding *Chanukah* candles. In light of this requirement, a host should give candles to his guest as a gift, and the guest should intend to acquire them. In *Yeinah Shel Torah* an inference is made from *Beith Yitzchak*, Vol. 1, No. 145, that it is sufficient to borrow candles. The *Beith Yitzchak* permits borrowing candles for the *mitzvah* of kindling *Chanukah* lights, which implies that this may also be done for *Shabbath* candles since there is no logical reason to distinguish these two *mitzvoth*.

Where to Light

40. Candles should be lit in a place where their light may be used. Otherwise the blessing has been said in vain, and the candles must be extinguished and re-lit (before sunset) in a proper place with a new blessing.[107]

Unless there is a special need to do so, the candles should not be moved after they have been lit, even in the same room or by someone who has not accepted *Shabbath*.[108]

41. Because the primary *mitzvah* is fulfilled where the *Shabbath* meal is eaten, the candles should be placed on the dining room table.[109] Some authorities maintain that they should not be placed on the table itself, but near it.[110]

---

107. *Remah* 263:10, and *Mishnah Berurah*. After they are lit, it is not effective to move them to a place where they will be used.

108. *Mishnah Berurah* 263:48. This applies even if they were lit in a place where their light could be used.

   The *Magen HaElef*, commenting on the *Mateh Ephrayim* 619:10, offers an example of a "time of need": bringing candles to the bedside of a sick person or of a woman who has just given birth and is unable to leave her bed. She may light the candles at her bedside and, after a few minutes, they may be moved to the dining table.

   The *Shulchan Arukh* 263:14, and the *Mishnah Berurah* 263:57, clearly state that in normal circumstances it is forbidden to move *Shabbath* candles after they are lit, even before *Shabbath*. Once they have been lit and set aside for the purpose of a *mitzvah*, it is forbidden to use them for any other purpose. The *Mishnah Berurah* goes as far as to forbid touching the candles lest their light be used for a purpose other than the *mitzvah*. He explains that because the restriction against touching *Shabbath* candles is not connected to the laws of *Shabbath*, it even applies to those who have not accepted *Shabbath*. But the *Shulchan Arukh HaRav* 263:22, in *Kuntres Acharon*, rules that touching the candles is permitted.

109. *Remah* 263:10, and *Mishnah Berurah*.

110. *KafHaChayim* 263:68, based on the *Zohar* and the *Ari. Ma'asey Rav*, No. 113, reports that the Vilna Gaon advised against placing candles

Some people are particular to place the candles on the south side of the dining room.[111]

42. The candles should not be placed where they might be extinguished by wind or the opening of a window or door.[112]

---

on the table, so that the table should not become *muktzeh*. This is based on the concept of *basis le'davar ha'asur*, which means that if *muktzeh* (e.g. the candles) is placed on a non-*muktzeh* surface, the "base" assumes the status of *muktzeh*. The principle of *basis* does not apply when there are non-*muktzeh* items more valuable than the *muktzeh* on the "base" at the start of *Shabbath*. Some authorities interpret the Vilna Gaon to have maintained that placing food on a table will not suffice to remove its *muktzeh* status because the food's value is less than the value of the candlesticks. On the other hand, HaGaon Rav Moshe Feinstein maintains that food for the *Shabbath* meal is more valuable than candlesticks. He rules that if *challoth* are placed on a table before the start of *Shabbath*, it does not become a *basis*.

Sefer Tiltuley Shabbath, Halachos of Muktzeh, p. 209, cites another ruling of HaGaon Rav Feinstein: If *challoth* are placed on the candlestick tray, the status of *basis* is not removed from the tray. HaGaon Rav Feinstein explains that a table is made to hold things; placing *challoth* on it makes it a base to both the *challoth* and the candlesticks. The tray, however, is primarily used as a base to the candlesticks; it is considered a *basis* only to them, even if *challoth* are also placed on it. HaGaon Rav Shlomo Zalman Auerbach, in a *responsum* cited at the end of *Sefer Tiltuley Shabbath*, rules to the contrary, maintaining that food placed on the candlestick tray removes the status of *muktzeh* from the tray.

111. This custom is cited in *Mishnath Chassidim* and *Tikuney Zohar*. It is based on the fact that the *Menorah* was placed on the southern side of the *Beith HaMikdash*. Those who follow this custom place the candlesticks on the southern side of the dining room or the southern side of the dining room table. One of the *Shabbath Zemiroth* composed by the *Ari* includes the phrase, "I will arrange the *menorah* in the south."

112. The *Shulchan Arukh* 277:1 explains that it is forbidden to open a window or door opposite a burning candle because the wind might

The Time for Lighting

43. In most communities, candles are lit about twenty minutes before sunset.[113] The custom in Jerusalem, Tiberias, and Petach Tikvah is to light about forty minutes before sunset.[114]

A woman who is traveling should light at the same time as the community in which she is staying.[115]

44. A woman may light earlier than the prescribed time, as long as she lights after *plag ha'minchah* (approximately one and a quarter hours before sunset).[116] Even when lighting early, she should accept *Shabbath* when she lights.[117] Some

---

blow it out. The *Mishnah Berurah* 277:3 and *Biur Halakhah* permit opening a window when necessary, for example, when a room is very warm, and only a slight breeze is blowing. The window should be opened gently.

113. The *Mishnah Berurah* 256:1 and 261:23, points out that the time for candle-lighting is towards evening, when the sun is just above the treetops: "Happy is he who lights twenty or thirty minutes before sunset." See also *Iggeroth Moshe, Orach Chayim*, Vol. 1, No. 96.

114. This custom is cited in *Ketzoth HaShulchan*, No. 73, note 14, and in HaGaon Rav Y.M. Tokitzinski's work, *Bein Hashmashoth*, Chapter 6. *Yabiah Omer*, Vol. 5, No. 21, reports that many Sephardic communities in Jerusalem have not accepted it.

115. When a community accepts *Shabbath* early, all its members must do so. See paragraph 26.

116. The "hour and a quarter" is calculated according to *sha'oth zemaniyoth* (proportional time): One "hour" is equal to one-twelfth of the time between sunrise and sunset; an hour and a quarter will be longer than seventy-five minutes in the summer and shorter than seventy-five minutes in the winter.

117. The *Shulchan Arukh* 263:4 rules that *Shabbath* candles should not be lit "early". This means that one should not light candles long before accepting *Shabbath*. When a woman accepts *Shabbath* immediately after lighting, she is not considered to have lit early, even if a

authorities rule that if she does not accept *Shabbath* when she lights, her husband should.[118]

A woman who lit after *plag ha'minchah* without accepting *Shabbath* has still fulfilled the *mitzvah*.[119]

45. When candles are lit before *plag ha'minchah*, the blessing has been said in vain. They must be extinguished and lit later, with a new blessing.[120] If a woman is in doubt as to

---

substantial amount of time remains before sunset. See the *Biur Halakhah*, beginning *Lo yakdim*.

If a woman needs to make a stipulation that she does not accept *Shabbath*, she should light when the community does; then, her lighting is not considered early even if she does not accept *Shabbath*.

118. *Shulchan Arukh HaRav* 263:11. As long as her lighting is accompanied by an acceptance of *Shabbath* — even her husband's — it is not considered early. Her husband's acceptance of *Shabbath* should not be delayed more than ten minutes after she lights. See *Kuntres Acharon* 263:2. As explained in note 117, when she lights at the same time as the community, she is not lighting early, even if she and her husband do not accept *Shabbath* at that time.

119. *Mishnah Berurah* 263:20. The *Biur Halakhah*, beginning *Mi'b'od yom*, cites this in the name of Rabbi Akiva Eiger, who explains that although the *Shulchan Arukh* emphasizes that a woman should not light candles early without accepting *Shabbath*, if she does light early, the *mitzvah* is still fulfilled. She should not extinguish the candles and re-light them, as this would render the blessing she already recited a blessing said in vain.

The *Shulchan Arukh HaRav* 263:6, on the other hand, maintains that the candles should be extinguished and re-lit. The *Ketzoth HaShulchan* 74, note 28, points out that even the *Shulchan Arukh HaRav* agrees that the blessing should not be repeated.

Lights in other rooms of the house should also be turned on after *plag ha'minchah*. If they were turned on beforehand, all agree that they need not be turned off and on again. See *Shevet HaLevi*, Vol. 1, No. 51.

120. *Remah* 263:4, *Mishnah Berurah*, and *Biur Halakhah*. This applies even if she has accepted *Shabbath* with her lighting. Since the time is before *plag ha'minchah*, such an acceptance is invalid, and she must light again with a blessing.

whether she lit the candles before or after *plag ha'minchah*, her husband should kindle additional candles without a blessing.[121]

46. It is absolutely forbidden to light candles during twilight.[122] Lighting candles after the community has accepted *Shabbath*[123] is also forbidden, even before sunset.[124] Once a

---

It should be noted that *Yabiah Omer*, Vol. 2, No. 17, and *Misgereth HaShulchan* 75:34 rule that she does not repeat the blessing when she re-lights.

121. *Sha'arey Teshuvah* 263:2. A blessing should not be said, since it is possible that she lit at a proper time, after *plag ha'minchah*. For the same reason, the woman herself may not light the candles; if she did light after *plag ha'minchah*, she has already accepted *Shabbath*.

122. *Shulchan Arukh* 261:1, and *Mishnah Berurah* 261:6. The *Mishnah Berurah* emphasizes that candles may not be lit during twilight, even if there is no other light, and it will be impossible to eat the *Shabbath* meal in the dark.

The *Shulchan Arukh* 261:1, and 342, rules that the Rabbinic prohibition against asking a non-Jew to perform *melakhah* for a Jew on *Shabbath* is waived during twilight for the needs of a *mitzvah*. When necessary, therefore, one may ask a non-Jew to light a candle during twilight, but he should only light one candle in the dining room, and one in each room where light is needed. See also the *Shulchan Arukh HaRav* 261:1 and the *Magen Avraham* 271:7.

The *Shulchan Arukh HaRav* 263:11 rules that a woman who asks a non-Jew to light during twilight should spread her hands over the candles and recite the blessing with the words *al hadlakath ha'ner* instead of the usual *le'hadlik ner shel Shabbath*.

The *Mishnah Berurah* 263:21 cites the contrary view of Rabbi Akiva Eiger: A non-Jew cannot act as a Jew's agent in fulfilling a *mitzvah*, so the blessing may not be recited.

123. See paragraph 26, that a woman follows the custom of her husband's synagogue. There is a question as to whether a family must accept *Shabbath* when the father's synagogue does if he is not in the synagogue at that time. See the *Orukh HaShulchan* 263:22.

Another question concerns a woman who regularly attends Friday night services in a synagogue other than her husband's: Which synagogue determines when she must accept *Shabbath*? It is reasonable to assume that she should still follow the custom of her

woman has declared her acceptance of *Shabbath*, she is no longer permitted to light candles.[125]

Some authorities maintain that a man should not accept *Shabbath* before his wife has lit the *Shabbath* candles.[126]

47. Although it is best to wear *Shabbath* clothes when lighting candles, weekday clothes should be worn if changing into *Shabbath* clothes will cause the candles to be lit after the prescribed time.[127]

48. If candle-lighting time is approaching, and a woman has not yet recited *Minchah*, she should light the candles and recite the *Ma'ariv Shemoneh Esrey* twice, with the intention that the second *Shemoneh Esrey* compensate for the missed *Minchah*.[128] When there is still time to recite *Minchah* before sunset, some authorities rule that she should light with the

---

husband's synagogue.

124. *Shulchan Arukh* 263:12. This applies even if the community accepts *Shabbath* very early, which is customary in many places during the summer. As explained in note 122, if she has not lit by this time, she may ask a non-Jew to light a candle for the needs of *Shabbath*. See the *Remah* 261:1, and the *Mishnah Berurah*.

125. *Shulchan Arukh* 263:11. The *Shulchan Arukh* 263:17 states that a person who accepts *Shabbath* may ask another person who has not accepted *Shabbath* yet to do *melakhah* for her. See paragraph 28.

126. See the journal *HaMaor, Kuntres* 124.

127. *Mishnah Berurah* 262:11.

128. The *Mishnah Berurah* 263:43 explains that once she accepts *Shabbath* through lighting, she may no longer recite the weekday *Shemoneh Esrey*. This ruling also applies to women who do not regularly recite *Ma'ariv* on Friday night.

   Yabiah Omer, Vol. 2, No. 16, cites authorities who draw a distinction between men and women, ruling that a man may recite *Minchah* after lighting *Shabbath* candles, but recommends that he stipulate that he does not accept *Shabbath* with candle-lighting. Other authorities do not make this distinction. See also *Lev Chayim*, Vol. 3, No. 57, and *Tehillah LeDavid* 263:8.

stipulation that she does not intend to accept *Shabbath* until after reciting *Minchah*.[129] Still others rule that *Minchah* can be said after accepting *Shabbath*.[130]

49. If the hour is late, and a woman will not have time to light candles before sunset, her husband should light them. He should not take his wife's feelings into account in this situation.[131]

The Procedure for Candle-Lighting

50. It is a beautiful custom to give money to charity before lighting candles.[132]

51. It is proper to designate a candle to be regularly used to kindle all the *Shabbath* candles.[133] A woman should light

---

129. *Kaf HaChayim* 263:35. When a woman makes a stipulation (See the *Mishnah Berurah* 263:44.), it should be complete, allowing her to perform all forms of *melakhah*. See note 65.

    According to *Eshel Avraham* (Butchach), if she remembers while lighting candles that she did not recite *Minchah*, a stipulation is assumed, and she may recite *Minchah* afterwards.

    A woman who recited *Minchah* and accepted *Shabbath* may go to the synagogue and answer to *Kaddish* and *Kedushah* during the repetition of the *Minchah Shemoneh Esrey*.

130. *Yabiah Omer*, Vol. 2, No. 16. The author still recommends making a stipulation.

131. *Mishnah Berurah* 262:11.

132. *Kitzur Shulchan Arukh* 75:2; *Ben Ish Chai, Shanah Sh'niah, Parshath Noach*. The *Kaf HaChayim* 263:34 writes that it is proper to give at least three *prutoth*.

133. *Biur Halakhah* 263, beginning *Sh'tey p'tiloth*, citing the *Eliyahu Rabbah*.

    The *Mishnah Berurah* 263:4 explains that according to the letter of the law one *Shabbath* candle may be used to light another. Since all

the candles with the intention to fulfill the *mitzvah* of Candle-lighting as part of *Kavod* and *Oneg Shabbath*.[134] Some people are accustomed to recite the prayer *LeShem yichud* before lighting.[135]

52. The blessing over the *mitzvah* of Candle-lighting is *LeHadlik ner shel Shabbath*.[136] Some conclude with *shel Shabbath Kodesh*.[137]

53. After candles are lit, the hands are placed over the eyes to delay deriving benefit from the light. The blessing is recited, then the hands are removed from the eyes so that benefit is derived from the light immediately following the blessing.[138] This is the custom of all Ashkenazic and many

---

the candles are part of the *mitzvah*, lighting one with another is not considered a degradation of the *mitzvah*. A match should not be lit from a *Shabbath* candle, even if it will be used to kindle other *Shabbath* candles.

134. According to the *Remah* 263:4, and the *Mishnah Berurah*, candles which were not lit for the sake of the *mitzvah* should be extinguished and re-kindled.

135. For the exact language of this prayer, see the *Kaf HaChayim* 263:34.

136. *Shulchan Arukh* 263:5. The *Mishnah Berurah* adds that the singular, *ner*, is used although more than one candle is kindled.

137. See the *responsum* of the Lubavitcher Rebbe in the journal *Yagdil Torah, Teshuvoth U'Biurim*, 5743, No. 76, and *Kuntres Shabbath Kodesh* of Rav Yitzchak Ginzburg, note 55: "This form of the blessing is found in the laws of candle-lighting in the *Ari*'s *Seder Tikuney Shabbath*." For a full discussion, see *Rivevoth Ephrayim*, Vol.1, No. 166.

138. This is the second opinion cited in the *Remah* 263:5 — *Shabbath* is accepted when the blessing is recited. If a woman were to recite the blessing before lighting, she would have already accepted *Shabbath*, and it would no longer be permissible for her to light the candles. In order to satisfy the general rule — a blessing over a *mitzvah* should precede its performance — she should place her hands over her eyes immediately after lighting the candles and avoid deriving benefit from them until she has recited the blessing. In this way, deriving

Sephardic women.[139]

Some Sephardic authorities maintain that the blessing should be recited before lighting candles. Whoever follows this practice should bear in mind to accept *Shabbath* with candle-lighting, not with the blessing. Women who regularly recite the blessing before lighting are assumed to have this intention and do not have to specifically bear it in mind every week.[140]

54. Women who recite the blessing before lighting should not extinguish the match or candle used to light the *Shabbath* candles. If a match is used, it should be put down gently so it will extinguish itself. If a candle is used, it should be left to burn.[141]

———————————

benefit from the light, part of the *mitzvah*'s purpose, follows the blessing.

139. *Bach* 263; *Ben Ish Chai, Shanah Shn'iah, Parshath Noach* 8; *Kaf HaChayim* 263:34.

A woman who does not accept *Shabbath* when she lights (See paragraph 26.) may recite the blessing before lighting. See the *Biur Halakhah* 263, beginning *Achar*, citing Rabbi Akiva Eiger and the *Chaye Adam*. The *Biur Halakhah* also cites the contrary view of the *Derekh HaChayim*: A woman should not change her usual custom. This case is similar to the one discussed in Chapter 17, note 22–23, concerning the blessing over candle-lighting on *Yom Tov*.

The *Orukh HaShulchan* 263:13 rules that a man should recite the blessing before lighting, since men do not accept *Shabbath* when they light.

140. *Yabiah Omer*, Vol. 3, No. 16, and *Ye'chaveh Da'ath*, Vol. 2, No. 33.

141. *Shulchan Arukh* 263:10. The *Orukh HaShulchan* 263:14 explains that this requirement only applies to women who recite the blessing before lighting. Since they accept *Shabbath* when they light, they must put down the match immediately. It is not necessary for women who first light and then accept *Shabbath* with the blessing to put down the match immediately. They may even extinguish it. *Yabiah Omer*, Vol. 3, No. 16, arrives at a similar conclusion.

Some women who recite the blessing after lighting are also careful not to extinguish the match.[142]

55. The candles should not be held while they are being lit. They should have already been placed in the candlesticks.[143]

The match should be held to the wick until most of the wick has caught fire.[144]

56. After lighting candles, it is customary to pray that one's children and grandchildren will merit to light up the world with Torah. Candle-lighting time is particularly propitious for supplicating God in prayer.[145]

Some authorities write that these special prayers should be said while gazing at the candles.[146]

---

142. *Ben Ish Chai, Shanah Sh'niah, Parshath Noach* 8; *Brith Olam*, p. 17. This accommodates those authorities who rule that a woman accepts *Shabbath* when she lights, not when she recites the blessing.

143. *Siddur Derekh HaChayim*. It should be apparent that the candles are being lit for the *mitzvah*.

144. *Shulchan Arukh* 264:8.

145. *Mishnah Berurah* 263:2. Tractate *Shabbath* 23a explains that those who faithfully observe this *mitzvah* will merit children who will become Torah scholars.

In his commentary on *Shemoth* 19:3, Rabbenu Bechaya points out that praying during the performance of a *mitzvah* is particularly effective. A number of authorities suggest that a barren woman, or one who has difficulty in childbirth, should say the first chapter of *Shmuel* I (the *haftorah* read in the synagogue on the first day of *Rosh HaShanah*) and the first ten verses of the second chapter after lighting *Shabbath* candles. The *Kitzur Shulchan Arukh*, citing the *She'lah*, adds that these verses should be recited with full devotion and understanding.

146. *Kaf HaChayim* 263:34. In order to derive benefit from the candles as quickly as possible after the blessing, any special prayers should be recited after the hands are removed from the eyes.

57. If one of the *Shabbath* candles blew out after they were all lit, some women are accustomed not to re-light it, even if they have not recited the blessing yet.[147] A family member who has not accepted *Shabbath* should be asked to re-light the candle.[148] If it blew out after the blessing, it is certainly forbidden for the woman to re-light it. If someone else re-lights it, the blessing is not repeated.[149]

A *Shabbath* candle that blew out on *Shabbath* may be used during the week.[150] Some people have a custom to light it on *motzo'ei Shabbath*.

58. The presence of undressed children in front of the *Shabbath* candles is a degradation of the *mitzvah*.[151] A baby's diaper should not be changed in a room where *Shabbath* candles are burning.

---

147. *Brith Olam*, p. 17. See note 142, concerning accommodating the view that *Shabbath* is accepted when a woman lights. *Ketzoth HaShulchan* 74, note 17, distinguishes the candles going out because they were improperly lit from the candles being blown out by some unforeseen cause. In the first case, the woman should re-light them before reciting the blessing. In the second case, some other person should re-light them.

148. The *Shulchan Arukh HaRav* 263, in *Kuntres Acharon* No. 3, rules that the *mitzvah* is only complete when some benefit is derived from the candles on *Shabbath* itself. We have therefore recommended that the candle that blew out be re-lit. If all the candles blew out, it appears that the *Shulchan Arukh HaRav* would require re-lighting them, as long as the sun has not set.

149. *Chovath HaDar*, p. 87.

150. *Magen Avraham* 154:20. In such a case, increasing the number of candles on future *Shabbathoth* is not necessary. It is only necessary when candle-lighting is omitted altogether. This is true even if they all blew out. See *Mor VeOhaloth*, No. 7.

151. *Remah* 275:12.

Some Miscellaneous Laws of Candle-Lighting

59. A woman who speaks after the blessing before lighting the first candle must repeat the blessing.[152]

60. A woman who normally follows the Ashkenazic custom of reciting the blessing after lighting the candles may light them after the blessing if she mistakenly recites it first.[153]

61. If it is before sunset, a woman who lit candles, but forgot to recite the blessing, may still recite it.[154] She should never light candles intending to recite the blessing later.[155]

62. A woman who is uncertain whether she recited the blessing should not recite it.[156]

---

152. This is the general rule for anyone who speaks between the blessing over a *mitzvah* and its performance. It is specifically applied to candle-lighting in the *Birkey Yosef* 263. Also see the *Ben Ish Chai, Shanah Sh'niah, Parshath Noach* 10.

153. *Torath Yekuthiel* (Rozenberger), No. 61. Those who light candles before the blessing usually accept *Shabbath* with the blessing. In this case, as she has not yet lit, her acceptance of *Shabbath* is assumed to be a mistake.

154. *Biur Halakhah* 263, beginning, *K'she'yadlik*, citing the *Eliyahu Rabbah*. The *Shulchan Arukh HaRav* 263, in *Kuntres Acharon*, par. 11, permits the blessing to be recited as long as the candles are burning, even if it is after nightfall. He explains that the *mitzvah* continues as long as benefit is being derived from the candles. (See note 148.) The blessing may be recited as long as the *mitzvah* is continuing.

155. *Mishnah Berurah* 263:21.

156. *Biur Halakhah, Ibid.*, based on *Siddur Derekh HaChayim. Nachalath Shivah*, No. 8, rules, in both this case and when she completely omitted the blessing, that it is not necessary for her to add a candle in the future. Even when the blessing is omitted, the *mitzvah* is fulfilled.

63. There is a question whether the blessing *She'he'che'yanu* should be recited the first time a woman fulfills the *mitzvah* of Candle-lighting.[157] Women are advised to wear a new garment and recite the blessing *She'he'che'yanu* over it, intending to include the *mitzvah* of Candle-lighting in the blessing.[158]

When a girl who is a minor lights candles for the first time, all authorities agree that she does not recite *She'he'che'yanu*, then or when she attains *bath mitzvah* age.[159]

Kiddush

64. The Torah requires men and women to recite *Kiddush* on *Shabbath*.[160] Since a woman's obligation is equal to a

---

157. This question is discussed in *Chatham Sofer, Orach Chayim*, No. 55, *Teshuvah MeAhavah*, Vol. 2, *Orach Chayim*, No. 239, and *Siddur Ya'avetz*. Its source is based in a ruling of the *Taz, Orach Chayim* 22:1, concerning a boy reciting *She'he'che'yanu* the first time he puts on *tefillin*. See also the *Shakh* and the *Pri Chadash* on *Yoreh De'ah* 28; *Ye'chaveh Da'ath*, Vol. 2, No. 31.

158. The *Biur Halakhah* 22 offers this advice regarding the *mitzvah* of *Tefillin*.

159. *Tzitz Eliezer*, Vol. 13, No. 24; *Az Nid'biru*, Vol. 7, No. 3.

160. *Shulchan Arukh* 271:2. Although *Kiddush* is a time-bound *mitzvah*, women are obligated to perform it, both at night and in the morning. As Rava explains in Tractate *Berakhoth* 20b, "The Torah obligates women in the *mitzvah* of *Kiddush*. As it states, '*Zakhor* (Remember [the *Shabbath*]) and *Shamor* (Guard [the *Shabbath*]).' Whoever is included in *Shamor* (the negative commandments of *Shabbath*) is also included in *Zakhor* (the positive commandments of *Shabbath*)."

Since women are forbidden to do *melakhah* on *Shabbath*, they must also fulfill its positive commandments. *Kiddush* is one of the seven time-bound positive *mitzvoth* women are obligated to fulfill.

man's, she may technically recite *Kiddush* for him[161] even after she has fulfilled the *mitzvah*.[162]

In practice, it is considered improper for a woman to recite *Kiddush* for a man who is not a member of her family[163] unless there is some pressing need.[164] Reciting *Kiddush* for

---

161. *Mishnah Berurah* 271:4, in accord with the *Taz*, *Magen Avraham*, and Vilna Gaon. The *Rashal* and the *Bach* rule to the contrary, that a woman cannot *motzie* a man.

A woman's ability to *motzie* a man in the *mitzvah* of *Kiddush* is based on the principle of *arvuth* (mutual responsibility). Two people equally obligated in a *mitzvah* are each responsible to ensure that the other carries it out. A corollary of *arvuth* permits one person to recite a *birkath ha'mitzvah* (blessing recited before the fulfillment of a *mitzvah*) on behalf of another, even if the reciter has already fulfilled the *mitzvah* or will fulfill it later. Since a woman's obligation to recite *Kiddush* is equal to a man's, she may recite it for him. With respect to other time-bound *mitzvoth* from which women are exempt (i.e., *Shofar*, *Sukkah*, and *Lulav*), she may not recite the blessing and *motzie* a man, even when reciting the blessing for herself.

162. *Mishnah Berurah* 271:5 and *Sha'ar HaTziyun* 271:9, based on the view of Rabbi Akiva Eiger, *responsum* No. 7, and glosses on the *Shulchan Arukh* 271. Rabbi Akiva Eiger maintains that when a *mitzvah* applies equally to men and women, the principle of *arvuth* operates for both of them. Just as a man who has already fulfilled a *mitzvah* may recite the blessing for someone who has not yet fulfilled it, so a woman may *motzie* a man in such *mitzvoth*.

In his commentary on the *Shulchan Arukh*, *Dagul Mer'vavah*, HaGaon Rav Yechezkiel Landau takes the opposing view, that the principle of *arvuth* is only relevant to men. The *Mishnah Berurah* himself, in *Biur Halakhah* 689, beginning *Ve'nashim*, appears to adopt the *Dagul Mer'vavah*'s position, ruling that a woman who has already heard the *Megillah* on Purim may not recite the blessing for another woman. But in the *Mishnah Berurah* 271:5, he agrees with Rabbi Akiva Eiger. For further discussion, see note 176.

163. *Mishnah Berurah* 271:4.

164. *Kaf HaChayim* 271:8. An example of a pressing need would be that of a hospitalized man who is too weak to recite *Kiddush*; a nurse may recite it for him.

her husband is also discouraged.[165]

Eating Before Kiddush

65. Once she has lit candles and accepted *Shabbath*, a woman may not eat or drink anything, including water, until after *Kiddush*.[166] If she stipulates that she is not accepting *Shabbath* with candle-lighting,[167] she may eat and drink until just before sunset.[168]

In case of an urgent need, for example, if she is in pain, she may drink water during twilight even without a stipulation.[169]

When necessary, young girls and boys may eat or drink before *Kiddush*.[170]

When a Husband is Away From Home

66. A woman whose husband is away for *Shabbath* is required to recite *Kiddush* herself.[171] If she does not know how, she may listen to it at someone else's home, but she

---

165. Tractate *Berakhoth* 20b: "In truth they said that a son may bless for his father, a slave for his master, and a woman for her husband. But the Sages have said that a curse will come to a man whose wife and children bless for him."

166. *Shulchan Arukh* 271:4, and *Mishnah Berurah*. Rinsing the mouth out with water is permitted.

167. See paragraph 25.

168. *Pri Yitzchak*, Vol. 2, No. 9.

169. *Minchath Shabbath, Hashmathoth*, No. 77:2; *Kuntres Ahavath Shalom* of the *Maharsham*, par. 11. *Pri Yitzchak, Ibid.*, permits food and other drinks as well.

170. *Mishnah Berurah* 269:1.

171. She is also obligated in this *mitzvah*. See note 160.

must eat at least a *kezayith* of cake or *revi'ith* of wine there.[172]

As an alternative, she may ask someone to come to her home to recite *Kiddush* for her. This may be done even if the person reciting *Kiddush* has already fulfilled the *mitzvah* and does not eat anything there.[173]

67. A woman may fulfill the *mitzvah* of *Kiddush* by listening to her son who is older than thirteen recite it. Listening to a minor recite it does not fulfill the *mitzvah*.[174] If

---

172. *Mishnah Berurah* 273:21–22. The *Shulchan Arukh* emphasizes that someone who is not fulfilling a *mitzvah* may recite the blessing for another person only if the other person is unable to recite it. For this reason, we have stated that a woman may ask someone to recite *Kiddush* for her only if she does not know how to recite it herself. The *Shulchan Arukh* concedes that the *mitzvah* is fulfilled even when she could have recited it herself.

173. *Shulchan Arukh* 273:4, and *Mishnah Berurah*. A person may *motzie* someone in the *mitzvah* of *Kiddush*, which includes the blessing *Borey pri ha'gafen* over wine, without drinking wine or eating.

Tractate *Rosh HaShanah* 29b explains that a person who is not obligated in a blessing may only recite a *birkhath ha'mitzvah* for another person, not a *birkhath ha'ne'henin* (blessing recited before physical pleasures, such as eating or drinking); because wine is needed for the *mitzvah* of *Kiddush*, its blessing is considered a *birkath ha'mitzvah*. The one fulfilling the *mitzvah* must drink some of the wine.

174. *Mishnah Berurah* and *Biur Halakhah*, commenting on the *Shulchan Arukh* 271:2. Since *Kiddush* is a Torah requirement, it must be firmly established that the child has reached the age of thirteen *and* attained "physical maturity", evidenced by the growth of a minimum of two pubic hairs. (See Chapter 11, paragraph 1.)

In reference to a minor reciting *Kiddush* for an adult, the *Mishnah Berurah* and *Biur Halakhah* cite the opinion of the *Magen Avraham*: The Torah requirement to make *Kiddush* may be fulfilled by reciting words in praise of *Shabbath*; *Ma'ariv* on Friday evening satisfies this criterion. Reciting *Kiddush* over wine is a Rabbinic requirement.

The *Magen Avraham* maintains, according to the *Mishnah Berurah*, that a minor may make *Kiddush* over wine for his mother if she has

only a minor is available, she should repeat *Kiddush* after him, word for word, with a cup of wine in her hand.[175]

Procedure

68. Most authorities agree that a man who has recited *Ma'ariv* on Friday night may recite *Kiddush* for his wife, although she has not recited *Ma'ariv* or marked the day as *Shabbath* with any other words.[176] The converse is also true:

---

recited *Ma'ariv*. Her remaining obligation, to recite *Kiddush* over wine, is Rabbinic; all his obligations, which stem from the *mitzvah* of *Chinukh*, are also Rabbinic. (For a similar case, see Chapter 3, note 29.)

The *Biur Halakhah* challenges the *Magen Avraham* on a number of points. He cites Rabbi Akiva Eiger's inference from the *Ran*, that reciting *Kiddush* over wine, or at a minimum over bread, is a Torah requirement. The *Rosh* appears to go even further in Tractate *Pesachim*, Chapter 10. He rules that the law that *Kiddush* must be recited where a person eats is also a Torah requirement. Moreover, Tractate *Pesachim* 117b teaches that the Exodus from Egypt must be mentioned during *Kiddush*; the Exodus is not mentioned in the Friday evening *Shemoneh Esrey*. Finally, people rarely intend to fulfill the *mitzvah* of *Kiddush* with *Ma'ariv*, and many authorities rule that a Torah *mitzvah* can only be fulfilled when performed with intention to fulfill it.

For these and other reasons, argues the *Biur Halakhah*, the *Magen Avraham*'s ruling is open to question, and a minor should not recite *Kiddush* for his mother, even if she has recited *Ma'ariv*. If the boy has reached the age of thirteen, without his physical maturity having been firmly established, we may rely on the *Magen Avraham*. He may recite *Kiddush* for his mother if she has recited *Ma'ariv*. When she recites *Ma'ariv*, it is advisable for her to intend to fulfill the Torah requirement of *Kiddush*.

175. *Mishnah Berurah, Ibid.*
176. *Mishnah Berurah* 271:5, and *Sha'ar HaTziyun* 271:9, based on *Responsa of Rabbi Akiva Eiger*, No. 7, and Rabbi Akiva Eiger's glosses on the *Shulchan Arukh* 271:6.

A woman who has recited *Ma'ariv* may recite *Kiddush* for a

The *Dagul Mer'vavah* rules to the contrary — a man or a woman who has recited *Ma'ariv* cannot recite *Kiddush* for a woman who has not recited *Ma'ariv*. The person who recited *Ma'ariv* has said words in praise of *Shabbath* and fulfilled the Torah requirement of *Kiddush*. His or her remaining obligation, to recite *Kiddush* over wine, is Rabbinic. The woman who has not recited *Ma'ariv* has not yet fulfilled the Torah requirement.

Although the principle of *arvuth* normally enables a person to *motzie* another in a *birkath ha'mitzvah* even after fulfilling the *mitzvah*, the *Dagul Mer'vavah* argues that women are not included in *arvuth*. He finds evidence for this in a statement of the *Rosh*, Tractate *Berakhoth*, Chapter 3, that a woman cannot recite *Birkath HaMazon* for a man, which he understands to exemplify a general rule: Women are not responsible to ensure that others carry out their obligations, so they cannot recite a blessing for others unless they are reciting it for themselves at the same time.

Carrying his argument further, the *Dagul Mer'vavah* explains that men have not accepted responsibility for the *mitzvoth* of women. A man who has already fulfilled a *mitzvah* may, therefore, not recite the blessing over that *mitzvah* for a woman. If a man has said *Ma'ariv* and fulfilled the Torah requirement to make *Kiddush*, he cannot *motzie* a woman who has not recited *Ma'ariv*.

In refuting the *Dagul Mer'vavah*, Rabbi Akiva Eiger brings many proofs that *arvuth* applies to women with respect to *mitzvoth* in which their obligation is equal to men's. He limits the *Rosh*'s ruling to *Birkath HaMazon*; a woman's obligation to perform it may be only Rabbinic, unlike a man's, which is definitely a Torah obligation. (See Chapter 3, paragraph 8.) Concerning a *mitzvah* such as *Kiddush*, the *Rosh* would concede that *arvuth* applies to women. Furthermore, the *Dagul Mer'vavah*'s premise that the Torah obligation to make *Kiddush* is fulfilled with the recitation of *Ma'ariv* is not at all clear. (See note 174.)

The text follows Rabbi Akiva Eiger's view, which is accepted by most authorities. See also the *Chatham Sofer*, *Orach Chayim*, Nos. 21 and 143, and *Minchath Yitzchak*, Vol. 3, No. 54.

man who has not recited *Ma'ariv*.[177] Furthermore, men or women who have already recited *Kiddush* over wine may repeat it for others.[178]

69. Those listening should stand or sit at the table, according to the family custom. They should not wander around the room.[179] They must have intention to fulfill the *mitzvah* through listening, and the reciter must have intention to *motzie* them.[180] It is proper for the person reciting *Kiddush* to remind them of this requirement before starting.[181]

Those listening should answer *amein* at the conclusion of each blessing. They should not say *Barukh hu u'varukh sh'mo* when they hear the Name of God.[182] If they do not answer *amein*, or do say *Barukh hu u'varukh sh'mo*, the *mitzvah* is still fulfilled.[183]

70. It is essential that those listening hear every word of *Kiddush*.[184] Some authorities maintain they should say each

---

177. *Ibid.*
178. See note 173.
179. *Mishnah Berurah* 271:46.
180. *Shulchan Arukh* 273:6.
181. *Mishnah Berurah* 271:5.
182. *Kitzur Shulchan Arukh* 77:4.
183. *Shulchan Arukh* 213:2; *Mishnah Berurah* 124:21. The *Birkey Yosef* 213 rules that it is not necessary to object when someone who is fulfilling her obligation through listening says *Barukh hu u'varukh sh'mo*.

   To the contrary, the *Shulchan Arukh HaRav* 124:2 maintains that a listener who answers *Barukh hu u'varukh sh'mo* does not fulfill the *mitzvah* since she interrupts with extra words not required by the Sages. He recommends cautioning people who are unaware of this law. See further in *Maharam Shick, Orach Chayim*, No. 51; *Iggeroth Moshe, Orach Chayim*, Vol. 2, No. 98.
184. As explained in the *Shulchan Arukh* 193:1, in reference to *Birkath HaMazon*. See Chapter 3, paragraph 10.

word silently with the person reciting it.[185] Others rule they should not do so without cups of wine in front of them.[186]

A listener who fails to hear every word has still fulfilled the *mitzvah* as long as she hears the main components of *Kiddush* — the beginning, the end, and the section which mentions the Exodus from Egypt.[187] Many authorities rule that a listener fulfills the *mitzvah* even if the blessing over wine is not heard.[188]

71. It is customary to rely on those who maintain that a listener fulfills the *mitzvah* of *Kiddush* even if she does not understand the words.[189] Since some authorities do insist

---

185. *Mishnah Berurah* 193:5, based on the *Shulchan Arukh* 183:7. Repeating each word of *Kiddush* will assure them of not missing a word.

Writing in *Hagadath Chazon Ovadiah*, p. 106, HaGaon Rav Ovadiah Yosef cautions those who repeat each word not to answer *amein* because it is an interruption between making the blessing and drinking the wine. The commentary *Tosafoth Chayim*, on the *Chaye Adam* 6, reminds them not to repeat the words so loudly that they will confuse the person reciting *Kiddush*.

186. *Mishnah Berurah* 271:3; *Biur Halakhah* 271, beginning *DeIthkash*, citing *Responsa of Rabbi Akiva Eiger*, No. 7. A woman who listens to *Kiddush* recited by someone who does not pronounce the words correctly should certainly repeat each word silently. If she cannot arrange for a cup of wine to be placed in front of her, she should make an effort to drink as quickly as possible from the host's cup.

187. *Biur Halakhah* 193:1, beginning *VeTzarikh*, and 271, beginning *DeIthkash*. The *mitzvah* is not fulfilled if she dozed off during *Kiddush*.

188. *Chelkath Yaacov*, Vol. 2, No. 146. *Iggeroth Moshe, Orach Chayim*, Vol. 2, No. 45, states that this is also the view of the *Shulchan Arukh HaRav*, in *Kuntres Acharon* 271:2. Also see *Har Tzvi, Orach Chayim*, No. 156. *Imrey Yosher*, Vol. 2, No. 173 rules, however, that if she does not hear the blessing over wine the *mitzvah* is not fulfilled because that blessing is an integral part of *Kiddush*.

189. *Mishnah Berurah* 193:5. The *Shulchan Arukh* 193:1 cites the conflicting views concerning this question. See Chapter 3, paragraph 11.

that a person who is only listening must understand the words, the listener should try to repeat each word silently; all agree that the *mitzvah* is fulfilled in this way, with or without comprehension. A cup of wine or loaf of bread should be placed in front of a listener who repeats the words silently.[190]

72. A person who normally prays and recites blessings with a certain Hebrew pronunciation may fulfill the *mitzvah* by listening to someone with a different pronunciation.[191]

73. One does not fulfill the *mitzvah* of *Kiddush* through listening to the recitation of a public desecrator of *Shabbath*.[192] In such a situation, the listener should repeat each word of

---

190. *Ibid.*
191. *Shevet HaLevi*, Vol. 1, No. 88; *Yesodey Yeshurun*, Vol. 1, p. 43.
192. We refer to a person who is classified in Jewish Law as a *mechalel Shabbath b'farhesya* (public desecrator of *Shabbath*). According to the *Mishnah Berurah* 385:4, a person is so classified if at least ten Jews know that he willfully transgresses a Torah prohibition of *Shabbath*. The transgression need not be in their presence. In his glosses on the *Shulchan Arukh*, *Yoreh De'ah* 2, Rabbi Akiva Eiger cites authorities who limit this classification to a person who transgresses *melakhoth* concerned with working the land, such as plowing or planting.

    Tosafoth Shabbath 385 cites authorities who rule that a person is not to be classified as a *mechalel Shabbath b'farhesya* if he would be embarrassed to transgress a Torah prohibition in the presence of a distinguished individual, such as a Rabbi or Torah scholar.

    A number of later authorities maintain that the laws pertaining to a *mechalel Shabbath b'farhesya* do not apply to most public desecrators of *Shabbath* today. Since their actions are based on lack of education rather than willfull disregard of the Torah, they are classified as "children who were taken into captivity", who are not held responsible for their actions. According to these authorities, only someone who received a proper Jewish education and rejected it can be a *mechalel Shabbath b'farhesya*. This is the view of *Binyan Tziyon (Chadashoth)*, No. 23, and *Iggeroth Moshe, Orach Chayim*, Vol. 3, No. 23, and Vol. 2, No. 19. The laws described in the text only

Kiddush silently to herself. If the reciter's wine has been cooked,[193] she may drink it.

If the wine has not been cooked, it is best to avoid embarrassment and strife by standing and listening to *Kiddush* with the intention not to fulfill the *mitzvah*. Either refrain from drinking the wine altogether or only appear to drink it. Afterwards, recite *Kiddush* unobtrusively over bread.[194] When necessary, *Kiddush* may be recited over bread even in the morning.[195]

---

apply to a desecrator of *Shabbath* who is classified as a *mechalel Shabbath b'farhesya*.

193. It is forbidden to drink wine which has been touched by a *mechalel Shabbath b'farhesyah* or by a non-Jew unless it has been "cooked". According to HaGaon Rav Moshe Feinstein, the normal pasteurization process, in which the wine or grape juice is heated to about 80° Celsius, fulfills the criterion of "cooked". HaGaon Rav Shlomo Zalman Auerbach and HaGaon Rav Yosef Sholom Eliashiv rule that the wine must actually be brought to a boil.

194. This advice is offered by HaGaon Rav Ben Zion Abba Shaul.

Generally, *Kiddush* may only be recited over bread if wine is unavailable. If possible, it should be recited over two whole loaves of bread (*lechem mishneh*), but it may also be recited over a piece the size of a *kezayith*. (See the *Mishnah Berurah* 274:2.) When there is a pressing need, it may even be recited over a product baked from one of the five species of grain — wheat, barley, oats, rye, or spelt — over which the blessing *Borey miney m'zonoth* is said. (See *Yabiah Omer*, Vol. 3, No. 19.)

The procedure for reciting *Kiddush* over bread follows: Wash the hands and recite the blessing *Al netilath yadoyim*. Place the hands on the bread and recite the paragraph beginning with *va'yikhulu*. Remove the cover from the bread, hold it, and recite the blessing *HaMotzie*. Re-cover the bread and recite the concluding blessing of *Kiddush*, *Asher kid'shanu b'mitzvothav v'ratzah vanu*. Break off a piece and eat it. (See the *Tur* 272 and the *Mishnah Berurah* 271:41.)

195. This is based on a ruling of HaGaon Rav Yosef Sholom Eliashiv.

74. Speaking during *Kiddush* is forbidden until the reciter or someone else at the table drinks a *maley lugmav* (cheek-full) of wine.[196] Whoever speaks during the actual recitation does not fulfill the *mitzvah*. Speaking between the conclusion of *Kiddush* and drinking the wine does not invalidate the *mitzvah*.[197]

75. Although not an obligation, it is a *mitzvah* for every person at the table to taste the wine.[198] Since they have

---

196. *Minchath Shabbath* 91:21.
197. *Mishnah Berurah* 167:45 and 271:76; *Sha'ar HaTziyun* 167:43.
198. *Shulchan Arukh* 271:14 and 271:16, *Mishnah Berurah* and *Sha'ar HaTziyun*.

Ideally, when wine over which a *mitzvah* was performed is drunk, the cup should not be *pagum*, i.e., none of the wine in the cup should have been drunk prior to its use for the *mitzvah*. One of the following safeguards will ensure that the listeners do not drink from a *pagum* cup.

a) Each person tastes the wine in the host's cup. Since they all drink from the same cup, the fact that the host began drinking from it does not make it *pagum*.

b) After reciting *Kiddush*, the host pours a small amount of wine from his cup into small cups before he drinks himself, and these cups are passed around to the company. The wine should not be poured out after the host drinks; since they do not all drink from the same cup, their cups will be considered *pagum*. At least a *revi'ith* of wine should remain in the host's cup after he pours for the company so he will have a sufficient amount to drink.

c) Full cups of wine are placed before each person. After *Kiddush*, everyone drinks from his own cup.

Following one of the first two procedures, the company should not drink from the host's wine until he does. If they follow the third procedure, and they do not drink from his wine, it is not necessary to wait.

already heard the blessing *Bor'ey pri ha'gafen*, they need not recite it before drinking. A person who speaks before drinking the wine must repeat the blessing unless the interruption concerned *Kiddush* or the meal.[199]

Some authorities rule that it is essential to taste the wine to fulfill the *mitzvah* of *Kiddush* in the morning.[200]

---

199. *Mishnah Berurah* 271:75, based on the *Magen Avraham*. Although one should not interrupt between the blessing and drinking even concerning matters related to *Kiddush*, such an interruption does not necessitate repeating the blessing.

200. In *Hagadah Mo'adim U'zmanim*, *Laws of Yom Tov*, par. 2, HaRav Moshe Sternbuch cites a difference of opinion between HaGaon Rav Naftali Tzvi Yehudah Berlin (the *Netziv*) and HaGaon Rav Chayim Soloveitchik of Brisk.

According to HaGaon Rav Chayim, the basic requirement of morning *Kiddush* is to drink wine before eating. Every person must drink, because drinking cannot be performed through an agent. At night, the basic requirement is the recitation of *Kiddush* over a cup of wine. Drinking the wine is not an integral part of the *mitzvah*, so everyone is not actually obligated to drink.

The *Netziv* argues that the basic requirement of morning *Kiddush* is for one member of the household to drink wine in honor of *Shabbath*. This can be compared to the *mitzvah* of kindling *Chanukah* lights, which one person may perform on behalf of the whole family.

When a man's wife is a *niddah*, he should take care not to pour wine for her or hand her the cup. One of the following options should be employed:

a) He may place his cup before her so she can pick it up herself. (*Misgereth HaShulchan*, commenting on the *Kitzur Shulchan Arukh* 153:12.)

b) When other people are seated around the table, he may pour wine from his cup into small cups. When everyone takes a cup, his wife also takes one.

c) He may pour wine from his cup into one large cup. Then his wife and the other people around the table pour wine for themselves from that cup. (*Sugah Ba'Shoshanim* 8:16, 11:9, and 25:3.)

Eating Before Kiddush Shabbath Morning

76. A woman who normally recites the *Shacharith Shemoneh Esrey* on *Shabbath* morning[201] may drink water, tea, or coffee before praying.[202] One who fulfills the *mitzvah* of *Tefillah* (Prayer) by reciting a short prayer[203] must make *Kiddush* before tasting anything, including water, once she has recited it.[204]

---

201. The question whether women are obligated to recite *Shemoneh Esrey* is discussed at length in Chapter 2, paragraph 1, note 1. We refer here to a woman who follows the ruling of the *Mishnah Berurah*, which obligates women to recite the *Shacharith* and *Minchah Shemoneh Esrey*s.

202. *Kaf HaChayim* 286:30, based on the *Pri Megadim*.

The *Shulchan Arukh* 89, and *Mishnah Berurah*, explain that once dawn has arrived, one may not eat or drink until after morning prayers except for medical reasons. One may drink water, tea, or coffee, and it is our custom to permit sugar in the tea or coffee. A very hungry or very thirsty person, who will be unable to pray with proper devotion without eating or drinking, may do so. For further details, see Chapter 2, paragraph 4.

The *Kaf Hachayim* explains that a woman whose normal custom is to recite *Shemoneh Esrey* is forbidden to eat a substantial amount of food before reciting it. Consequently, her obligation to make *Kiddush* has not yet begun. Drinking water, tea, or coffee, is not a transgression of the prohibition against tasting any food or drink before *Kiddush* because this prohibition only begins once the time for reciting *Kiddush* arrives. This ruling also applies to a woman who has recited a short prayer but does not intend to fulfill the *mitzvah* of *Tefillah* with it. See note 204.

203. According to the view of the *Rambam*. See Chapter 2, notes 1–3.

204. *Pri Megadim*, *Eshel Avraham* 289:4; *Tosafoth Shabbath* 286, and 289:3, based on the *Shulchan Arukh* 289:1 and *Mishnah Berurah* 289:6.

The *Magen Avraham* reports in his time many women had adopted the view of the *Rambam*, fulfilling their daily prayer obligation with a short prayer. Such women are permitted to eat after reciting the short prayer. The obligation to recite *Kiddush* then

A woman who is so weak that she is permitted to eat a *ke'betzah*[205] of bread or cake before prayers is required to recite *Kiddush* before eating.[206]

77. When a woman who does not know how to recite *Kiddush* needs to eat, some authorities permit her to eat before praying without reciting *Kiddush*.[207]

Some authorities rule that a woman who needs to eat before praying, and whose husband has not recited *Shacharith* yet, may eat without reciting *Kiddush*.[208] But if she has already recited *Shacharith*, she may not eat before *Kiddush* even if her husband has not prayed.[209] This ruling applies to married women. Single girls must recite *Kiddush* before

---

takes effect, along with the restriction against tasting any food or drink, even water, before *Kiddush*. See also *Minchath Yitzchak*, Vol. 4, No. 28:3.

Yay'na shel Torah, Shabbath Kodesh, p. 95, cites the ruling of the Admor of Belz, Rebbe Aharon of Blessed Memory, that a woman who intends to fulfill her prayer obligation by reciting *Birkath HaTorah* is forbidden to taste anything once she has recited it.

205. Approximately 40-45 grams of bread or cake.
206. *Minchath Yitzchak, Ibid.*, quotes the *Biur Halakhah* 289, beginning *Chovath Kiddush*: "A person who is given permission to eat and drink before prayers for medical reasons must certainly recite *Kiddush* before doing so." This ruling is supported by *Minchath Shabbath*, No. 77:35, and *Az Nid'biru*, Vol. 1, Nos. 9–10.

HaGaon Rav Moshe Feinstein writes in *Iggeroth Moshe, Orach Chayim*, Vol. 2, No. 26: "In regard to the question of *Kiddush* for a weak person who needs to eat before morning prayers, according to my inadequate knowledge, it seems if a person must eat bread or cake, *Kiddush* must be recited, in keeping with the ruling of the *Mishnah Berurah* in *Biur Halakhah*."

207. *Minchath Yitzchak*, Vol. 4, No. 28, rules that in a time of need a woman may rely on the view of the *Rashba*, which exempts women from the *mitzvah* of reciting *Kiddush* in the morning.
208. See note 202.
209. *Iggeroth Moshe, Orach Chayim*, Vol. 4, No. 101:2, cites the ruling in *Shulchan Arukh, Evven HaEzer* 70:2, which requires a couple to eat

eating, even if their fathers have not recited *Shacharith*.[210]

Shalosh Seudoth and Lechem Mishneh

78. The *mitzvah* of eating three *Shabbath* meals is an obligation for men and women,[211] as is the recitation of the blessing *HaMotzie lechem min ha'aretz* over two whole loaves of bread (*lechem mishneh*) at each meal.[212]

A woman should intend to fulfill the *mitzvah* of *lechem*

---

the *Shabbath* meal together. If a man is not permitted to eat because he has not recited *Shacharith* yet, his wife is not required to make *Kiddush*. If she is weak, she may eat before prayers without reciting *Kiddush*. *Iggeroth Moshe* cautions, however, that if she has already prayed, she may not eat before *Kiddush*, even if her husband has not prayed yet. Since it is usually forbidden to eat after praying until *Kiddush* is recited, exceptions are not made for unusual situations.

210. *Ibid.* A daughter is not required to eat with her parents on *Shabbath*, even if they want her to. The law is not different for her than for men. If she is given permission to eat before praying, she must recite *Kiddush* before she eats.

211. *Shulchan Arukh* 291:6, and the *Mishnah Berurah*.

"And Moses said, 'Eat it [the manna] *today*, for *today* is *Shabbath* unto God. *Today* you will not find it in the field'" (*Shemoth* 16:25). The three-fold repetition of the word *today* is the source for the obligation to eat three meals on *Shabbath*. The *Maharam* of Rothenberg 473 cites the opinion of Rabbenu Tam that women are obligated to eat three *Shabbath* meals because they, too, were included in the miracle of the manna.

212. *Mishnah Berurah* 274:1; *Biur Halakhah* 291, beginning, *Nashim*.

The *mitzvah* to recite *HaMotzie* over two loaves of bread commemorates the double portion of manna that fell on Friday to provide food for *Shabbath*. The fact that women benefited from the manna obligates them in the *mitzvah* of *Lechem Mishneh*. The *Orukh HaShulchan* 274:4, citing the *Mordekhai*, adds that *Lechem Mishneh* is one of the positive commandments of *Shabbath*, and women are obligated in all the positive commandments of *Shabbath*. See note 160.

mishneh when she listens to her husband, father, or host recite *HaMotzie*. The person reciting the blessing should intend to *motzie* her in this *mitzvah*.[213]

79. A woman who is fulfilling the requirement of *lechem mishneh* through her husband, father, or host, should not recite the blessing *HaMotzie*.[214] Some authorities do permit her to recite her own blessing,[215] but she should not eat the bread before the head of the house does.[216]

80. Some authorities rule that a person who has not yet washed her hands fulfills the obligation of *lechem mishneh* by listening to *HaMotzie* recited over two loaves of bread. She then washes her hands and recites *HaMotzie* over one piece of bread.[217]

---

213. *Chaye Adam*, cited in the *Mishnah Berurah* 291:21; *Shulchan Arukh HaRav* 274:4.
214. *Mishnah Berurah* 274:2 and 291:21.
215. *Eshel Avraham* (Butchach) 274. *Melamed Le'Ho'il*, No. 24, observes that this was the custom in many Hungarian, Polish, and Russian communities. The author reports that many people would converse between the host's blessing and eating bread, disqualifying themselves from fulfilling their obligation through his blessing. To prevent people from eating without reciting a blessing, the custom was initiated for each person to recite his or her own blessing. People who follow this custom are assumed not to intend to fulfill their obligation through the host's blessing.
    In a letter re-printed in the journal *Yagdil Torah*, *Nissan* 5739, No. 72, the Lubavitcher Rebbe writes that this is the practice among Lubavitch Chassidim. See also the *Shulchan Arukh HaRav* 167:18.
216. *Shulchan Arukh* 167:15. Since they all fulfill the *mitzvah* with the host's bread, they should wait to eat until he does. See note 198. If each one is given his or her own *lechem mishneh*, they may eat before the host.
217. *Eshel Avraham, Ibid.* Nevertheless, the *Orukh HaShulchan* 274:4 states that the host should wait until everyone has taken a seat around the table before reciting the blessing.
    The *Mishnah Berurah* 274:2 states that the person reciting the

Some Miscellaneous Laws of Shabbath

81. *Chazal* describe the laws of *Shabbath* as "mountains hanging by a hair's breadth."[218]. Clearly, it is beyond the scope of this book to present an exhaustive summary of all the complex laws of *Shabbath* which relate to women.

It is extremely important for every woman to learn thoroughly the laws of cooking, selecting, preparing food, caring for clothing, and house-cleaning. She must also familiarize herself with the problems of baby and child care. Fortunately, our generation has been blessed with many important and valuable works in these areas.[219]

We will limit our discussion to some laws of body care on *Shabbath* which are particularly relevant to women.

Care of the Hair

82. A special brush, with very soft bristles to smooth the

---

blessing should first say *Birshuth* (with your permission [I will recite the blessing]). But it is reported in *Ma'asey Rav*, No. 78, that the Vilna Gaon considered this an unnecessary interruption.

218. *Mishnah*, Tractate *Chagigah* 1:8. *Sefer Yesod V'Shoresh HaAvodah*, *Sha'ar* 6, Chapter 3, states, "Every person is obligated to become expert in the laws of *Shabbath*, for they are like mountains [of laws] hanging by a hair. [The bulk of the laws of *Shabbath* are derived from the Oral Law; very few of them are actually written in the Torah]...and the punishment [for transgressing them] is great."

219. It is worthwhile to note the astonishing words of HaGaon Rav Yehonasan Aibeshitz in *Ya'arath D'vash*: "Someone who has not thoroughly studied the laws of *Shabbath* at least two or three times cannot avoid desecrating *Shabbath* by performing an act forbidden by the Torah or by the Sages. It is crucially important to review these laws constantly with a competent authority, who can clarify obscure points...Happy is he who follows this [advice], as it will protect him from punishment like a shield."

hair, should be set aside for *Shabbath*.[220] Using a regular comb or a brush with hard or thick bristles is forbidden;[221] this also applies to their use on a wig.[222]

83. Hair may only be parted with the fingers.[223] A woman may scratch her head gently or remove something stuck to it, as long as she is careful not to detach any hairs in the process.[224]

84. One may not braid or unbraid hair on *Shabbath*.[225]

---

220. *Mishnah Berurah* 303:86-87, and the *Sha'ar HaTziyun*. Brushing with the same brush used during the week has the character of "weekday activity", which is forbidden by Rabbinic Law.
221. *Shulchan Arukh* 303:27. Using a thick comb or a hard brush inevitably results in detaching hair, a *melakhah* of *Shabbath*. Generally, acts which result in unintentional *melakhah* are permitted; however, if the *melakhah* is inevitable, the act which will cause it is forbidden. Even if some of the comb's bristles are removed, it is still likely that hairs will be detached.
    A woman who plans to immerse in the *mikvah* on Friday night or *Yom Tov* night must comb her hair before sunset. If she forgets, she should consult a competent halakhic authority.
222. *Egley Tal, M'lekheth Gozez*, par. 10. *Beith Yitzchak, Orach Chayim*, No. 15, explains that combing a wig is included under the Rabbinic prohibition against "repairing a utensil". See also *Ketzoth HaShulchan*, No. 143, note 6, and No. 146, note 21; *Shemirath Shabbath KeHilkhethah* 14:46.
223. *Shulchan Arukh* 303:26-27, and the *Mishnah Berurah* 303:84. According to the *Mishnah Berurah*, parting hair with a comb is forbidden because of the possibility of detaching hairs. The *Ketzoth HaShulchan*, No. 146, note 21, relates parting hair to the *melakhah* of "building". See note 225. *Shemirath Shabbath KeHilkhethah*, Chapter 14, note 130, points out that, according to the *Mishnah Berurah*, parting the hair with a soft brush which has been designated for *Shabbath* may be permitted. But according to the *Ketzoth HaShulchan*, it would be forbidden.
224. *Minchath Shabbath*, No. 80:117, and No. 86:6.
225. *Shulchan Arukh* 303:26. The *Mishnah Berurah* 303:82 explains: "This

Curling[226] and teasing hair are also forbidden.[227] A woman may gather hair with her hands and straighten it out.[228] She may also tie her hair with a permissible knot, using a ribbon,[229] rubber band, beret, or the like,[230] and attach decorative pins and combs to hold it in place.[231]

Makeup

85. Cosmetics may not be used on *Shabbath*.[232] Although some authorities permit the use of makeup powder which does not adhere to the face,[233] it is best to refrain from using it.[234]

---

is a Rabbinic prohibition because it is similar to building. We expound on the verse, 'And God *built* the rib' (*Bereshith* 2:22): This teaches that God braided Chava's [hair] and brought her to Adam." (The Aramaic words for "braiding" and "building" share the same root.)

Braiding a wig is forbidden because of its similarity to weaving. See the *Mishnah Berurah, Ibid.*

226. *Ketzoth HaShulchan*, No. 146. Curling children's *pey'oth* (sidelocks) on *Shabbath* is forbidden unless they have already been curled on Friday.

227. *Biur Halakhah* 303, beginning *La'chof*. It is forbidden to spray hair in order to keep it in place. *Shemirath Shabbath KeHilkhethah* 14:50 forbids applying a liquid to hold a wig in place.

228. *Ketzoth HaShulchan*, No. 146, note 21.

229. The laws of tieing and untieing knots on *Shabbath* are discussed in *Shemirath Shabbath KeHilkhethah* 15:49–58.

230. *Ketzoth HaShulchan, Ibid.*

231. *Shemirath Shabbath KeHilkhethah, Ibid.,* par. 47.

232. *Shemirath Shabbath KeHilkhethah* 14:57–60.

233. See *Iggeroth Moshe, Orach Chayim,* Vol. 1, No. 114.

234. *Shemirath Shabbath KeHilkhethah* 14, note 158, citing the view of HaGaon Rav Shlomo Zalman Auerbach, who rules that as long as the powder is added for coloring, even for a short time, there is no basis for permitting it.

Care of the Fingernails

86. Dirt attached to the fingernails may be removed, as long as the fingernails themselves are not cut.[235]

A woman who attends the *mikvah* on *Shabbath* may remove fingernail polish with water or acetone, but not with cotton.[236]

Perfume

87. One may apply perfume to the hands or other parts of the body, but not to a garment or handkerchief.[237] Spraying perfume on wigs is forbidden.[238]

---

235. *Biur Halakhah* 161, beginning *Hu tzarich*, and the *Mishnah Berurah* 340:3. A woman who forgets to cut her fingernails before going to the *mikvah* on Friday night or *Yom Tov* night should consult a competent halakhic authority.

236. *Shemirath Shabbath KeHilkhethah* 14:61. The use of cotton is prohibited due to the likelihood that it will be squeezed out.

237. *Mishnah Berurah* 322:18 and 128:23. *Chazal* prohibit introducing fragrance into utensils or clothing on *Shabbath* and *Yom Tov*. This prohibition does not apply to fragrance applied to the body. The *Mishnah Berurah* 511:26 forbids applying fragrance to clothing even if it has already been applied before *Shabbath* or *Yom Tov*. *Shemirath Shabbath KeHilkhethah* 15, note 137, cites the ruling of HaGaon Rav Shlomo Zalman Auerbach that only the introduction of a new fragrance is forbidden. One may add more of the same fragrance.

The *Kaf HaChayim* 128:44, and the *Shulchan Arukh HaRav* 511:7, forbid adding fragrance to the body with the intention to perfume the body. In their opinion, one may only sprinkle fragrance on the body in order to smell the fragrance, not to give the body a fragrant smell. *Minchath Yitzchak*, Vol. 6, No. 26, rules that Sephardim should be stringent in this matter. HaGaon Rav Ben Zion Abba Shaul, however, allows Sephardic women to use perfume.

238. *Mishnah Berurah* 322:18. This is prohibited according to all opinions because the fragrance is applied to an artificial substance.

Havdalah

88. It is debatable whether the *mitzvah* to prolong *Shabbath* applies to women.[239]

89. Eating or drinking anything except water before making *Havdalah* over wine on *motzo'ei Shabbath* is forbidden. This is so even if the paragraph beginning with the words *atah chonantanu* in the *Ma'ariv Shemoneh Esrey*, or the words *barukh ha'mavdil bein ha'kodesh u'vein ha'chol* (Blessed is He who makes a separation between the sacred and the profane.), have been said.[240] Although some authorities permit women to eat after saying *barukh ha'mavdil*,[241] in practice their view is not accepted.[242]

90. *Melakhah* is forbidden on *motzo'ei Shabbath* until *Havdalah* is made.[243] If a woman recites *Ma'ariv* and includes

---

239. See paragraph 12.
240. *Shulchan Arukh* 299:1, and *Mishnah Berurah* 299:35. The *Kaf HaChayim* 299:46 reports that some people refrain from drinking water before *Havdalah*.

   The *Biur Halakhah* rules that one should not start a meal during twilight. (Twilight begins with sunset.) Those who permit starting a meal during twilight may be relied on only when there is an urgent need. A meal that is started before sunset may be continued into the night.
241. *Ezer Me'kudash*, commenting on the *Shulchan Arukh, Evven HaEzer* 62:8.
242. *Mishneh Halakhoth*, Vol. 6, No. 62, responds to a question concerning a man who does not return home immediately after services on Saturday night and whose wife finds it difficult to wait for him: "The best advice is that his wife eat the third *Shabbath* meal toward evening so she will not be hungry, and she will be able to wait for him to come home and recite *Havdalah*. In this way everything can be arranged peacefully."
243. *Shulchan Arukh* 299:10, and the *Mishnah Berurah*. Acts forbidden on

the paragraph *Atah chonantanu*, or if she says the words *barukh ha'mavdil bein ha'kodesh u'vein ha'chol*, she may do *melakhah* before hearing *Havdalah* recited over wine.[244]

A woman who does not know the *barukh ha'mavdil* formula may listen to someone else say it.[245]

91. Some authorities report that women are accustomed to refrain from *melakhah* on Saturday night, but this custom is not mentioned by most authorities and it is not practiced today.[246]

92. There is a dispute as to whether women are obligated to recite *Havdalah*.[247] Because women may be exempt, they

---

Shabbath by Rabbinic Law may not be performed before *Havdalah*. Discussing business or plans for the week, however, is permitted although such discussions may not be held on *Shabbath* itself. See the *Shulchan Arukh HaRav* 297:15.

244. *Remah* 299:10; *Mishnah Berurah* 299:39. When *Yom Tov* occurs on Saturday night, preparations such as cooking and setting the table may not begin until after *barukh ha'mavdil bein kodesh l'kodesh* (Blessed is He who makes a separation between one type of sanctity and another.) is said. See the *Mishnah Berurah* 299:36.

245. *Ba'er Heytev* 299:12. Whoever recites *barukh ha'mavdil* should keep in mind that it is being recited for the listener, and the listener should intend to fulfill her obligation by listening.

246. This custom is found in the *Avudraham*, at the end of *Seder Motzo'ei Shabbath*, and is mentioned in the *Magen Avraham* 229:15. But the *Orukh HaShulchan* 299:21 states, "We have not heard of this custom, which contradicts the Talmud *Yerushalmi*...Our women wait until after *Havdalah* and then perform all manner of work. This is the proper custom." Nevertheless, some women are accustomed to refrain from sewing on *motzo'ei Shabbath*.

247. The *Rambam*, *Hilkhoth Shabbath* 30:1, includes *Havdalah* in the *mitzvah* of *Zakhor eth yom HaShabbath* (Remember the *Shabbath*): "It is a positive commandment of the Torah to sanctify *Shabbath* with words. As it states, 'Remember the *Shabbath* day to sanctify it' — Remember it [with words of sanctification] when it enters and when it leaves. When it enters,[remember it] with *Kiddush*, and when

should listen to a man's recitation instead of reciting it themselves.[248]

A man may only recite *Havdalah* for a woman if he is also reciting it for himself. If he has already heard *Havdalah*, he may only recite it for her if other men or boys are fulfilling their obligations through his recitation.[249] It follows that a

---

it leaves, with *Havdalah.*"

Clearly, the *Rambam* categorizes *Kiddush* and *Havdalah* as two parts of the same *mitzvah*; women, who are required to make *Kiddush*, are also required to make *Havdalah*. The same view is expressed in the *Sefer HaChinukh* and by the *Smag*. The *Shulchan Arukh* 296:8 cites this view, as well as the dissenting one of the *Rash MiShantz*, according to which women are exempt from *Havdalah*. The *Mishnah Berurah* 296:34 cites the *Pri Megadim*, who explains how the *Rash MiShantz* does not categorize *Havdalah* as a *Shabbath mitzvah*; since it is recited after *Shabbath*, it is not governed by the juxtaposition of *zakhor v'shamor* (See note 160.), and the usual exemption of women from time-bound *mitzvoth* applies.

It would appear according to the *Remah*, who permits women to recite blessings over time-bound *mitzvoth*, that Ashkenazic women should be permitted to recite *Havdalah* whether they are obligated or not. The *Magen Avraham* argues to the contrary: When a *mitzvah* consists entirely of a blessing, such as *Havdalah*, one who is exempt from the *mitzvah* should not recite it; the *Remah*'s ruling applies only to blessings over *mitzvoth* that involve an act, such as *Shofar* and *Lulav*.

Har Tzvi, Orach Chayim, Vol. 1, No. 154, cites HaGaon Rav Issur Zalman Meltzer, who brings forward an additional reason why women refrain from reciting *Havdalah*. He argues that if women are not obligated to recite *Havdalah*, their recitation of the concluding blessing constitutes an interruption between the blessing over wine and drinking it.

The *Kaf HaChayim* 296:24 concludes, "Although the *Shulchan Arukh* cites authorities who obligate women in *Havdalah*, since there are conflicting views, one should be lenient with regard to questionable blessings."

248. *Remah, Ibid.* Since women *may* be exempt, they may not recite *Havdalah* for a man. See the *Shulchan Arukh HaRav* 296:19.

249. *Mishnah Berurah* 296:36. The *Birkey Yosef* 296:7 and *Orukh*

man should not intend to fulfill the *mitzvah* when listening to *Havdalah* in the synagogue if he plans to recite it at home for his wife when there are no other males present.[250]

A woman who cannot find a man to recite *Havdalah* for her should recite it herself.[251]

When a Woman Recites Havdalah

93. A woman who recites *Havdalah* should say the blessings over wine, spices and the concluding blessing, *HaMavdil bein kodesh le'chol*.[252] There is a dispute over whether she should recite the blessing over fire, *Borey me'orey ha'eish*.[253] Some Sephardic authorities rule that

---

HaShulchan 296:5 maintain that since many authorities rule that women are obligated to recite *Havdalah*, the principle of *arvuth* (mutual responsibility) applies, and a husband may recite *Havdalah* for his wife after fulfilling the *mitzvah* himself. (See note 161.) But the *Mishnah Berurah* concludes that we must take into account those authorities who exempt women from the *mitzvah*.

250. *Yabia Omer*, Vol. 4, *Orach Chayim*, No. 23–24.
251. *Mishnah Berurah* 296:35.
252. *Biur Halakhah* 296, beginning *Lo yavdilu*.
253. The *Magen Avraham*'s view — whenever a *mitzvah* consists entirely of a blessing, someone who is exempt from the *mitzvah* should not recite the blessing — is discussed in note 247. Even if women are required to recite *Havdalah*, the blessing over fire is not part of this *mitzvah*. The blessing over fire on Saturday night commemorates the tradition that *Adam HaRishon* discovered fire on *motzo'ei Shabbath*; since it is not connected to *Shabbath*, it is a time-bound *mitzvah*. According to the *Magen Avraham*, women should not perform this *mitzvah*, because it consists entirely of a blessing.

Nevertheless, the *Birkey Yosef* 693:1, *Kaf HaChayim* 296:55, *Yabia Omer*, Vol. 4, *Orach Chayim*, Nos. 23–24, and *Be'er Moshe*, Vol. 4, No. 28, all rule that women may recite the blessing over fire. One of their reasons is that it is not a *birkath ha'mitzvah*, but a blessing in praise of God, which relates to women as much as to men. HaGaon Rav Moshe Feinstein arrives at the same conclusion

women should recite the blessing *HaMavdil bein kodesh le'chol* without *shem* and *malkhuth*.[254]

94. Although it is not customary for women to drink *Havdalah* wine,[255] a woman who recites *Havdalah* should.[256]

95. Some authorities rule that a woman who is unable to hear *Havdalah*, for example a hospital patient, may listen to it over the telephone.[257]

---

in *Iggeroth Moshe, Evven HaEzer*, Vol. 4, No. 65.

254. *Kaf HaChayim* 296:55.

255. *Mishnah Berurah* 296:6, citing the *Magen Avraham*. This custom, found in the *She'lah*, is based on the tradition that the tree of knowledge, through which Eve caused *Adam HaRishon* to sin, was a grapevine. See also *Ta'amey HaMinhagim* 417 and *Har Tzvi, Orach Chayim*, Vol. 1, No. 154.

The *Orukh HaShulchan* 296:5 reports that many women are not particular about this custom. In fact, *Leket Yosher* observes that his teacher, the author of the *Terumoth HaDeshen*, was accustomed to give his wife *Havdalah* wine to drink.

256. *Mishnah Berurah, Ibid. Shevet HaLevi, Orach Chayim*, Vol. 4, No. 56, writes, "[A woman who recites *Havdalah* herself] has no reason to fear tasting the wine...for this is only a custom and cannot override the requirements of the law [that one who recites *Havdalah* must drink some of the wine]."

257. *Iggeroth Moshe, Orach Chayim*, Vol. 4, No. 91:4, based on *Iggeroth Moshe, Orach Chayim*, Vol. 2, No. 108, which rules that in a time of need, a person can fulfill the *mitzvah* of hearing the *Megillah* on *Purim* by listening to it over a loudspeaker. According to this view, one should answer *amein* to a blessing heard over a telephone or loudspeaker. Other authorities, such as *Shevet HaLevi, Orach Chayim*, Vol. 4, No. 56, *Tzitz Eliezer*, Vol. 4, No. 26:2, and *Yabia Omer*, Vol. 1, *Orach Chayim*, No. 19:18, in the name of HaGaon Rav Shlomo Zalman Auerbach, rule that a voice heard over the telephone or loudspeaker is not the true voice, and a person cannot fulfill the obligation of listening to a recitation in this way. See *Ha'Tefillah B'Tzibur*, Chapter 5, note 31.

Of course, the woman should say *Barukh ha'mavdil bein ha'kodesh u'vein ha'chol* before picking up the telephone.

Listening to Havdalah

96. A woman should stand or sit (according to the family custom) in one place, near the person reciting *Havdalah*. She should not wander around the room.[258]

When the blessing over fire is recited, the listeners should stand close enough to the candle to derive benefit from its light.[259]

97. The listeners must intend to fulfill the *mitzvah* by listening. They must be careful to hear every word of the blessings and answer *amein. Barukh hu u'varukh sh'mo* should not be said.[260]

98. The listeners should not speak until the person reciting *Havdalah* has drunk from the cup of wine.[261] If a person hears the blessing *HaMavdil bein kodesh le'chol*, but not the

---

258. *Mishnah Berurah* 296:27; *Ben Ish Chai, Shanah Rishonah, Parshath VaYetze* 21.

259. *Mishnah Berurah* 297:13 and 298:13. See the *Shulchan Arukh* 298:4 and 298:15, which rules that a person should stand close enough to see the flame and derive benefit from its light. The *Kaf HaChayim* 298:22 rules that one who heard the blessing in a place where she could not derive benefit from the light need not repeat it.

260. See note 183.

261. *Iggeroth Moshe, Orach Chayim*, Vol. 4, No. 70, raises the possibility that the *mitzvah* might not be fulfilled if listeners speak before the person reciting *Havdalah* drinks some wine. It is important to caution listeners not to interrupt, even with *shavu'a tov* (a good week), until after wine has been drunk.

The *Mishnah Berurah* 297:14 objects to people who engage in reciting the blessings over spices and fire while the person reciting *Havdalah* is saying the blessing *HaMavdil bein kodesh le'chol*: "Since they intend to fulfill the *mitzvah* by listening, they must concentrate on hearing the concluding blessing of *Havdalah* without reciting other blessings at that time."

blessing over wine, the *mitzvah* is fulfilled.[262]

99. Some people are accustomed to recite their own blessings over the fire and spices although they only listen to the rest of *Havdalah*.[263] This is not recommended.[264]

100. A woman who is a *niddah* may hold the candle while her husband recites *Havdalah* and derives benefit from the candle's light.[265] It is reasonable to assume that he may also smell spices while she holds them.[266]

---

262. *Mishnah Berurah* 296:33; *Shulchan Arukh HaRav* 296:18. Also see *Imrey Yosher*, Vol. 2, No. 173.
263. This custom is cited in *Va'yaged Moshe, Laws and Customs of the Seder*, p. 293; *Mateh Ephrayim* 600:4; *Orukh HaShulchan* 297:7 and 298:9; *Ketzoth HaShulchan*, No. 96, note 6.
264. The *Mishnah Berurah* 297:13 explains that there is a greater glory to God when many people participate in the recitation of a blessing than when each person recites the blessing separately. See also the *Shulchan Arukh* 298:14.
265. *Iggeroth Moshe, Yoreh De'ah*, Vol. 2, No. 83, cites the *Pithchey Teshuvah, Yoreh De'ah* 195:3, which forbids a man to light a fire or warm himself with a candle held by his wife when she is a *niddah*. *Iggeroth Moshe* explains, "He is deriving benefit from heat which is connected to her body. This is considered deriving physical pleasure from his wife. The blessing over fire at *Havdalah* is recited over benefit obtained from the *light*, not the heat. Since the light is not connected to her body, he receives no physical pleasure from her, and it is permitted."
266. This is based on other arguments mentioned in *Iggeroth Moshe, Ibid*. Since her husband only derives momentary pleasure, without touching her hand, it is permitted. This ruling does not contradict the law stated in the *Shulchan Arukh* 217:4, and the *Mishnah Berurah* 217:16, forbidding a man to smell his wife's perfume when she is a *niddah*. Here he does not intend to smell his wife's fragrant body, only to smell the *Havdalah* spices.

Melaveh Malkah

101. Men and women are included in the *mitzvah* to make a *melaveh malkah*, a meal to escort the *Shabbath* Queen on *motzo'ei Shabbath.*[267] Some authorities state that the *mitzvah* of *Melaveh Malkah* is a *segulah* for easy childbirth.[268]

102. Women should not become involved in time-consuming work until after the *melaveh malkah.*[269] Some are particular not to take off their *Shabbath* clothes until after this meal.[270]

---

267. *Machatzith HaShekel* 300; *Ma'asey Rav*, No. 16. See also the *Pri Megadim, Eshel Avraham* 300. *Tosafoth Ma'asey Rav*, par. 39, reports that the Vilna Gaon attached great importance to the *melaveh malkah:* "He was accustomed to eat radish and fresh bread at the *melaveh malkah.* Once he became sick and vomited his food. When he recovered, he asked those who were standing around him to check if there was still time before dawn so that he could eat a *kezayith* of bread in order to fulfill the *mitzvah* of *Melaveh Malkah.* On another occasion, his wife undertook to fast. She interrupted the third *Shabbath* meal [to begin her fast] and went to sleep immediately after *Havdalah.* When the Gaon heard of this, he sent for her [and said that] all the fasts a person observes cannot rectify one omitted *melaveh malkah.* She then got up from bed and ate."
268. This is cited in the name of the Saintly R. Elimelech of Lizansk, in the additional notes to *Minchath Shabbath* 96:30. The author also advises one to say, "This is for the sake of the *mitzvah* of *Melaveh Malkah,*" before eating.
269. *Mishnah Berurah* 300:2.
270. *Yesod V'Shoresh HaAvodah, Sha'ar* 8, citing the *Ari Zal; Kaf HaChayim* 300:6.

103. Cooking a special dish for the *melaveh malkah* is praiseworthy.[271] It is customary to eat bread, meat, or some other cooked dish,[272] and a hot drink.[273]

---

271. *Sha'arey Teshuvah* 300, citing the *Maharsha*.
272. *Mishnah Berurah* 300:1.
273. *Eshel Avraham* (Butchach), *Mahadura Tinyana* 300. This is based on Tractate *Shabbath* 119b: "Hot food on *motzo'ei Shabbath* is therapeutic." The *Maharsha* explains that this refers to food heated on Saturday night: "The reason for this [custom] is that it is proper to escort *Shabbath* out by preparing something after *Shabbath* that could not have been prepared on *Shabbath*, such as a hot drink or fresh bread. Because cold foods and drinks eaten on *Shabbath* are not beneficial to sick people, we say that hot food served at the *melaveh malkah* is therapeutic."

CHAPTER 16
Rosh Chodesh

Its Significance for Women

1. *Rosh Chodesh* is considered a minor holiday for women, a reward for their righteousness in not contributing ornaments for the golden calf.[1]

---

1. *Tur* 417, based on the Talmud *Yerushalmi*, Tractate *Ta'anith*, Chapter 1, and *Pirkey D'Rabbi Eliezer*, Chapter 45. *Me'am Loez, Shemoth*, p. 1115, offers a number of interpretations of the relationship between the sin of the golden calf and *Rosh Chodesh*. The *Levush* emphasizes the great reward promised women in the merit of their not donating ornaments for the golden calf. The *Darkey Moshe* cites an additional reason for this custom in the name of the *Ohr Zarua* (2:454): "Because women immerse themselves in the *mikvah* each month and endear themselves to their husbands, they are renewed like the moon...[*Rosh Chodesh*] is therefore treated as a holiday by them."

The *Ben Ish Chai, Shanah Sh'niah, Parshath VaYikra*, states, "Women should be extremely conscientious to observe the sanctity of *Rosh Chodesh*. Although they are secondary to men in many *mitzvoth*, this is one of the *mitzvoth* in which women play a more significant role than men do." *Shibuley HaLeket*, No. 169, traces the

Some women are accustomed to wear special clothes on *Rosh Chodesh*.[2]

Refraining from Work

2. It is an old, established custom for women to refrain from everyday chores on *Rosh Chodesh*.[3] Refraining from sewing, weaving, laundering, and ironing is customary.[4]

---

observance of *Rosh Chodesh* as a holiday to the days of *Moshe Rabbenu*. Due to the festive nature of the day, the *Shulchan Arukh* 420 forbids crying over a deceased person on *Rosh Chodesh*.

In many Sephardic communities it is customary for women to light candles on the night of *Rosh Chodesh* (without a blessing). They refrain from sewing, weaving, and embroidering while the candles are burning. The Babylonian custom of lighting two candles is cited in *Yalkut Minhagim LeShivtey Yisrael*.

2. *Kaf HaChayim* 419:6. *Ma'asey Rav*, No. 149, reports that the Vilna Gaon wore his *Shabbath* hat in honor of *Rosh Chodesh*.

3. *Shulchan Arukh* 417. The *Mishnah Berurah* 417:4 discusses the question whether the custom to refrain from work applies to one or both days of *Rosh Chodesh* in months in which two days are observed. After citing authorities who rule that a woman follows the custom of her community, he adds that those who refrain from work for only one day of *Rosh Chodesh* should refrain on the second day, since that is the first calendar day of the new month.

Although *Mor U'Ketziah* rules that all forms of work are permitted at night, the *Biur Halakhah* 417 is uncertain that this is the accepted practice.

4. *Ibid*. Housework necessary for that day may be done. See *Eshel Avraham* (Butchach) 417.

Women who refrain from doing laundry on *Rosh Chodesh* should not launder clothes in a washing machine.

A related custom, cited in the *Sefer HaChinukh* 403, forbids women to launder linen garments when the new moon appears (the *molad ha'levanah*). This custom is also cited in *Sha'arey Teshuvah* 426 and the *Ben Ish Chai, Shanah Sh'niah, Parshath VaYikra* 33.

3. In keeping with the above, a man may not demand that his wife carry out these chores on *Rosh Chodesh*. She may prepare meals as usual; indeed, it is a *mitzvah* to serve a festive meal on this day.[5]

4. A woman who is employed is not obligated to refrain from her normal work on *Rosh Chodesh*.[6]

The Rosh Chodesh Meal

5. Ideally, one should eat a meal with bread in honor of *Rosh Chodesh*. It is a *mitzvah* to have a larger meal than usual.[7] Those who are particular in the fulfillment of

---

5. Contrary to paragraph 2, the *Bach* 417 explains that the custom only prohibits a husband from demanding that his wife work; she may work if she wishes.

    The *Biur Halakhah* 417 points out that men who refrain from work on *Rosh Chodesh* are acting incorrectly. Whoever adopts this practice is not considered to have taken a vow, so annulment is unnecessary.

6. *Orukh HaShulchan* 419:10: "Women who have a profession go to work on *Rosh Chodesh*. They did not accept the custom [to refrain from work on *Rosh Chodesh*] when it conflicts with their livelihood."

7. *Shulchan Arukh* 419:1, and *Mishnah Berurah*. Although not obligatory, eating bread on *Rosh Chodesh* is a *mitzvah*. Whoever spends extra money for a festive *Rosh Chodesh* meal is praiseworthy, as explained in the *Midrash Rabbah*, *Parshath Emor* 20: "On *Rosh HaShanah*, a person's sustenance for the whole year is determined with the exception of money spent on food for *Shabbath*, *Yom Tov*, *Rosh Chodesh*, and *Chol HaMoed*." (A similar reading is found in Tractate *Betzah* 16a, but *Rosh Chodesh* and *Chol HaMoed* are omitted. See the glosses of HaGaon Rav Betzalel Ransburg on Tractate *Betzah*.) The *Midrash* explains that the *mitzvah* of eating a festive meal applies primarily during the day.

mitzvoth prepare a special dish in honor of the day. Even when *Rosh Chodesh* occurs on *Shabbath*, they prepare an extra dish in its honor.[8]

Hallel and Mussaf

6. Women are not required to recite *Hallel* on *Rosh Chodesh.*[9] Ashkenazic women are permitted to recite *Hallel* with its blessings.[10] Sephardic women who wish to recite *Hallel* should omit the blessings.[11]

7. There is a debate as to whether women are obligated to recite *Mussaf.* Both Ashkenazic and Sephardic women may recite it if they wish.[12]

---

8. *Mishnah Berurah* 419:2. A woman who forgets to add an extra dish on *Shabbath* in honor of *Rosh Chodesh* should prepare a larger than usual *melaveh malkah.*

9. *Biur Halakhah* 422, beginning *Hallel.*

10. *Biur Halakhah, Ibid.* See also Chapter 2, paragraph 39. The Ashkenazic practice follows the ruling of the *Remah*, which allows women to recite blessings over *mitzvoth* from which they are exempt.

In most Sephardic and some Ashkenazic communities, men do not recite the blessing over *Hallel* on *Rosh Chodesh.* The recitation of *Hallel* on *Rosh Chodesh* is a *minhag* (custom); these communities follow the view that a blessing is not recited over a *minhag.* Clearly, women in these communities should not recite the blessing over *Hallel.*

11. Sephardic women follow the view of the *Beith Yosef*, which forbids women to recite blessings over time-bound *mitzvoth.* (See the Introduction, paragraph 8.) As explained in note 10, there is a more compelling reason for Sephardic women to omit the blessing: Even men do not recite the blessing over *Hallel* on *Rosh Chodesh* in most of their communities.

12. See Chapter 2, note 78, for a detailed discussion.

Kiddush Levanah

8. Women are exempt from reciting *Kiddush Levanah*, the blessing to the Creator of the moon.[13] Some authorities

---

13. *Magen Avraham* 70:1, 296:11, and 426:1, cited in the *Mishnah Berurah* 70:1 and 106:4. *Kiddush Levanah* is only recited during the waxing of the moon, therefore it is categorized as a time-bound *mitzvah*. Although Ashkenazic women are generally permitted to recite blessings over time-bound *mitzvoth* (See note 10.), a variety of reasons are offered why it is not customary for them to recite *Kiddush Levanah*.

The *Shelah* explains that women refrain from reciting the blessing over the moon's renewal because Eve's sin contributed to its diminution.

The *Magen Avraham* postulates, "It is possible that the *Remah* only permits women to recite blessings over *mitzvoth* that involve an action. If [the *mitzvah*] consists entirely of a blessing, they are not permitted [to recite it]. Perhaps this is the reason why they do not recite *Kiddush Levanah*." The *Magen Avraham*'s theory is cited in Chapter 15, note 247, as the reason why women do not recite *Havdalah*.

In his glosses on the *Shulchan Arukh* 426, the *Chokhmath Shlomoh* questions the *Magen Avraham*'s premise that *Kiddush Levanah* is a time-bound *mitzvah*. He argues that *Kiddush Levanah* cannot be compared to *mitzvoth* such as *Shofar*, *Sukkah*, and *Lulav*. The actions involved in these *mitzvoth* could hypothetically be carried out any time of the year. The fact that the Torah requires their performance at particular times makes them time-bound. *Kiddush Levanah*, which praises God for the moon's renewal, can *only* be recited during the first half of the month, when the moon is undergoing renewal. Its timing coincides with natural factors, not halakhic ones. *Kiddush Levanah*, therefore, is not categorized as a time-bound *mitzvah*. The recitation of *She'he'che'yanu* over a fruit that has just come into season is similar. No one argues that women should not recite this blessing because it is "time-bound", i.e., it can only be recited at the beginning of the season.

The *Chokhmath Shlomoh* supports his argument by citing the *Turey Evven*'s explanation of Tractate *Megillah* 20b. The *Turey Evven* explains that women are obligated to bring first fruits

maintain that a woman should listen to a man say the blessing or recite the blessing *Me'chadesh chodashim* without *shem* and *malkhuth*, but this is not the general custom.[14]

It is customary for women to recite the special prayer *Mi she'asah nissim*, announcing the arrival of *Rosh Chodesh* on the *Shabbath* before *Rosh Chodesh*, but they are not obligated to do so.[15]

(*Bikurim*) to Jerusalem, in spite of the fact that this *mitzvah* can only be fulfilled between *Shavuoth* and *Chanukah*, because the time factor is a function of the growing season and not intrinsic to the *mitzvah*. In spite of its time limits, it is not a time-bound *mitzvah*. This logic applies to *Kiddush Levanah* as well.

In *Mishmereth Chaim*, p. 30, HaGaon Rav Chaim Pinchus Sheinberg defends the view of the *Magen Avraham*. According to Hagaon Rav Sheinberg, the time-orientation of *She'he'che'yanu* and *Bikurim* is certainly based on seasonal factors, but *Kiddush Levanah* could hypothetically be recited even during the waning of the moon. The blessing is recited over the phenomena of waxing and waning, and there is no intrinsic reason to recite it only during the moon's waxing; *Chazal mandated* that the blessing be said during the moon's waxing, for halakhic rather than natural considerations. It is thus classified as time-bound. See further in *HaElef LeKhah Shlomoh, Orach Chayim,* No. 193, and *Teshuvoth Maharil Diskin, Kuntres Acharon,* 5:26.

An additional reason why women do not recite *Kiddush Levanah* is brought forward by *Salmath Chayim*, Vol. 1, No. 98, who cites the *Chatham Sofer* on kindling *Chanukah menorah*s. The *Chatham Sofer* writes that *menorah*s were traditionally lit outdoors. It was considered unseemly for a woman to stand among a group of men outside at night, and for this reason, it became customary for women not to light their own *menorah*s. (See Chapter 21, note 3.) *Kiddush Levanah* is also recited outdoors in a public gathering.

The *Yeshuoth Yaqcov, Orach Chayim* 426:1, links *Kiddush Levanah* with the study of the Oral Law; since women do not usually study the Oral Law they do not recite *Kiddush Levanah*.

14. *Orukh HaShulchan* 426; *Kaf HaChayim* 426:1.

15. *Pri Megadim* 426; *Kethav Sofer, Orach Chayim,* No. 34. This prayer simply reminds people which day *Rosh Chodesh* will fall on so they will remember to say *Hallel* and *Mussaf.* See the *Mishnah Berurah* 417:1.

CHAPTER 17
Yom Tov

Introduction

1. All categories of *melakhah* forbidden on *Shabbath* are also forbidden on *Yom Tov*, with the exception of certain *melakhoth* connected to the preparation of food, and the *melakhah* of carrying. A woman must be well-versed in the differences between *Shabbath* and *Yom Tov*, especially in regard to food preparation, lighting a fire, and preparing on *Shabbath* for *Yom Tov* and vice versa. Otherwise, she may be mistakenly lenient in actions which involve a transgression of Torah Law.

Eiruv Tavshilin

2. When *Yom Tov* occurs on *Erev Shabbath*, it is forbidden to cook or prepare food on *Yom Tov* for *Shabbath* unless an *eiruv tavshilin* is prepared.[1] An *eiruv* prepared by the master

---

1. The *mitzvah* of *Eiruv Tavshilin* is fulfilled by preparing two cooked

or mistress of the house allows all members of the family to cook and prepare for *Shabbath*; there is no need for other members of the family to make their own *eiruvs*.[2]

Guests — individuals or families — may rely on their host's *eiruv tavshilin*.[3]

3. A woman who lives alone must prepare an *eiruv tavshilin*.[4] If she does not know how to make one, or forgets

---

foods and reciting the blessing *Al mitzvath eiruv*, followed by the words, "Through this *eiruv* may it be permitted for us to bake, cook, keep food warm, kindle lights, and do anything on the Festival in preparation for *Shabbath*, for us and all who live in this city." The *eiruv* is then set aside to be eaten on *Shabbath*, customarily at the third *Shabbath* meal.

In Tractate *Betzah* 15b, two reasons are given for *Chazal* legislating *Eiruv Tavshilin*. Rava explains that when *Yom Tov* occurs on Friday, people are apt to spend all their energies on *Yom Tov* and forget that *Shabbath* immediately follows; they might neglect to set aside food for *Shabbath*, neglecting the *mitzvah* of *Kavod Shabbath*. *Chazal* therefore require food to be set aside for *Shabbath* before the onset of *Yom Tov*, "so that one will choose a good portion for *Shabbath* and a good portion for *Yom Tov*."

Rav Ashi ascribes the law of *Eiruv Tavshilin* to *Chazal*'s fear that if people are permitted to cook freely on *Yom Tov* for *Shabbath*, they might come to cook on *Yom Tov* for the week, an act forbidden by the Torah. *Chazal* therefore permit cooking on *Yom Tov* for *Shabbath* only if an *eiruv tavshilin* is prepared beforehand, "So people should say that one may not cook on *Yom Tov* for *Shabbath* [except with an *eiruv*]; certainly one may not [cook] on *Yom Tov* for the week."

2. *Mishnah Berurah* 527:56. Since everyone eats together, one *eiruv* is sufficient.

3. *Eshel Avraham* 527. It is improper to prepare additional *eiruv tavshilins* when one is sufficient because such preparation would entail recitation of unnecessary blessings.

4. *Shulchan Arukh* 527:7; *Kitzur Shulchan Arukh* 102:6. Since women are obligated in the *mitzvah* of *Kavod Shabbath* and cautioned against cooking on *Yom Tov* for the week, both of the reasons for

to do so, she may rely on the *eiruv* which the Rabbi or Rabbinical Court of the city prepares on behalf of the city's residents.[5]

A group of women who are spending *Yom Tov* together must make individual *eiruv tavshilin*s if each woman eats her own food.[6]

4. The *eiruv tavshilin* should be prepared before lighting *Yom Tov* candles. If the candles were already lit, it can still be prepared anytime before nightfall.[7]

5. If an *eiruv tavshilin* was not prepared by the family, and the Rabbi of the city did not prepare one on behalf of the city's residents,[8] only one candle may be lit for *Shabbath*. But if someone who made an *eiruv* is found, a number of candles

---

Eiruv Tavshilin in note 1 apply to them. The fact that *Eiruv Tavshilin* is a time-bound *mitzvah* does not exempt women from it. See *Sho'el U'meishiv, Tinyana*, Vol. 2, No. 55, and *Sdeh Chemed, Ma'arekheth HaMem*, No. 135.

5. *Shulchan Arukh* and *Remah* 527:7; *Orukh HaShulchan* 527:14.

Although the Rabbi of the city intends to include all its residents in his *eiruv*, the *Shulchan Arukh* and *Mishnah Berurah* explain that the Rabbi's *eiruv* may only be used by someone who fails to make an *eiruv* due to pressing circumstances, someone whose *eiruv* was lost before *Shabbath* preparations were complete, or someone who does not know how to make an *eiruv*. A person who neglects to make an *eiruv* due to laziness or willfull neglect may not rely on the Rabbi's *eiruv*. The *Mishnah Berurah* adds that a person who forgets to make an *eiruv* twice in a row is deemed negligent.

6. *Eshel Avraham* 527.

7. *Biur Halakhah* 527, beginning *Safek*. The *Remah* 527:1 rules that an *eiruv tavshilin* may be prepared during twilight. The *Mishnah Berurah* limits the *Remah*'s ruling to a person who has not accepted *Yom Tov* yet. Since it is uncertain whether women accept *Yom Tov* when they light (See note 15.), the *Biur Halakhah* concludes that one who forgets to prepare an *eiruv* before candle-lighting may prepare it afterwards.

8. See note 5.

may be given to him as a gift and he may light them.[9]

6. The wicks of *Shabbath* candles should not be singed on *Yom Tov*, nor should the wax on the bottoms of the candles be melted to hold them in place.[10] People who use oil should prepare the wicks before *Yom Tov*.[11]

Candle-lighting

7. Lighting candles for *Yom Tov* is as much an obligation as lighting candles for *Shabbath*. When *Yom Tov* occurs during the week, the blessing for candle-lighting is *LeHadlik ner shel Yom Tov*.[12] This blessing is repeated when lighting candles on the second day of *Yom Tov* outside *Eretz Yisrael*. When *Yom Tov* occurs on *Shabbath*, the blessing is *LeHadlik*

---

9. *Shulchan Arukh* 527:12; *Mishnah Berurah* 527:55.

10. *Shulchan Arukh* 514:9. The *Mishnah Berurah* 514:18 explains that melting the wax may result in smoothing it, a sub-category of the *melakhah* of *me'machek* (scraping).

   The *Chaye Adam* 92:2 points out that although wax may be removed from the candlesticks, it is better to use other candlesticks that do not have to be cleaned out.

   All these rules also apply to lighting candles on the second night of *Yom Tov* outside *Eretz Yisrael*.

11. *Shulchan Arukh, Ibid.* The *Mishnah Berurah* 501:34 advises those who use wicks to prepare new ones for the second night of *Yom Tov*. If new wicks are not available, it is best to kindle the other end of the old wick, which was not lit the previous night.

12. *Shulchan Arukh* 263:5, and *Mishnah Berurah. Ye'chaveh Da'ath*, Vol. 1, No. 27, reports that the Yemenite custom is to omit the blessing over candle-lighting on *Yom Tov*. This is based on the fact that the *Rambam* only mentions a blessing when discussing *Shabbath* candle-lighting. See *Pe'ulath Tzadik*, Vol. 3, No. 270. *Ye'chaveh Da'ath* advises Yemenite women who settle in *Eretz Yisrael* to adopt the prevailing custom and recite the blessing.

ner shel Shabbath V'Yom Tov.[13]

8. Some women are accustomed to postpone candle-lighting on weekday *Yamim Tovim* until their husbands return from the synagogue.[14] Others light towards evening, just as on *Erev Shabbath.*[15] Candles should certainly be lit early if a room is dark.[16]

9. When *Yom Tov* falls on *motzo'ei Shabbath*, it is forbidden to light the candles, cook, or prepare for *Yom Tov* in any way until the conclusion of *Shabbath*, and then only after reciting *Ma'ariv,*[17] or the words *Barukh ha'mavdil bein kodesh le'kodesh.*[18]

10. On the second night of *Yom Tov* outside *Eretz Yisrael*, candles should not be lit until after dark.[19] If there are no

---

13. *Mishnah Berurah* 263:24 and 514:48. *Yom Tov* candles which blow out before the meal should be re-kindled without a blessing.
14. *Mateh Ephrayim* 625:33; *Chatham Sofer*, novellae on Tractate *Shabbath* 23b. Also see the glosses of HaGaon Rav Y.S. Natanson on the *Shulchan Arukh* 263.
15. The *Prishah*, in the introduction to his commentary on the *Tur*, *Yoreh De'ah*, in the name of his mother. See also *Pri Yitzchak*, Vol. 1, No. 6.
    The *Biur Halakhah* 527, beginning *safek*, is uncertain whether a woman accepts *Yom Tov* when she lights candles. (See Chapter 15, paragraph 25, where it is explained that a woman certainly accepts *Shabbath* when she lights *Shabbath* candles.) In fact, this question is debated by earlier authorities. In his novellae on Tractate *Shabbath* 23b, the *Chatham Sofer* rules that a woman accepts *Yom Tov* when she lights candles. HaGaon Rav Shlomo Kluger rules to the contrary in *U'vacharta Ba'Chayim*, No. 83.
    A woman who recites the blessing *She'he'che'yanu* when she lights candles definitely accepts *Yom Tov*. See paragraph 14.
16. *Mateh Ephrayim* 625:33.
17. *Mateh Ephrayim* 599:10.
18. *Mishnah Berurah* 299:36.
19. See the *Prisha*'s introduction to his commentary on the *Tur*, *Yoreh*

electric lights burning and the dining room is dark, candles may be lit before nightfall.[20]

11. Most authorities agree that even women who light *Shabbath* candles before reciting the blessing[21] should recite the blessing before lighting *Yom Tov* candles.[22] Some rule that they should not deviate from their usual custom, and should therefore light and then recite the blessing.[23]

Some commentators note that the proponents of both views agree that if a woman lights after dark, the blessing

---

De'ah. Lighting candles before dark is considered "preparing" for the next day; preparing on the first day of *Yom Tov* for the next day is forbidden.

20. *Eliyahu Rabbah* 485:7; *Mishnah Berurah* 514:33. In this case, the candle-light will be used on the first day of *Yom Tov*, and lighting the candles is not an act of preparation for the next day. Candles which will be lit after dark should not be placed in the candlesticks before dark; this is also considered preparing for the second day.

21. See Chapter 15, paragraph 53.

22. This appears to be the conclusion of the *Mishnah Berurah* 263:27. It is based on an halakhic insight of the *Prishah*'s mother.

   It is explained in Chapter 15, note 138, that the custom to light *Shabbath* candles before making the blessing is based on the view that a woman accepts *Shabbath* when she recites the blessing. The *Prisha*'s mother reasons that since candles may be lit after the start of *Yom Tov*, it is best to follow the general procedure and recite the blessing prior to the performance of the *mitzvah*. This is also the conclusion of the *Dagul Mer'vavah* and Rabbi Akiva Eiger in their glosses on the *Shulchan Arukh* 263, as well as the *Chaye Adam* 5:11, and the *Orukh HaShulchan* 263:13.

23. The *Magen Avraham* 263:12, *Shulchan Arukh HaRav* 263:8, and *Kitzur Shulchan Arukh* 75:4, maintain that women should not depart from their normal procedure. Since the blessing is recited after lighting *Shabbath* candles, the same procedure should be followed on *Yom Tov*.

   Women who are accustomed to recite the blessing before lighting *Shabbath* candles (See Chapter 15, paragraph 53.) should certainly follow the same procedure on *Yom Tov*. See *Ye'chaveh Da'ath*, Vol. 1, No. 27.

should precede the lighting.[24]

12. A woman should light the same number of candles for *Yom Tov* that she lights for *Shabbath*.[25] Candles which blow out should not be used for any other purpose during *Yom Tov*.[26]

13. Many women are accustomed to recite the blessing *She'he'che'yanu* when they light *Yom Tov* candles.[27] Some

---

24. *Mateh Ephrayim* 625:33. Lighting *Yom Tov* candles after dark is not similar to lighting *Shabbath* candles, which may never be lit after dark. Therefore, the principle "One must not deviate from the usual procedure" does not apply.

25. *Az Nid'biru*, Vol. 3, No. 5. There is no source which distinguishes the number of candles to be lit for *Shabbath* from the number to be lit for *Yom Tov*. The *Shulchan Arukh* 514:24 rules that lighting one candle satisfies the minimum requirement for *Yom Tov*. The *Pri Megadim, Mishbetzoth Zahav* 514:12, explicitly states that a woman who lights two candles for *Shabbath* should also light two candles for *Yom Tov*. The *Kaf HaChayim* 263:9 rules that a woman who lights seven candles for *Shabbath*, equal to the number of people called to the Torah on that day, should light five candles on *Yom Tov*, equal to the number called to the Torah on that day.

26. *Shulchan Arukh HaRav* 514:24. *Yom Tov* candles, which have been "set aside" for a *mitzvah*, may not be used for any other purpose. When oil is used instead of candles, any which spills or is leftover may not be used for any other purpose. While they are burning, the candles may be moved for their light. Only using them for a purpose other than light is forbidden.

27. *Eliyahu Rabbah* 600:3; *Mateh Ephrayim* 581:54, and 619:4; *Ben Ish Chai, Shanah Sh'niah, Parshath Noach* 8.

In *Hagadath Mo'adim U'Zmanim, Hilkhoth Hadlakath HaNer*, par. 4, HaRav Moshe Sternbuch points out that women who recite the blessing before lighting *Yom Tov* candles should recite *She'he'che'yanu* after lighting so as not to make an interruption between the blessing over the *mitzvah* of Candle-lighting and its performance. See also *Pri HaSadeh*, Vol. 3, No. 159, and the article of HaGaon Rav Shmuel Aharon Yudelevitz, in the journal *Moriah*, *Adar*, 5729.

authorities rule that they should not recite *She'he'che'yanu* then, but listen to their husbands recite *She'he'che'yanu* with *Kiddush.*[28] A woman who recited it when she lit candles should not repeat it if she recites *Kiddush* herself.[29]

Some authorities rule that a woman who recites *She'he'che'yanu* when she lights candles should not answer *amein* when she hears the blessing at *Kiddush.*[30]

---

28. *She'ilath Ya'avetz*, Vol. 1, No. 107, cited in the *Mishnah Berurah* 263:23, fails to find any source mandating the recitation of *She'he'che'yanu* when lighting *Yom Tov* candles. Nevertheless, the *Mishnah Berurah* concludes that one need not object to this custom. Also see *Ye'chaveh Da'ath*, Vol. 3, No. 34, and the glosses of Rabbi Akiva Eiger on the *Shulchan Arukh* 263.

   Hagadah Shel Pessach Mi'Beith Levi (Brisk), p. 70, reports that HaGaon Rav Yitzchak Ze'ev Soloveitchik cautioned women against this practice, maintaining that they should listen to *She'he'che'yanu* at *Kiddush* just as men do.

   HaGaon Rav Ben Zion Abba Shaul rules that although many Sephardic authorities maintain that women should not recite *She'he'che'yanu* when they light candles, a woman who does recite it need not change her custom. There are recognized authorities on whom she can rely.

29. *Mateh Ephrayim* 619:4; *Kaf HaChayim* 514:112. *She'he'che'yanu* recited at candle-lighting refers not only to the sanctity of the day but also to the particular *mitzvoth* of the Festival. There is therefore no reason for her to repeat the blessing when she recites *Kiddush*.

30. *Har Tzvi, Orach Chayim*, No. 154; *Ye'chaveh Da'ath*, Vol. 3, No. 34. Answering *amein* to a blessing which she has already made constitutes an unnecessary interruption between *Kiddush* and drinking the wine. See *Rivevoth Ephrayim*, Vol. 1, No. 182, for a full discussion.

   To the contrary, HaGaon Rav Moshe Feinstein decides, in *Iggeroth Moshe, Orach Chayim*, Vol. 4, No. 21:9, that a woman may answer *amein* to *She'he'che'yanu*, even if she already recited it. He reasons that if answering *amein* to the blessing is an interruption, early authorities who allow women to recite *She'he'che'yanu* at candle-lighting would have cautioned them not to answer *amein* to *She'he'che'yanu* at *Kiddush*.

14. A woman who stipulates that she does not accept *Yom Tov* with candle-lighting[31] should not recite *She'he'che'yanu* at that time.[32]

15. When *Yom Tov* occurs on *Shabbath* and a woman forgets to mention *Shabbath* or *Yom Tov* in her blessing, she need not repeat it. This is so even when she mistakenly says *le'hadlik ner shel Shabbath* on a *Yom Tov* which occurs during the week.[33]

A third view is held by HaGaon Rav Shmuel Wossner in *Shevet HaLevi*, Vol. 3, No. 69. Agreeing in principle with the view of *Har Tzvi*, he offers a suggestion as to how women may answer *amein* to *She'he'che'yanu* at *Kiddush* on *Pessach* and *Sukkoth*: *She'he'che'yanu* should be recited at candle-lighting with the intention that it refer only to the general sanctity of the day, not to the unique *mitzvoth* of the Festival, i.e., sitting in the *sukkah* and the *mitzvoth* of the *Seder*. She may then answer *amein* to *She'he'che'yanu* at *Kiddush* with the intention that it refer to the unique *mitzvoth* of the holiday.

The reason this advice does not apply to *Shavuoth*, *Rosh HaShanah*, or *Shemi'ni Atzereth*, is these holidays have no unique *mitzvoth*. (The *mitzvah* of blowing the *shofar* on *Rosh HaShanah* is marked with a special *She'he'che'yanu* in the morning.)

31. See Chapter 15, paragraph 25.
32. *Orchoth Chayim* 263:6, citing *Sefer Me'orey Ohr*. Tractate *Eruvin* 40b explains that the blessing *She'he'che'yanu* ushers in the sanctity of the day. The *Kaf HaChayim* 514:112 also rules that once a person recites *She'he'che'yanu*, she may no longer perform any *melakhah* which is forbidden on *Yom Tov*.
33. *Responsa of Maharam Brisk*, Vol. 2, No. 45. Support for this view is found in *Rashi*'s commentary on Tractate *Betzah* 17a, which notes that the term *Shabbath* includes *Yom Tov*. Although *Hithoreruth Teshuvah*, Vol. 1, No. 112, is inclined to require the blessing to be repeated, since there is a doubt, we are lenient in practice. See also *Shevet HaLevi*, Vol. 4, No. 28.

In general, when a person corrects a blessing within the length of time it takes to say, *Shalom alekha, Rabbi u'Mori* (Greetings to you, my Teacher and Master), the correction is valid, and the obligation fulfilled.

Kiddush

16. A number of authorities obligate women in the *mitzvah* of reciting *Kiddush* on *Yom Tov*.[34] When *Yom Tov* occurs on Saturday night, they may drink from the *Kiddush* cup even though the wine also serves for *Havdalah*.[35]

17. If *Yom Tov* occurs during the week, a woman may fulfill the *mitzvah* of *Kiddush* by listening to a boy or girl who has attained *bar* or *bath mitzvah* age, even if his or her

---

34. *Shulchan Arukh HaRav* 271:5. HaGaon Rav Moshe Feinstein discusses women's obligation to recite *Kiddush* on *Yom Tov* in *Iggeroth Moshe, Orach Chayim*, Vol. 4, No. 100. He quotes the *Rambam*'s formulation of this *mitzvah* in *Hilkhoth Shabbath* 29:18: "Just as we recite *Kiddush* on the night of *Shabbath* and *Havdalah* on *motzo'ei Shabbath*, we are [required to] recite *Kiddush* on the night of *Yom Tov*...for they [the days of *Yom Tov*] are also referred to [by the Torah] as *Shabbathoth* to God."

HaGaon Rav Feinstein infers from this passage that the *mitzvah* to make *Kiddush* on *Yom Tov* is included in the *mitzvah* of *Zakhor eth yom HaShabbath le'kadsho*. (Remember the *Shabbath* day to sanctify it.) It follows that women are included in the *mitzvah* to make *Kiddush* on *Yom Tov* just as they are included in the *mitzvah* of *Zakhor*.

Among authorities who exempt women from the *mitzvah* of *Kiddush* on *Yom Tov* is Rabbi Akiva Eiger, in *Hashmatoth* (additions) to *responsum* No. 1. In the *responsum* itself, Rabbi Akiva Eiger discusses whether women are obligated in the positive *mitzvoth* of *Kavod* and *Oneg Yom Tov*. He brings evidence from *Tosafoth*, Tractate *Kiddushin* 34a, that they are exempt from the positive *mitzvoth* of *Yom Tov*. Reasoning that the juxtaposition of *Zakhor* and *Shamor*, which obligates women in the positive *mitzvoth* of *Shabbath*, does not apply to *Yom Tov*, he categorizes the *mitzvoth* of *Kavod* and *Oneg Yom Tov* as time-bound. See note 39. In the *Hashmatoth*, Rabbi Akiva Eiger employs this reasoning to exempt women from *Kiddush* on *Yom Tov*.

For further discussion, see *Minchath Chinukh* 31; *Maharsham*, Vol. 3, No. 226; *Torath Raphael* No. 90.

35. *Sovah Semachoth* 4:196. See Chapter 15, paragraph 92.

36. Most authorities rule that the *mitzvah* of *Kiddush* on *Yom Tov* is

physical maturity has not been firmly established.[36]

Because some authorities exempt women from the *mitzvah* of *Kiddush* on *Yom Tov*, a woman should not recite it for a man.[37]

The Yom Tov Meal

18. The debate over whether women are required to recite *Kiddush* on *Yom Tov* also calls into question their obligation to eat a meal with bread on *Yom Tov*.[38] Since women may be exempt from eating bread on *Yom Tov*, a woman who omits *Ya'a'leh v'yavo* from *Birkath HaMazon* need not repeat it.[39]

Rabbinic. With respect to Rabbinic *mitzvoth* we may assume that a child who has reached *bar* or *bath mitzvah* age has also attained physical maturity. See Chapter 11, note 1.

It should be noted that according to Rabbi Akiva Eiger's view cited in note 34, exempting women from the *mitzvah* of *Kiddush* on *Yom Tov*, it is one of those *mitzvoth* which women fulfill voluntarily. Accordingly, it may be possible for a minor to recite *Kiddush* for a woman on *Yom Tov*.

37. See note 34.
38. Contrary to Rabbi Akiva Eiger's position, the *Pri Megadim, Eshel Avraham* 328:10, indicates that women are obligated in all the *mitzvoth* of *Yom Tov*. The *Pithchey Teshuvah* of *Mahariya* of Vilna, commenting on the *Shulchan Arukh* 188:6 rules this way explicitly. See also *Sdeh Chemed, Asifath Dinim, Ma'arekheth Yom Tov* 2:6.
39. *Responsa of Rabbi Akiva Eiger, Ibid.* Tractate *Berakhoth* 49b explains that when a person fails to mark a special occasion, *Birkath HaMazon* must be repeated only if the person was required to eat bread at that meal. Since, according to Rabbi Akiva Eiger, women are exempt from the *mitzvah* of eating a *Yom Tov* meal, they need not repeat *Birkath HaMazon* if they omit *Ya'aleh v'yavo*. See Chapter 3, paragraph 17. The same conclusion is reached by the *Maharsham* and *Be'er Moshe,* Vol. 3, No. 38, par. 9 and 17. All authorities agree that women who omit *Ya'aleh v'yavo* at the *Pessach Seder* are obligated to repeat *Birkath HaMazon*; women are required to eat *matzah* on the first night of *Pessach*.

19. Women are included in the *mitzvah* to rejoice on *Yom Tov*.[40]

Hallel

20. Women are not required to recite *Hallel* on *Yom Tov*.[41] Ashkenazic women who wish to recite *Hallel* may recite the preceding and concluding blessings.[42]

---

40. *Shulchan Arukh* 529:2; *Mishnah Berurah* 529:15; *Kaf HaChayim* 529:15. "And you shall rejoice on your festivals, you and your sons and daughters" (*Devarim* 16:14).

The *Rambam, Hilkhoth Yom Tov* 6:17–18, describes this *mitzvah*: "Included in the *mitzvah* of rejoicing is gladdening the hearts of one's wife and children, according to their needs. How is this [accomplished]? Children are given toasted grains, nuts and sweets. Clothes and attractive ornaments are bought for the women, in accordance with one's financial means." The *Biur Halakhah* 529 adds, "If a person cannot afford [expensive clothing and ornaments], he should at least buy new shoes for his family in honor of the holiday."

In the days of the *Beith HaMikdash*, there was an added element to rejoicing on Festivals. Everyone who came to Jerusalem on pilgrimage would offer a special sacrifice, known as *shalmey simchah*, a peace-offering of joy. The *Rambam, Hilkhoth Chagigah* 1:1, rules that women were obligated to offer this sacrifice. The *Ra'avad* disagrees: "[She is] not required to offer a sacrifice, only to rejoice with her husband by accompanying him to Jerusalem." For a full discussion see *Sha'agath Aryeh*, No. 63.

41. See Chapter 2, paragraph 1.

42. *Ibid.* Men who do not recite the blessing over *Hallel* on *Rosh Chodesh* (See Chapter 16, note 10.) do recite it on *Yom Tov*. Reciting *Hallel* on *Rosh Chodesh* is a *minhag*, reciting it on *Yom Tov* an obligation. The blessing is said by all men and by Ashkenazic women, who follow the view of the *Remah* which permits them to recite blessings over the voluntary fulfillment of time-bound *mitzvoth*.

It should be noted that half-*Hallel* recited on the intermediate days of *Pessach* is also a *minhag*. Those who do not recite the blessing on *Rosh Chodesh* do not recite it on these days either.

A Visitor to Israel on the Second Day of Yom Tov

21. An unmarried woman who temporarily resides in *Eretz Yisrael* is required to continue observing two days of *Yom Tov*.

Some authorities rule that she continues to observe two days of *Yom Tov* even if she intends to remain in *Eretz Yisrael* permanently because her ultimate decision will depend on her choice of a husband. They only allow her to adopt the custom of *Eretz Yisrael* to observe one day of *Yom Tov* if her decision is final, and she will not consider living outside of *Eretz Yisrael* under any circumstances.[43]

Other authorities allow a woman who intends to live in *Eretz Yisrael* permanently to observe one day of *Yom Tov* even though it is possible that she may change her decision after marriage.[44]

22. When the second day falls on Friday, a woman who observes two days of *Yom Tov* in *Eretz Yisrael* must make an *eiruv tavshilin* on *Erev Yom Tov* with its appropriate blessing.[45]

---

43. This is the view of HaGaon Rav Chaim Pinchus Sheinberg. Her final decision as to a permanent residence is dependent on her husband. She cannot be considered one who has "no intention of returning" to live outside *Eretz Yisrael*.

   HaGaon Rav Sheinberg concedes that a woman who was instructed by a competent halakhic authority to observe one day of *Yom Tov* should continue this practice although he personally disagrees with such an opinion.

44. This is the view of HaGaon Rav Yosef Shalom Eliashiv.

   In *Minchath Shlomo*, No. 19:6, HaGaon Rav Shlomo Zalman Auerbach rules that a minor who attains *bar* or *bath mitzvah* age while his or her parents are temporarily residing in *Eretz Yisrael* is required to observe two days of *Yom Tov*, like his parents, even though he never observed two days outside *Eretz Yisrael* after attaining majority.

45. A person who observes two days of *Yom Tov* in *Eretz Yisrael* is

If she forgets to make an *eiruv*, she may not cook on Friday for *Shabbath*. A neighbor who observes one day of *Yom Tov* may not cook the woman's food for her, but when the neighbor cooks her own food for *Shabbath* she may add extra for her.[46]

23. When the second day falls on Friday, a woman who observes one day of *Yom Tov* may cook food for *Shabbath* for a guest from outside *Eretz Yisrael* even if the guest has not prepared an *eiruv tavshilin*. But the guest is forbidden to assist her hostess unless she has prepared an *eiruv tavshilin*. Similarly, if the guest wishes to light *Shabbath* candles, she must prepare an *eiruv tavshilin* on *Erev Yom Tov*.[47]

24. Although it is generally forbidden to prepare food during *Chol HaMoed* for after the Festival, a woman who observes one day of *Yom Tov* may prepare food during *Chol HaMoed* to serve a guest on her second day of *Yom Tov*, even though that day is not part of the Festival for the hostess.[48]

25. A person who visits *Eretz Yisrael* and observes two days of *Yom Tov* may not ask someone who observes one day to perform *melakhah* for her.[49] Moreover, a person who

---

required to fulfill all its details.

46. *Shulchan Arukh* 527:20; *Mishnah Berurah* 527:58–59.
47. See the *Kaf HaChayim* 527:113.
48. HaGaon Rav Shlomo Zalman Auerbach explains in *Minchath Shlomo*, p. 138, that assisting guests from outside *Eretz Yisrael* to rejoice on their second day of *Yom Tov* is considered a holiday need, and it may be done on *Chol HaMoed*.
49. *Sha'arey Teshuvah* 496:2; *Mishnah Berurah* 624:16. Also see *Iggeroth Moshe, Orach Chayim*, Vol. 3, No. 73.
   Shemirath Shabbath KeHilkhethah, Chapter 31, note 80*, cites HaGaon Rav Shlomo Zalman Auerbach's explanation of why this situation is different from the ruling in the *Shulchan Arukh* 263:17, which permits a person who has accepted *Shabbath* to ask another person to perform *melakhah* for her: "In that case, although the

observes one day of *Yom Tov* should not perform *melakhah* for one who is observing two days even if she was not asked to do so.[50]

A visitor to *Eretz Yisrael* should not join a resident of *Eretz Yisrael* on a bus or in a car on the second day of *Yom Tov*.[51]

26. A visitor to *Eretz Yisrael* may cook on the second day of *Yom Tov* for a resident of *Eretz Yisrael*, even though that day is a normal weekday for the resident of *Eretz Yisrael*.[52]

27. A person who is accustomed to sit in the *sukkah* on *Shemini Atzereth* outside of *Eretz Yisrael* should not do so when visiting *Eretz Yisrael*.[53]

---

person herself has accepted *Shabbath*, the community has not, and she herself knows that it is not actually *Shabbath* yet... But with respect to the second day of *Yom Tov*, it is considered as if she is actually in doubt whether the day is *Yom Tov* or not." Nevertheless, HaGaon Rav Auerbach concludes, "In practice, many people act leniently today, since [two days of *Yom Tov*] are only observed in order to continue the custom of our forefathers [who kept two days of *Yom Tov* out of doubt (See Tractate *Betzah* 4b.)], and the guest realizes that it is definitely a weekday for the residents of *Eretz Yisrael*. Therefore, in combination with the view of the *Chacham Tzvi* [who rules that a guest in *Eretz Yisrael* is only required to observe one day of *Yom Tov* in any case], they are lenient."

It should be noted that in *Minchath Shlomo*, No. 19:3, HaGaon Rav Auerbach clarifies that this argument is only intended to be a justification for the prevailing practice, not his personal halakhic opinion.

50. *Tur* 624.
51. *Shemirath Shabbath KeHilkhethah* 31:13.
52. *Sha'arey Teshuvah* 496:2. Also see the *responsum* of Rabbi Akiva Eiger to R. Isaac Segal, printed in *Sefer Drush V'Chidush* at the end of the *Ma'arakhoth* on Tractate *Kethuboth*.
53. See *Minchath Shlomo*, p. 137.

Isru Chag

28. *Melakhah* may be performed on *Isru Chag* (the day following a *Yom Tov*).[54] In communities where people refrain from certain types of work on *Isru Chag*, the custom should be respected.[55]

It is customary to prepare a festive meal on *Isru Chag* in honor of the day.[56]

---

54. *Magen Avraham* 494:3.
55. *KafHaChayim* 494:49. The extent of this prohibition depends on the custom of the community.
56. *Remah* 429:2.

CHAPTER 18
Chol HaMoed

Rejoicing on the Festival

1. To rejoice and be happy on *Chol HaMoed* (the intermediate days of *Pessach* and *Sukkoth*) is a positive *mitzvah* which is also incumbent on women.[1] Holiday garments are worn during these days,[2] and it is customary for a festive tablecloth to be spread on the dining table.[3]

---

1. *Shulchan Arukh* 429:2, based on *Devarim* 16:14: "And you shall rejoice on your holidays, you, your sons, and your *daughters*."
2. *Mishnah Berurah* 530:1. The *Ba'er Heytev* notes that the *Maharil* wore *Shabbath* clothes during *Chol HaMoed*. The *Pri Megadim*, commenting on the *Magen Avraham* 530:1, rules that wearing *Shabbath* clothes on *Chol HaMoed* is in fact an obligation. The *Sha'ar HaTziyun* 530:4 finds evidence that wearing *Shabbath* clothes on *Chol HaMoed* is not obligatory. He claims that wearing clean and neat garments, more formal than regular weekday clothes, is sufficient.
3. *Orukh HaShulchan* 530:4.

Food Preparation During Chol HaMoed

2. Food may be cooked and prepared[4] in the normal manner.[5] This is so even if the same food could have been bought pre-cooked.[6] A cook may accept wages for working.[7] One may even cook food to sell to people for their holiday needs.[8]

3. A woman may plan in advance to cook during *Chol HaMoed*, even if she could have prepared extra food before *Yom Tov*.[9] She may not cook extra food during *Chol HaMoed* to have leftovers available after the Festival,[10] unless no extra effort or *melakhah* is involved.[11] If cooking extra food improves the flavor of the food prepared for *Chol HaMoed*, it may be done, even if it requires more effort and *melakhah*.[12]
On *Chol HaMoed* one may not cook for non-Jews.[13]

---

4. *Shulchan Arukh* 533:1.
5. *Mishnah Berurah* 533:11 and 537:52. This applies even if the "normal manner" is professional and involves a great deal of time and effort. See the *Mishnah Berurah* 530:1, 533:4 and 537:15.
6. *Shulchan Arukh* 537:15.
7. *Biur Halakhah* 542, beginning *Afilu*.
8. *Shulchan Arukh* 537:4; *Mishnah Berurah* 537:14.
9. *Chaye Adam* 106:2.
10. *Shulchan Arukh* 533:1; *Mishnah Berurah* 533:6.
11. *Biur Halakhah* 533, beginning *Shari*; *Mishnah Berurah* 533:23; *Sha'ar HaTziyun* 533:7. These rules also apply to cooking on *Yom Tov*. Although it is forbidden to cook for the week on *Yom Tov*, a woman may add extra food to a pot if no extra effort is involved and the extra food is placed in the pot before it is put on the fire (to avoid extra *melakhah*).
12. When adding extra food improves the flavor, i.e., filling a pot with meat, the food may be added after the pot has been placed on the fire; the extra *melakhah* is considered to be for the needs of the Festival. See the *Shulchan Arukh* 503:2 and the *Mishnah Berurah* 503:14.
13. A Jew may only cook on *Yom Tov* for other Jews. Not only is

Body Care

4. Although cutting hair is forbidden, a married woman whose hair is protruding from her head-covering may cut it.[14] Combing, braiding, and caring for the hair in general is permitted.[15]

5. Powders, perfumes, and cosmetics may be used.[16]

---

cooking for non-Jews forbidden on *Yom Tov*, but it is forbidden to add food for a non-Jew to a pot which is already on the fire. The *Chaye Adam* 106:11 extends this prohibition to *Chol HaMoed*. See also the *Kaf HaChayim* 542:2.

As a safeguard against cooking for a non-Jew, *Chazal* prohibit inviting a non-Jew to a *Yom Tov* meal. This prohibition applies to *Chol HaMoed* as well. If a non-Jew visits a Jew without being invited, he may be fed providing no extra *melakhah* or effort is involved. For example, one can fill a pot with water and place it on the fire in order to prepare two cups of tea, one for the Jew, and the other for the non-Jew, but it is forbidden to add water to a pot which is already on the fire, since this is a separate *melakhah* which is performed exclusively for the non-Jew. See the *Shulchan Arukh* 512:1, and the *Mishnah Berurah*.

14. *Shulchan Arukh* 531:2; *Mishnah Berurah* 531:3 and 546:16; Glosses of the *Maharsham* on the *Shulchan Arukh* 531; *Orchoth Chayim* (Sphinka) 531:1.

A woman who needs to cut her hair should do so in private, not at the hairdresser. The *Orukh HaShulchan* 531:5 explains that other people may not realize that she has a valid reason to cut her hair and come to take the prohibition against haircuts lightly. She may ask a Jew to cut her hair and even pay a wage for it. Shaving hair from parts of the body other than the head is permitted. See the *Biur Halakhah* 531, beginning *Ein*, 542, beginning *Afilu*, and the *Shulchan Arukh* 542:1.

15. *Remah* 531:8 and the *Biur HaGra*.

16. *Shulchan Arukh* 546:5; *Biur Halakhah* 546, beginning *Kol takh'shi'te'ha*.

6. Wigs may be combed. Some authorities forbid setting a wig, even one which is being worn during *Chol HaMoed*,[17] while others permit it.[18]

7. It is customary for Ashkenazic women not to cut fingernails if they were not cut before the Festival. A woman who attends the *mikvah* may cut her fingernails.[19] Many Sephardic women follow the view which permits cutting fingernails during *Chol HaMoed*.[20]

Clothes and Laundry

8. A button that falls off may be sewn back on a garment which is needed for the Festival. A garment that tears may be repaired, but some authorities rule that a change should be made in the normal manner of sewing.[21]

---

17. This is the ruling of HaGaon Rav Moshe Feinstein, cited in *Zikhron Shlomoh* (Hebrew section), p. 34. *Chazal* prohibit haircuts during *Chol HaMoed* so people will not postpone them until then and thus celebrate the first days of *Yom Tov* in a dishevelled state. This concern is also a reason for prohibiting women from setting wigs. Furthermore, setting a wig involves a certain amount of expertise. Actions that entail expertise are generally forbidden on *Chol HaMoed*, even those which are for the needs of the Festival.
18. HaGaon Rav Moshe Stern, cited in *Zikhron Shlomoh* (Hebrew section), p. 52: "I am accustomed to rule leniently [with respect to setting a wig], which is one of a woman's ornaments. The *Shulchan Arukh* 546 rules that parting hair is permitted on *Chol HaMoed*. What difference is there between the hair of the head and the hair of a wig? The prohibition against haircuts...applies only to hair that is connected to the head, not to a wig."
19. *Remah* 532:1; *Mishnah Berurah* 532:4.
20. This is the view of the *Shulchan Arukh* 532:1.
21. *Remah* 541:4; *Orukh HaShulchan* 541:4. Generally, work which is necessary for the Festival and does not entail any special skill is permitted; it must be *ma'aseh hedyot* (the work of an amateur), not

9. A sufficient quantity of freshly-laundered clothes should be prepared in advance for the entire Festival.[22] During *Chol HaMoed* clothes may not be laundered, even for the concluding days of *Yom Tov*[23] or by a non-Jew.[24]

Clothes should not be brought to a non-Jewish laundry even if they will be picked up after the Festival.[25]

10. When necessary, the following garments may be

---

ma'aseh uman (the work of a craftsman). There are situations in which the classification of a particular act as *ma'aseh hedyot* or *ma'aseh uman* depends on the skill of the person doing it. One such example is sewing. When a person who is unskilled in sewing repairs a garment, the work is considered a *ma'aseh hedyot*, due to its inferior quality. When a person skilled in the art of sewing performs the same work, it is considered a *ma'aseh uman* due to its professional quality.

If a craftsman sews in an unusual way, i.e., he sews a button on loosely or through only two of the four openings in the button, the work is considered a permissible *ma'aseh hedyot*. Since they are usually well-versed in the art of sewing, women must sew in an unusual way. A man who does not know how to sew may sew a button on a garment in any way he can.

22. *Shulchan Arukh* 529:1; *Mishnah Berurah* 529:3–4, and 534:1. Wearing freshly laundered clothes is one of the ways of honoring the Festival.

23. *Shulchan Arukh* 529:1; *Mishnah Berurah* 531:3, and 534:2.

24. *Mishnah Berurah* 534:14. *Zikhron Shlomoh* (Hebrew section), p. 49, cites a *responsum* of HaGaon Rav Moshe Stern concerning a family which entertains a number of guests during the first days of *Yom Tov* and runs out of linen. As additional guests are expected for the last days of *Yom Tov*, the question is raised whether sheets may be laundered for them. HaGaon Rav Stern's response: "Sheets may be laundered, preferably by a non-Jew in his home, but they may not be sent out to a non-Jewish laundry. A non-Jew may be asked to purchase new sheets or, if this is not possible, the Jew may purchase them. Purchasing new sheets is preferable to laundering old ones, even through a non-Jew."

25. *Mishnah Berurah* 543:10.

laundered: Diapers and baby clothes[26] in any quantity;[27] essential children's clothes;[28] socks, underwear, stockings, handkerchiefs, kitchen towels, and the like, as needed.[29]

---

26. *Remah* 534:1. Since diapers are soiled many times a day, no limit is imposed on cleaning them. *Zikhron Shlomoh* (Hebrew section), p. 49, cites a ruling of HaGaon Rav Moshe Stern that a woman who normally uses disposables may not wash diapers during *Chol HaMoed*. She should purchase enough disposables for the entire Festival.

27. *Remah, Ibid.* Since it is impossible to predict how many diapers will be needed, they may be laundered all at one time. A similar ruling exists in regard to washing dishes on *Shabbath*. Any number of dishes may be washed on Friday night for *Shabbath* morning since it is impossible to know exactly how many dishes will be needed. See the *Shulchan Arukh* 323:6.

28. *Shulchan Arukh* 534:1; *Mishnah Berurah* 534:7 and 11.

    HaGaon Rav Moshe Feinstein, cited in *Zikhron Shlomoh* (Hebrew section), p. 34, permits washing children's clothes even when enough clothes for the whole Festival could have been purchased in advance.

    HaGaon Rav Feinstein adds, "A person who is going away for the Festival and has enough clothes for the children need not bring along all the clothes in order to limit the amount of laundering to be done." HaGaon Rav Moshe Stern disagrees, maintaining that all the children's clothes should be brought on the trip. See *Zikhron Shlomoh* (Hebrew section), p. 48.

    Although in reference to washing children's clothes the *Remah* states, "one should only wash what is needed, one piece [at a time]," HaGaon Rav Moshe Stern, *Ibid.*, limits the *Remah*'s rule to the days when laundry was done by hand. Today it is better to wash all the children's clothes in the washing machine at one time than wash them as they are needed, which would involve more time and effort.

    Zikhron Shlomoh (Hebrew section), p. 34, cites another ruling of HaGaon Rav Moshe Feinstein regarding laundering children's clothes: "It is permitted to wash a child's garment even if he has a clean one that is not quite as nice as the soiled one. Once *Chazal* permit laundering children's clothes, it may be done in all circumstances."

29. *Shulchan Arukh* 537:1; *Mishnah Berurah* 537:4. These garments become soiled very quickly, so they are treated like children's clothes.

11. A washing machine may be used for laundering.[30] Adult clothes should not be added to a load of children's clothes.[31] A washing machine which breaks down may not be repaired.[32]

12. Stains may be removed from garments,[33] but they should not be brought to a dry cleaners for general cleaning.[34]

13. Wet clothes may be hung out to dry. We are not worried that an onlooker might suspect that they were laundered in disregard of the law.[35]

14. Clothes needed for the holiday may be ironed,[36]

---

30. If possible, one should avoid washing clothes in view of neighbors or visitors.

31. HaGaon Rav Moshe Feinstein, cited by *Zikhron Shlomoh* (Hebrew section), p. 34. *Chazal* prohibit laundering to prevent people from putting it off until *Chol HaMoed*, thereby celebrating the first days of *Yom Tov* in soiled clothes. There is no reason to distinguish washing clothes separately from washing them with children's clothes.

32. This ruling may be inferred from the *Magen Avraham* 545:26, which permits repairing a quill pen only because it does not require any special skill. Repairs requiring specialized skill would be forbidden.
    It can be inferred from the *Shulchan Arukh* 540:7 that stoves or gas ovens may be repaired during *Chol HaMoed*, even if they require a craftsman, because they are essential to food preparation. See the *Mishnah Berurah* 540:18.

33. *Zikhron Shlomoh* (Hebrew section), p. 34, in the name of HaGaon Rav Moshe Feinstein.

34. *Zikhron Shlomoh, Ibid.* The *Mishnah Berurah* 534:9 explains that laundering clothes is forbidden even if a person has only one garment.

35. *Emek Halakhah, Orach Chayim*, No. 146, explains that hanging wet clothes out to dry is only forbidden on *Shabbath*, when no laundry of any kind may be done.

36. *Remah* 541:3; *Mishnah Berurah* 541:9.

providing no new creases are formed.[37]

15. Many authorities permit polishing shoes during *Chol HaMoed*,[38] although others forbid it.[39]

Mopping and Sweeping During Chol HaMoed

16. Mopping and sweeping the floor is permitted.[40] Some authorities forbid sweeping floors which are not usually swept daily.[41] A straw broom may be used to clean the yard.[42]

---

37. *Mishnah Berurah* 541:8. Making new pleats or creases is classified as a *ma'aseh uman. Sefer Mo'adey HaShem*, B'ney Brak, 5741, *Hilkhoth Chol HaMoed*, par. 29, includes pants among garments that may not be ironed on *Chol HaMoed*.
38. *Melamed L'Ho'il, Orach Chayim* No. 113:10, reports that HaGaon Rav Wolf Hamburger permitted polishing shoes. The same ruling is found in *Chelek HaLevi, Orach Chayim*, No. 182, *Yagel Yaacov, Orach Chayim*, No. 25, and corroborated by HaGaon Rav Moshe Feinstein in *Zikhron Shlomoh* (Hebrew section), p. 33. HaGaon Rav Feinstein adds, "One should polish normally, without giving the shoes an extra shine, unless they were shined before the first days of *Yom Tov*."
39. *Levushey Mordekhai, Orach Chayim T'litha'i*, No. 1:2; *Ye'chaveh Da'ath*, Vol. 4, No. 34. *Zeh HaShulchan*, Vol. 2, No. 534, reports the *Chazon Ish* maintained that it is customary not to polish shoes on *Chol HaMoed*.
40. *Minchath Yom Tov*, No. 104. The author concludes, "Only light cleaning to remove the dirt and dust is permitted. To rub thoroughly, the way one does during the week, is forbidden."
41. *Beith Avi*, No. 29, Vol. 1. The author explains that today, when it is common to clean certain rooms every day, especially the kitchen and the dining room, a housewife may be uncomfortable if a room is not clean. Cleaning these rooms may be considered a Festival need, but this does not apply to rooms which are not normally cleaned every day.
42. *Shulchan Arukh* 540:2. This applies even if pieces of straw may break

Musical Instruments

17. Playing musical instruments to enjoy the holiday is permitted.[43] If an instrument which can easily be repaired breaks, a non-craftsman may repair it.[44] A music teacher should not give lessons during *Chol HaMoed*.[45]

---

off the broom, or if the yard has a dirt floor and sweeping will level the holes in the ground.

43. *Sha'arey Teshuvah* 534:5; *Ye'chaveh Da'ath*, Vol. 1, No. 71.
44. *Sha'arey Teshuvah, Ibid.* For example, replacing a broken guitar string.
45. HaGaon Rav Moshe Feinstein, cited in *Zikhron Shlomoh* (Hebrew section), p. 33: "It is forbidden to play musical instruments for a livelihood on *Chol HaMoed*, but playing for pleasure or for a *mitzvah* is permitted."

CHAPTER 19
Yamim Nora'im

Selichoth

1. It is customary to recite *Selichoth* (special penitential prayers) the week prior to *Rosh HaShanah*. Although these prayers are normally recited in the synagogue, women may also say them privately, omitting the Thirteen Attributes of God's Mercy. A woman who knows how to chant these verses the way they are chanted for the Torah reading may chant them.[1]

---

1. *Shulchan Arukh* 565:5; *Mishnah Berurah* 565:13 and 581:4; *Kitzur Shulchan Arukh* 125:9. The Thirteen Attributes are found in *Shemoth* 34:6–7. When read in the form of a prayer, they have the same status as *Kaddish* and *Kedushah*, that is, they may only be recited in a *minyan*. Chanting them similar to the Torah reading has the character of Torah study, which is permitted in private.

   Mishneh Halakhoth, Vol. 4, No. 78, rules that even when a large group of women gather together to recite *Tehillim* for a sick person or a great Torah scholar, they may not recite the Thirteen Attributes.

All prayers in Aramaic should be omitted when *Selichoth* are recited privately.[2]

2. A woman who is a *niddah* may attend the synagogue during *Selichoth* even if she is not accustomed to do so the rest of the year.[3]

Erev Rosh HaShanah

3. It is customary to pray at the graves of the righteous on *Erev Rosh HaShanah.*[4] Some authorities rule that a woman

---

2. *Mishnah Berurah* 581:4, based on Tractate *Shabbath* 12b, which explains that the ministering angels do not understand Aramaic. Since they are not capable of assisting a person's prayer in Aramaic, such prayers should only be recited in a *minyan*, where they are considered so potent that they do not require assistance from the angels.

  The *Kaf HaChayim* 581:26 is astonished: "What difference does it make if the angels do not understand? If someone's native tongue is Aramaic, and he requests something from God, will not his words be heard? Is it not written, 'Who is like *Hashem* our God, however we call out to Him?'" See also *Yabiah Omer*, Vol. 1, *Orach Chayim,* No. 35.

3. *Remah* 88; *Magen Avraham* 88:3; *Chaye Adam* 3:38. The *Remah* explains that these women will become despondent when they see everyone gathering in the synagogue while they remain outside. Also see *Menachem Meishiv, Orach Chayim,* No. 22, and the *Chatham Sofer, Orach Chayim*, No.65. It should be noted that the *Chaye Adam* maintains that there is no sound basis for the custom of a *niddah* not entering the synagogue. See Chapter 2, paragraph 47.

4. *Remah* 581:4, and *Mishnah Berurah.* Prayers recited at the grave of a righteous person are particularly effective. It is customary to give charity to the poor at this time.

  Drashoth Maharil, Hilkhoth Ta'anith, cautions those who pray at the graves of the righteous not to fall into the category of one who makes requests of the dead.The prayer should request that God be merciful in the merit of the righteous person.

  The *Kaf HaChayim* 581:96 reports that when the *MaHaRash* prayed at a grave, he said only, "May it be Your Will that [this person] have an honorable resting place and his merit stand for us."

who is a *niddah* should not visit a cemetery.[5] Others rule that women should not visit cemeteries at all.[6]

4. Some people fast on *Erev Rosh HaShanah*.[7]

5. It is customary to annul vows, both those taken knowingly and those taken unknowingly, on *Erev Rosh HaShanah*. A woman may designate her husband her agent for annulling vows.[8] Some women annul their vows themselves in the presence of three men.[9]

6. As a reminder of the seriousness of the Day of Judgement, a woman should not wear silk or embroidered clothes on *Rosh HaShanah*, only simple white garments. Where completely white clothes are not worn, extravagant dress should still be avoided.[10]

---

5. *Chaye Adam* 3:38; *Chamudey Daniel*, cited by the *Pithchey Teshuvah*, *Yoreh De'ah* 195:19. See Chapter 12, paragraph 7.

   Shulchan Melakhim, Shalom V'Emeth, par. 5, states that a woman may visit a cemetery during the days of *Selichoth* for the same reason that the *Remah* permits a woman who is a *niddah* to enter the synagogue during these days. (See note 3.) The *Mishnah Berurah* and the *Chaye Adam* do not distinguish these days from the rest of the year.

6. See Chapter 12, note 12. Some women enter the cemetery, but do not approach closer than four *amoth* (approximately seven feet) of the graves.

7. The *Mishnah Berurah* 581:16 notes that girls older than *bath mitzvah* age are also accustomed to fast.

8. *Shulchan Arukh, Yoreh De'ah* 234:56; *Kitzur Hilkhoth HaMo'adim*, Vol. 1, p. 11.

9. This is the custom of many communities in Jerusalem. A vow may be annulled in the presence of three laymen. They may be related to the person who seeks annullment and to one another. A husband, however, may not be one of the men in whose presence his wife's vows are annulled. See the *Shulchan Arukh, Yoreh De'ah* 234:57.

10. *Mishnah Berurah* 581:25; *Mateh Ephrayim* 581:55. A woman should not wear any gold or silver on *Rosh HaShanah*.

7. Care should be taken to change into *Yom Tov* clothes before sunset. The candles should be lit and the table set with a holiday tablecloth before the men return from the synagogue. Beginning *Rosh HaShanah* with the home neatly arranged is an auspicious sign for a good year.[11]

Rosh HaShanah Eve

8. On the night of *Rosh HaShanah* it is customary to greet neighbors with the words, *Le'shanah tovah teikatheiv v'teichatheim* (May you be written and sealed for a good year). The feminine form of the greeting is, *teikatheivi v'teichatheimi*.[12]

9. *Chazal* urge people to eat a festive meal on *Rosh HaShanah*.[13] It is customary to eat foods whose names

---

11. *Kaf HaChayim* 583:1.
12. *Shulchan Arukh* 582:9; *Mishnah Berurah* 582:25. The custom of adding *v'teichatheimi* (and may you be sealed) is based on the *Magen Avraham* and the *Chaye Adam* 139:5. According to the Vilna Gaon and *Shulchan Arukh HaRav*, one does not mention *chathimah* on *Rosh HaShanah* because even the righteous are not sealed for a good year until *Yom Kippur*. Their ruling is based on *Tosafoth*'s interpretation of a Talmudic passage in Tractate *Rosh HaShanah* 16a. The *Magen Avraham*'s view is based on the *Ramban*'s interpretation of the same passage.

    According to the *Magen Avraham*, the special *Rosh HaShanah* greeting is used until the afternoon of the first day. The *Taz* rules that it should also be used on the second night. The *Levush*, citing the tradition that the righteous are inscribed during the first three hours of the day, rules that the greeting should not be used once the first day's morning prayers are concluded. Greeting a friend with the words "May you be inscribed" after this time indicates that the person is not assumed to be righteous. But the *Shulchan Arukh HaRav* 582:17 states that the greeting may be used until the afternoon of the second day, because some people are not inscribed until then.
13. *Mishnah Berurah* 529:11 and 597:1. This is based on the verse, "Go eat sumptuously and drink sweet beverages" (*Nechemiah* 8:10), which was said to the people of Jerusalem on *Rosh HaShanah*. Although it is a

symbolize blessing and merit.[14]

In Jerusalem, the custom is as follows: The bread over which *Ha'motzie* is said is dipped into honey and eaten. A blessing is then recited over a date with the intention that it exempt other fruits which are to be eaten. Afterwards, a pomegranate, an apple dipped in honey, pumpkin (*kara*), black-eyed peas (*rubiah*), leeks (*karti*), beets or spinach (*silka*), and a fish or sheep head are eaten.[15] No separate blessing is required for the vegetables, but it is preferable to eat them together with a little bit of bread.[16]

A short prayer is customarily said before eating each of these foods.[17]

Day of Judgement, the *mitzvah* to rejoice on a Festival applies. One should not indulge to the extent that it compromises the subdued attitude that exemplifies the seriousness of the day.

14. *Shulchan Arukh* 583. Contrary to the view of *B'ney Yisaskhar, Tishrei* 2:11, the *Eliyahu Rabbah* 583:1 reports that these foods are also eaten on the second night of *Rosh HaShanah*. The *Mateh Ephrayim* 597:4 recommends eating them at the morning meal, and the *Ben Ish Chai, Shanah Rishonah, Parshath Nitzavim* 4, reports that this was the custom in his home.

15. The order of eating the food in the text follows the one printed in many prayer books. The *Kaf HaChayim* 583:25 presents a slightly different order.

16. *Kitzur Hilkhoth HaMo'adim.*

17. When dipping the apple in honey it is customary to say, "May it be Your Will to renew for us a good and sweet year." Over the dates (*tamri*) one says, "May our enemies be destroyed (*yitamu*)", and over the pomegranate, "May our merit be increased like[the seeds of] a pomegranate". The prayer said when eating pumpkin(*kara*) is,"May our evil decree be torn (*yikara*)", for black-eyed peas (*rubiah*), "May our merit be increased (*yirbu*)", for leeks (*karti*), "May our enemies be cut off (*yikhritu*)", and for spinach or beets (*silka*), "May our enemies be removed (*yistalku*)." When eating the fish or sheep head it is customary to say, "May we be as a head and not as a tail."

The *Mishnah Berurah* 583:4 and the *Shulchan Arukh HaRav* explain that one should take a bite of the apple and then recite the short prayer. Reciting the prayer before eating would constitute an

Blowing the Shofar

10. Although women are exempt from the time-bound *mitzvah* to hear the *shofar* blown on *Rosh HaShanah*,[18] they may blow the *shofar* for themselves, or a man may blow it for them. A woman who fulfills the *mitzvah* of *Shofar* receives the reward for the voluntary fulfillment of a *mitzvah*.[19] Ashkenazic

---

interruption between the blessing over the apple and eating it. But in the journal *Yagdil Torah*, No. 90, the Lubavitcher Rebbe rules that the prayer is said before eating the apple.

The *Mishnah Berurah* further cites the *Shelah*, who advises people to meditate on repentance while eating these foods.

Although the *Mishnah Berurah* maintains that God's Name is included in the prayer, the custom in Jerusalem is to omit it.

The Talmudic source for eating the symbolic foods on *Rosh HaShanah* (*Horiyoth* 12a) makes no mention of praying or making a request while eating them. It appears that the auspicious "sign" is expressed simply by eating them. This view is expressed by the *Beith Yosef*, in his commentary on the *Tur* 583. But in the *Shulchan Arukh*, the custom of Rav Hai Gaon that a short prayer is recited over each item is cited.

The *Kaf HaChayim* 583:6 points out that if a person does not wish to eat one of the foods, having it on the table is sufficient. He further rules that any one of the prayers may be recited even when the food alluding to that prayer is missing. The prayer is nothing more than a supplication that can be said by anyone.

The *Mishnah Berurah* describes other customs of the night of *Rosh HaShanah*. One should not cook with vinegar or eat foods that have vinegar in them, such as *borsht*. It is customary to refrain from eating nuts. They cause a person to cough and may interfere with hearing the *shofar* the next morning. Also, the numerical value of the Hebrew word *egoz* (nut) is equivalent to the word *chet* (sin). The *Mishnah Berurah* 600:4 cites the Vilna Gaon, who advises people to refrain from eating grapes on *Rosh HaShanah*.

18. *Shulchan Arukh* 589:3.

19. *Shulchan Arukh* 589:6, and *Mishnah Berurah*. Blowing a *shofar* is generally forbidden on *Yom Tov* because of the Rabbinic prohibition against *uvdin d'chol* (weekday activity). This relatively minor prohibition is waived to give women the opportunity to fulfill the *mitzvah*.

women may recite the blessing.[20] Some authorities maintai:
that Sephardic women may also recite the blessing, but other
disagree.[21]

The *Kaf HaChayim* 589:24 cites the *Pri Megadim*, who rules that
after the *mitzvah* is fulfilled, it is forbidden for men or women to blow
the *shofar*. To imbue them with love for *mitzvoth*, children are
permitted to blow the entire day. See Tractate *Rosh HaShanah* 33a.

20. *Remah* 589:6, based on the view of Rabbenu Tam permitting women
to recite blessings over the voluntary fulfillment of *mitzvoth*. See the
Introduction, paragraph 8.

21. The *Shulchan Arukh, Ibid.*, states, "They may not recite the blessing,
nor may [a man] recite it for them." The *Mishnah Berurah* explains
that since the blessing contains the word *v'tzivanu* (and has commanded
us), women, who are not commanded to perform the *mitzvah*, may not
recite it. See also the *Kaf HaChayim* 589:23 and 34.

The *Ben Ish Chai, Shanah Rishonah, Parshath Nitzavim* 17 states, "If
a woman cannot attend synagogue services, a man may come to her
home to blow the *shofar* for her...but she should not recite the
blessing... This is the custom in my home." *Ye'chaveh Da'ath*, Vol. 2,
No. 70, arrives at the same conclusion.

The *Chida*, in *Birkey Yosef* 654:2 and *Yosef Ometz*, No. 82, is one of
the Sephardic authorities who permit women to recite the blessing
over the *Shofar*. He cites the passage in Tractate *Rosh HaShanah* 16a,
"Say before me *malkhiyoth* to proclaim me King; *zichronoth* so that I
will remember you for good. With what? With the *Shofar*." Since the
themes of accepting God's Kingship and His remembering all our
deeds on *Rosh HaShanah* relate to women, they may recite the blessing
although they are not obligated in the *mitzvah*. See Chapter 20, note
26, regarding the blessing over the *mitzvah* of *Lulav*. A number of
authorities report that both Ashkenazic and Sephardic women recite
the blessing over *shofar*. See *Tzitz Eliezer*, Vol. 9, No. 2, and *Yabia
Omer*, Vol. 1, *Orach Chayim*, Nos. 40–42, and Vol. 5, *Orach Chayim*,
No. 22.

A woman may certainly not blow the *shofar* on behalf of a man.
Since she is not obligated in the *mitzvah*, she cannot *motzie* a
man. See the *Shulchan Arukh* 589:1.

Although some authorities rule that one woman may blow the *shofar* for another woman,[22] others advise against it.[23]

11. Some authorities report that women have accepted the *mitzvah* of *Shofar* as an obligation.[24] A woman who is accustomed to hear the *shofar* every year is considered to have taken a vow. If she will be unable to hear it a particular year, she should anul the vow on *Erev Rosh HaShanah.*[25]

12. Some authorities forbid carrying a *shofar* to be blown for women on *Rosh HaShanah*[26] through an area which is not encompassed by an *eiruv*.[27] Others permit it.[28]

---

22. *Mikra'ey Kodesh, Yamim Nora'im*, p. 79, contrary to the view of *Yad HaMelekh*. See the notes of Rav Yosef Cohen, *Ibid.*
23. *Sha'agath Aryeh*, No. 105, cited by the *Sha'arey Teshuvah* 589:1. If a man is not available to blow the *shofar* for her, she may certainly blow it herself.
24. *Responsa of Rabbi Akiva Eiger, Hashmatoth* to *responsum* No. 1. "Most women act strictly. They are diligent and careful to fulfill time-bound *mitzvoth* such as *Shofar* and *Lulav*. These are considered obligatory for them." See also the *Chaye Adam* 1:7 and the *Ben Ish Chai, Shanah Rishonah, Parshath Nitzavim* 17.
25. *Ben Ish Chai, Ibid.,* cited in the *Kaf HaChayim* 589:34. *Yabia Omer,* Vol. 2, *Orach Chayim*, No. 30, rules that it is not necessary for a woman who is unable to hear the *shofar* one year to annul her vow. Annulment is only necessary if she plans to discontinue her practice permanently. The *Ben Ish Chai* requires annulment even if only one year is to be skipped.
26. *Sha'agath Aryeh*, No. 106, cited in the *Sha'arey Teshuvah* 589:1. Carrying is permitted on *Yom Tov* only for a holiday need. Since women are not obligated in the *mitzvah* of *Shofar*, the *Sha'agath Aryeh* maintains that carrying a *shofar* to them is not a holiday need.
27. An *eiruv* is an imaginary enclosure which permits carrying within its bounds on *Shabbath*. It is usually marked by a series of vertical poles connected by a horizontal string, wire, or something similar.
28. *Yosef Ometz*, No. 82, based on the view of the *Rosh* and the *Ravi'ah* that carrying for the voluntary fulfillment of a *mitzvah* is a holiday need. Also see the *Tur* 589. In *Iggeroth Moshe, Orach Chayim*, Vol. 3,

13. Since women are not actually obligated in the *mitzvah*, it is advisable that small children stand near their mothers during the blowing of the *shofar* in the synagogue to avoid disturbing the men.[29]

14. A woman who is unable to remain in the synagogue for the entire *Mussaf* service should hear the *tekioth d'm'yushav*[30] in preference to the *tekioth d'm'umad*.[31]

No. 94, HaGaon Rav Moshe Feinstein also concludes that it is our custom to permit carrying a *shofar* to women.

29. *Mishnah Berurah* 587:20. Once a boy has reached the age of *chinukh*, he should be brought into the men's section of the synagogue to hear the *shofar*. He should be cautioned not to disturb the congregation and to pay attention to the sounds of the *shofar*.

   Congregants should refrain from conversation during the blowing of the *shofar*.

30. Literally, "sitting blasts". This refers to the thirty sounds that are blown before the silent *Mussaf Shemoneh Esrey*.

   The *mitzvah* of *Shofar* is fulfilled by blowing several combinations of three sounds: *teki'ah*, a straight unbroken sound; *shevarim*, three short broken sounds; and *teru'ah*, a stacatto sound. These sounds are blown in sets, each set beginning and ending with a *teki'ah*. The *tekioth d'm'yushav* consists of thirty sounds divided into the following sets:

   a) Three sets of *tashrat* – *teki'ah*, *shevarim-teruah* (the two broken sounds combined into one), *teki'ah* (total of 12 sounds);

   b) three sets of *tashat* – *teki'ah*, *shevarim*, *teki'ah* (total of 9 sounds);

   c) three sets of *tarat* – *teki'ah*, *teruah*, *teki'ah* (total of 9 sounds).

   Although it is customary to stand during *tekioth d'm'yushav*, they are called the "sitting" blasts because standing is not a legal requirement. See note 32.

31. Literally, "standing blasts". This refers to the sounds blown during the *Mussaf* service. In Talmudic days, *tekioth d'm'umad* were blown during the silent *Mussaf Shemoneh Esrey* and during its repetition. In order to avoid confusing the worshippers, many communities today have discontinued the practice of blowing during the silent *Shemoneh Esrey*. They only blow *tekioth d'm'umad* during the repetition of *Mussaf*. These communities compensate for the omitted *tekioth* by blowing thirty sounds after the *Kaddish* following *Mussaf*.

A woman who listens to the *tekioth d'm'yushav* knowing that she will not be able to remain for the *tekioth d'm'umad* is required to stand during the *tekioth*.[32]

15. A woman who stands outside the synagogue, or in her home near the synagogue, can fulfill the *mitzvah* as long as she hears the true sounds of the *shofar* with the intention to fulfill the *mitzvah*. The *ba'al tokey'ah* (the person who blows the *shofar*) of the synagogue is assumed to *motzie* anyone who can hear the sound.[33]

A man who blows the *shofar* in private for a woman is not assumed to intend to *motzie* anyone else who may hear it. Someone in another room or a nearby house cannot fulfill the

---

The *Rosh HaShanah Mussaf* includes a special three-part section that describes various themes of *Rosh HaShanah*. These themes are *Malkhiyoth*, accepting God's Kingship over the world; *Zikhronoth*, *Rosh HaShanah* as a Day of Remembrance on which God passes judgement over all mankind and remembers all their deeds; and *Shofroth*, the *shofar* in Jewish history — at God's revelation on Mt. Sinai and in the future, heralding the arrival of *Mashiach*.

At the conclusion of each section, a set of *tashrat*, followed by *tashat* and *tarat* is blown. Since standing is required, they are called the "standing" blasts.

Since *tekioth d'm'umad* is a communal obligation (See paragraph 20.), and *tekioth d'm'yushav* an individual one, a woman who cannot hear both should try to hear *tekioth d'm'yushav*.

32. *Mishnah Berurah* 585:2. The reason why *Chazal* do not require standing during the *tekioth d'm'yushav* is that *tekioth* will be heard while standing later during *Mussaf*. Consequently, someone who will not remain for *Mussaf* should stand for *tekioth d'm'yushav*.

As explained in note 30, it is customary to stand for *tekioth d'm'yushav* as well. See the *Mishnah Berurah, Ibid.*

33. *Shulchan Arukh* 589:9; *Mishnah Berurah* 589:16. Those who are present in the synagogue fulfill the *mitzvah* without a specific intention to do so. Coming to hear the *shofar* itself creates the assumption of an intention to fulfill the *mitzvah*. A woman who stands outside, however, is not automatically assumed to intend to fulfill the *mitzvah*. See the *Kaf HaChayim* 589:47.

mitzvah unless the *ba'al tokeyah* was asked to *motzie* her.[34]

16. Since some authorities maintain that a person who stands outside a synagogue only hears an echo (and not the true sound), it is recommended that women come inside for the *shofar* blowing. A woman who heard the *shofar* outside, and has the opportunity to hear it again later, should do so without repeating the blessing. If she is certain that she only heard an echo, she should recite the blessing when she listens to the *shofar* later.[35]

17. Each sound must be heard in its entirety. It is not sufficient to hear part of a *teki'ah*, even if it is long enough to constitute a whole *tekiah*.[36]

18. An Ashkenazic woman who arrives in the synagogue after the blessing over the *shofar* has been recited should recite it before the *ba'al tokey'ah* begins blowing the *tekioth d'm'yushav*.[37] Even if she arrives in time to hear the conclusion of the blessing, she should not respond with *amein*,[38] but recite the blessing herself.

A woman who arrives in the synagogue in the middle of *tekioth d'm'yushav* may only recite the blessing if she plans to remain there until enough of the *tekioth d'm'umad* will be blown so that she will have heard the minimum thirty sounds necessary to fulfill the *mitzvah*.

---

34. *Mishnah Berurah* 589:17.
35. *Mishnah Berurah* 587:7.
36. A *tekiah* consists of a minimum of nine beats. The *Shulchan Arukh* 587:3 cites conflicting views regarding someone who hears this amount of a longer *teki'ah*. The *Mishnah Berurah*, citing the *Magen Avraham* and Vilna Gaon, decides in favor of the stringent opinion.
37. *Kaf HaChayim* 589:36.
38. See the *Shulchan Arukh* 124:8 and the *Biur Halakhah* 124, beginning *V'zeh*.

It is questionable whether a woman who heard *all* the *tekioth d'm'yushav* without reciting the blessing may recite it before *tekioth d'm'umad*. Some authorities advise her to silently think the words of the blessing.[39]

19. A man who has already fulfilled the *mitzvah* may blow the *shofar* for a woman.[40] If she is Ashkenazic, she should recite the blessing herself. (See paragraph 10 concerning a Sephardic woman reciting the blessing.) If the man intends not to fulfill the *mitzvah* of *Shofar* in the synagogue he may recite the blessing when he blows it for a woman because he will also be fulfilling his own obligation at that time.

A man may blow the *shofar* before synagogue services for a woman who is ill and finds it difficult to wait. Some authorities rule that it is preferable that he intend to fulfill the *mitzvah* himself at this time and recite the blessing for both of them.[41]

---

39. *Kaf HaChayim* 585:36 and 39.
40. The *Mishnah Berurah* 589:11 cites the *Magen Avraham*, who discourages a man from blowing the *shofar* before synagogue services. He cites the *Maharil*, who explains that the *shofar* should not be blown during the first three hours of the morning, the time when God sits in judgement. A man who blows the *shofar* for a woman in private should do so after synagogue services.

    An adult should not blow the *shofar* for a girl younger than *bath mitzvah* age. Since she will not be obligated in the *mitzvah* when she grows up, *Chazal* do not waive the Rabbinic prohibition of blowing the *shofar* on *Yom Tov* while she is a minor. See *Chanokh Le' Na'ar*, Chapter 22, note 7.

    Although children are permitted to blow the *shofar* all day long, a woman does not fulfill the *mitzvah* by listening to a child blow the *shofar*. See *Mo'adim U'Zmanim*, Vol. 1, No. 2.
41. In *Mikra'ey Kodesh*, *Yamim Nora'im*, p. 25, HaGaon Rav Tzvi Pessach Frank cites the *Darkey Moshe*, who explains that a man may blow the *shofar* during the first three hours of the day for a woman who finds it difficult to wait. Citing the *Mateh Ephrayim*, HaGaon Rav Frank advises the man to intend to fulfill the *mitzvah* at this time, to

20. When the *mitzvah* of *Shofar* is fulfilled in private, only the thirty sounds of *tekioth d'm'yushav* are blown. *Tekioth d'm'umad* are only blown during *Mussaf* in a *minyan*.[42] A woman who does not attend the synagogue to hear *tekioth d'm'umad* is still considered to have fulfilled the *mitzvah* of *Shofar*.[43]

21. Although a woman's obligation to recite *Mussaf* on *Shabbath* and *Yom Tov* is questionable,[44] all authorities agree that they are obligated to recite it on *Rosh HaShanah* and *Yom Kippur*.[45]

22. A woman who feels weak may eat before hearing the *shofar*.[46] If she has already recited the *Shacharith Shemoneh Esrey* she must recite *Kiddush* before eating.[47]

Tashlikh

23. It is customary to go to a river or some other body of water on the afternoon of the first day of *Rosh HaShanah* (or

---

accommodate the view of the *Pri Chadash* that a man may not blow the *shofar* for a woman if he is not also fulfilling the *mitzvah* himself. HaGaon Rav Frank reminds the man to listen to the blessing later in the synagogue as well, since it covers the *tekioth d'm'umad*, which he has not heard yet.

42. *Shulchan Arukh* 592:2; *Mishnah Berurah* 592:6.
43. *Chazon Ish, Orach Chayim*, No. 137:3.
44. See Chapter 2, paragraph 36.
45. *Hithoreruth Teshuvah*, Vol. 3, No. 66; *Yabiah Omer*, Vol. 2, *Orach Chayim*, No. 6. Since we ask for God's mercy in these prayers, women are obligated to recite them. See Chapter 2, note 82.
46. *Kitzur Shulchan Arukh* 129:19; *Eshel Avraham* (Butchach), *Hilkhoth Shofar*.
47. *Shulchan Arukh* 286:3; *Mishnah Berurah* 286:7.

the second day if the first day falls on *Shabbath*) to recite special prayers. This custom is based on the verse, "And You shall throw (*tashlikh*) all their sins into the sea" (*Michah* 6:19). Men and women should not walk to *tashlikh* in a mixed group. Some authorities rule that it is better not to go at all than to go in a mixed group.[48]

The Second Night of Rosh HaShanah

24. It is forbidden to make any preparations on the first day of *Rosh HaShanah* for the second day.[49] Candles for the second day should be lit only after nightfall. But if the dining room is dark, and the light of the candles will be used on the first day itself, they may be lit before nightfall.[50]

25. On the second night of *Rosh HaShanah*, a woman who recites *She'he'che'yanu* when she lights *Yom Tov* candles should wear a new garment or place a fruit that she has not eaten that season in front of her with the intention that the *She'he'che'yanu* include the garment or the fruit.[51]

---

48. *Orukh HaShulchan* 583:4. The *Mateh Ephrayim* 598, *Elef HaMagen*, par. 7, states, "The custom for women to attend *tashlikh* should be abolished, for it turns into a mixed social gathering... Woe to the eyes that behold this on such a holy day... It is the responsibility of the community leaders to supervise and make all possible objections."
49. See the Introduction to the commentary of the *Prishah* on the *Tur*, *Yoreh De'ah*. All forms of preparation, i.e., washing the dishes or setting the table, are forbidden.
50. See Chapter 17, note 19.
51. *Mishnah Berurah* 600:4; *Eliyahu Rabbah* 600:3. The question whether women recite *She'he'che'yanu* when they light *Yom Tov* candles is discussed in Chapter 17, paragraph 13. See also the *Kaf HaChayim* 600:6 and 263:40.

A woman who does not have a new garment or a new fruit may still recite *She'he'che'yanu.*[52]

The Ten Days of Repentance

26. During the Ten Days of Repentance between *Rosh HaShanah* and *Yom Kippur*, it is customary to act more stringently than during the rest of the year, especially in regard to forbidden foods. For example, although eating kosher bread baked by a non-Jew is not actually prohibited, one

---

The need to include a new fruit or garment for *She'he'che'yanu* on the second night of *Rosh HaShanah* is based on the halakhic principle of *kedushah achath* (one sanctity), which means that the *halakhah* views the two days of *Rosh HaShanah* as one long day. This concept leads certain authorities to the conclusion that *She'he'che'yanu* should be omitted on the second night of the holiday. Most authorities rule that the second night of *Rosh HaShanah* is no different than other *Yamim Tovim*, on which *She'he'che'yanu* is required both nights. To accommodate both views, it is customary to take a new garment or fruit with the intention that *She'he'che'yanu* also be made over it.

Nevertheless, the *Kaf HaChayim* explains that a woman may recite *She'he'che'yanu* when she lights candles although she will not eat the fruit until after *Kiddush*. Since the majority view mandates the recitation of *She'he'che'yanu* on the second night, and the function of the fruit is only to accommodate a minority view, we may rely on another minority view, which permits saying *She'he'che'yanu* on *seeing* a new fruit even if it is not eaten. See the *Shulchan Arukh* 225:3.

The *Mateh Ephrayim* 599:9 advises a woman who uses a new fruit for *She'he'che'yanu* on the second night to light as close to the time of the meal as possible.

52. *Shulchan Arukh* 600:2; *Mishnah Berurah* 600:5. The *Mishnah Berurah* explains that although in *halakhah* the two days have "one sanctity", they are still separate days, and *She'he'che'yanu* is said. Since this is the majority view, the blessing should be recited even if a new garment or fruit is not available. *Ma'asey Rav*, par. 213, reports that the Vilna Gaon ruled that no special effort need be made to find a new fruit for the second night. This is also the conclusion of *Birkey Yosef* 600:2.

should refrain from eating it during the Ten Days of Repentance.[53]

Kaparoth

27. In communities where the custom of *kaparoth*[54] is carried out with live chickens, a woman should use a hen. A pregnant woman uses a hen and a rooster. In some places, pregnant women use two hens and one rooster.[55]

28. When there is a shortage of chickens, one rooster may be used for all the males in the family and one hen for all the females. The master of the house should first wave the rooster around his own head and then around the heads of the members of his family. A man may wave the chicken around his wife's head when she is a *niddah* as long as he is careful not to touch her.[56]

---

53. *Shulchan Arukh* 603:1, and *Mishnah Berurah*. If a Jew participates in the baking, for example by adding wood or lighting the fire, the bread is no longer considered "non-Jewish". See the *Shulchan Arukh, Yoreh De'ah* 114.

   Challah is not separated from bread kneaded by a non-Jew even when a Jew purchases the dough and bakes it. See the *Mishnah Berurah, Ibid.*

   The *Kaf HaChayim* 603:26 advises women to make a special effort to fulfill the *mitzvah* of *Challah* during the Ten Days of Repentance.

54. *Kaparoth* (literally, "atonement") is an ancient custom. A person takes a chicken and symbolically transfers his transgressions to it. The chicken is waved over the head three times while a special prayer is recited. In Israel the custom is still widely observed in its original form. In many communities, the chicken is given to the poor for their *se'udah ha'mafseketh*. In other places it has become customary to use money for *kaparoth*, which is then given to charity.

55. *Beith Yosef* 605, citing the *Tashbatz*; *Remah* 605:1; *Mishnah Berurah* 605:3.

56. *Kitzur Shulchan Arukh* 136. The *Shulchan Arukh* 605 notes that it is customary to throw the liver and the innards to the birds.

In many communities, *kaparoth* is performed with money which is then given to charity. The money is waved around the head three times while reciting a special prayer found in most prayer books.

Erev Yom Kippur

29. Although the *mitzvah* to eat on *Erev Yom Kippur* is time-bound, most authorities obligate women in it. A woman who is sick or has just given birth and will therefore not be able to fast on *Yom Kippur* is exempt from this *mitzvah*.[57]

When necessary, a woman who is a *niddah* can wave the chicken around her husband's head, as long as she is careful not to touch him. See *Sugah BaShoshanim* 38:1.

57. *Kethav Sofer, Orach Chayim*, No. 112; *Responsa of Rabbi Akiva Eiger, Psakim*, No. 16; *Minchath Chinukh* 313; *Sdeh Chemed, Ma'arekheth Yom HaKippurim*, No. 1.

"'On the ninth of the month [of *Tishrey*] in the evening, from evening unto evening you shall rest.' (*VaYikra* 23:32). Do we fast on the ninth? Is it not on the tenth [of the month] that we fast? But this teaches that anyone who eats and drinks on the ninth of *Tishrey* is considered to have fasted on the ninth and the tenth" (Tractate *Rosh HaShanah* 9a).

The source for obligating women in this *mitzvah* is *Rashi*'s commentary on Tractate *Berakhoth* 5b. *Rashi* explains that the purpose of eating on *Erev Yom Kippur* is to "prepare yourselves on the ninth so you will be able to fast on the tenth." Since women are obligated to fast on *Yom Kippur*, they are included in the *mitzvah* to prepare by eating on the ninth. It is known that the *Maharal* permitted a woman who had taken a vow only to eat meat on *Shabbath* and *Yom Tov* to eat meat on *Erev Yom Kippur* also.

Sephardic authorities such as *Torah Lishmah*, No. 164, and *Ye'chaveh Da'ath*, Vol. 1, No. 58, also conclude that women are obligated in this *mitzvah*.

Rashi's explanation also explains why women who will be unable to fast on *Yom Kippur* are exempt from the *mitzvah* to eat on *Erev Yom Kippur*. In *Mikra'ey Kodesh, Yamim Nora'im*, No. 37, HaGaon Rav

30. To avoid complacency and arrogance, easily digestible foods should be served on *Erev Yom Kippur.* Intoxicating beverages should also be avoided.

At the *se'udah ha'mafseketh* (the final meal before the fast), dairy dishes, onions and garlic should not be served. It is customary to eat chicken.[58]

Authorities attach great significance to eating fish on *Erev Yom Kippur.*[59]

31. It is customary for men to immerse in the *mikvah* on *Erev Yom Kippur.*[60] Some authorities rule that unmarried women over *bath mitzvah* age should immerse,[61] but this is not

---

Tzvi Pessach Frank rules that a woman who is permitted to eat in small quantities on *Yom Kippur* is obligated to eat on *Erev Yom Kippur*; she will partially observe the fast.

58. *Shulchan Arukh* 608:4. The *Mishnah Berurah* cites a custom reported in the *Pri Megadim* to eat chicken for lunch.

59. The *Tur* 604 relates this story from the *Midrash*: "Once [on *Erev Yom Kippur*] the ruler of a city asked his servant to buy him some fish. The servant found one fish in the market which he was about to purchase for a gold coin. A Jewish tailor appeared, offered five gold coins, and bought the fish. When the servant returned to his master and told him what had happened, the ruler of the city sent for the tailor, and asked him why he had purchased a fish worth one gold coin for five gold coins and why he had bought it away from his servant? 'How could I not buy it even for ten gold coins,' responded the tailor, 'to have on this day when we are commanded by God to eat and drink, trusting that He will cleanse us of all our sins?' 'If so,' answered the ruler, 'you have done well.' And he sent him away in peace."

The *Mateh Ephrayim* 608:1 states that fish should be eaten at lunch, not at the *se'udah ha'mafseketh*. Also see the *Kaf HaChayim* 604:3.

60. *Shulchan Arukh* 606:4. Two purposes are put forward for this custom: to be ritually pure for the *Yom Kippur* prayers, and as a means of repentance. For ritual purity, one immersion is sufficient, and there is no need to recite the confessional prayer. As a means of repentance, a person should immerse three times and recite the confessional prayer.

61. *Mishnah Berurah* 606:17; *Shulchan Arukh HaRav* 606:12; *Kitzur Shulchan Arukh* 131:6; *Kaf HaChayim* 606:55.

the general practice.[62]

32. Some authorities permit leaving food on a fire on *Erev Yom Kippur* in order to have warm food available immediately

---

The *Kaf HaChayim* 581:24 notes that in many Sephardic communities it is customary for women to immerse in the *mikvah* on *Erev Rosh HaShanah* as well.

The *Ben Ish Chai, Shanah Rishonah, Parshath Nitzavim* 3, and *Parshath VaYelekh* 8, states that a woman should comb her hair and inspect herself before immersion so that there be no *chatzitzah* (separation) between her body and the water.

Rav Pe'alim, Vol. 4, No. 16, rules that a married woman who is a *niddah* may also immerse on *Erev Yom Kippur*. She must realize that this immersion does not permit her to have relations with her husband; at the end of her seven clean days she must immerse again.

Minchath Yitzchak, Vol. 6, No. 146, discusses the case of a woman who has completed her seven clean days, but has not yet been able to immerse in the *mikvah*. He rules that even if she immerses on *Erev Yom Kippur* in honor of the holiday she must immerse again after *Yom Kippur*. The blessing over the immersion is recited at that time, not on *Erev Yom Kippur*.

62. *Sdeh Chemed, Ma'arekheth Yom HaKippurim* 1:6; *She'arim Metzuyanim BeHalakhah*, commenting on the *Kitzur Shulchan Arukh* 131:13.

K'tzeh HaMateh, commenting on the *Mateh Ephrayim* 606:14–15, cites many authorities who object to unmarried women immersing in the *mikvah* on *Erev Yom Kippur*. This is based on the general hesitation of allowing unmarried women to immerse.

Once a woman has experienced her first menstrual period, she has the status of a *niddah* until she immerses in a *mikvah*. The punishment for sexual relations with a *niddah* is *kareth*, one of the severest in the Torah. When asked if unmarried women who engage in sexual relations should immerse in a *mikvah* to remove the punishment of *kareth*, the *Rivash, responsum* No. 425, answered: "On the contrary, allowing unmarried women to immerse would only lead to an increase in promiscuity. People would deal lightly with the prohibition [against sexual relations with an unmarried woman who is not a *niddah*, the punishment for which is much lighter than the punishment for sexual relations with a woman who is a *niddah*]."

after the fast.[63] Others forbid keeping food warm over *Yom Kippur*, even if it is placed on the fire the morning of *Erev Yom Kippur*.[64] If someone mistakenly keeps food warm over *Yom Kippur* it may be eaten immediately after the fast.[65]

Food may be left on a fire for children or a sick person who is permitted to eat.[66]

Lighting Candles and Accepting the Fast

33. Lighting candles for *Yom Kippur* depends on the custom of the community. When *Yom Kippur* coincides with *Shabbath*, it is an obligation to light candles, as for other *Shabbathoth* of the year.[67]

---

63. *Shulchan Arukh* 609:1. As long as the preparation is carried out during the week, there is nothing wrong with preparing for the conclusion of the fast.

64. The *Remah, Ibid.*, citing the *Maharil*. The *Mishnah Berurah* explains that these authorities forbid keeping food warm over *Yom Kippur* because it has the appearance of preparing for the week on *Yom Kippur*. The *Sha'ar HaTziyun* adds that it appears ravenous to arrange to have warm, fully cooked food ready the moment the fast ends.

65. *Pri Megadim*, cited by the *Mishnah Berurah, Ibid.*

66. The laws for keeping food warm on *Yom Kippur* are identical to the laws of *Shabbath*. Food, even if it is fully cooked, may not be placed on a fire on *Yom Kippur* to warm up for a child. A *blech* should be used for food placed on a fire before *Yom Kippur*, just as for *Shabbath*.

67. *Shulchan Arukh* 610:1. Since there is no meal on *Yom Kippur*, *Chazal* did not mandate candle-lighting. Nevertheless, the *Mishnah, Pesachim* 4:4, states, "Where it is customary to light candles on *Yom Kippur*, they are lit." The *Gemara* explains that this custom is a safeguard against marital relations, which are forbidden on *Yom Kippur*. The *Mishnah Berurah* 610:3 cites the Talmud *Yerushalmi*, which prefers lighting candles, and concludes that this practice should be adopted in a city that has no established custom.

In many communities married men light a candle on *Erev Yom Kippur* in the synagogue which will burn the entire day. This candle, called *ner chayim* (candle of life), is not lit by women. See the *Mishnah Berurah* 610:10–11.

It is a *mitzvah* to accept the fast of *Yom Kippur* a short time before sunset. The *mitzvah* of *Tosafoth Yom Kippur* (adding to *Yom Kippur*) is incumbent on men and women.[68]

34. In many communities the blessing *LeHadlik ner shel Yom HaKippurim* is recited when lighting candles. When the fast falls on *Shabbath*, the blessing is *LeHadlik ner shel Shabbath v'shel Yom HaKippurim*.[69]

In some Sephardic communities the blessing is omitted.[70] The blessing should also be omitted in a community that does not have an established custom.[71]

35. Since *Kiddush* is not recited on *Yom Kippur*, *She'he'che'yanu* is recited by the entire congregation in the synagogue after *Kol Nidrey*. A woman who recites *She'he'che'yanu* when she lights candles should not repeat it in the synagogue. She should only answer *amein* to the blessing of the prayer leader.[72]

36. A woman accepts *Yom Kippur* when she lights the candles. Therefore, once she has lit, she may not eat, drink, or

---

68. *Shulchan Arukh* 608:1; *Mishnah Berurah* 608:1–3; *Pri Megadim, Mishbetzoth Zahav* 608:1.

69. *Shulchan Arukh* and *Remah* 610:2; *Mishnah Berurah* 610:7.

The *Mateh Ephrayim* 619:4 explains that someone who does not light candles when *Yom Kippur* occurs on a weekday should only mention *Shabbath* in the blessing when *Yom Kippur* falls on *Shabbath*.

70. *Kaf HaChayim* 610:12, based on the view cited in the *Shulchan Arukh* 263:5.

71. *Sha'ar HaTziyun* 610:5 cites the view of the Vilna Gaon and *Pri Chadash* that no blessing was established over the *custom* of lighting candles on *Yom Kippur*. He concludes that the Vilna Gaon's view should be adopted where there is no established custom.

72. *Mateh Ephrayim*, cited by the *Sha'ar HaTziyun* 619:7; *Chaye Adam* 144:14.

perform any *melakhah*. Leather shoes should be removed before candle-lighting.[73]

Additional Preparations

37. Although eating is forbidden on *Yom Kippur*, and hence there is no *mitzvah* of *Oneg* (Enjoying *Yom Kippur* through food and drink), there is a *mitzvah* of *Kavod* (Honoring *Yom Kippur*). We are commanded to honor *Yom Kippur* in the same way we honor *Shabbath*. The house should be put in order and a clean *Shabbath* tablecloth placed on the table.[74]

38. Women do not wear a *kittel* on *Yom Kippur*. They often wear white garments in honor of the day.
Shabbath and *Yom Tov* ornaments are not worn on *Yom Kippur*. Garments with gold embroidery should also not be worn.[75]

39. In many homes, it is customary for a father to bless his children just before the start of *Yom Kippur*. Many mothers also bless their children at this time.[76]

40. Women are encouraged to recite the prayer *Tefillah Zakah*, found in most *machzorim*, before *Kol Nidrey*.

---

73. *Mateh Ephrayim* 610:8.
74. *Remah* 610:4; *Mishnah Berurah* 610:15.
75. *Mishnah Berurah* 610:16.
76. *Mateh Ephrayim* 619:2. The commentary *Magen HaElef* lists a number of holy books which encourage parents to bless their children before *Yom Kippur*. The traditional blessing is found in the *Chaye Adam* 144:19 and the *Kitzur Shulchan Arukh* 131:16. It is also printed in many *machzorim*.

Yom Kippur

41. Women are obligated to fast and observe all the other laws of *Yom Kippur*.[77] For women who have recently given birth or who are pregnant or nursing, the laws pertaining to eating are complex. In certain situations, they may eat normally, in others only small amounts at a time or not at all. A competent halakhic authority should be consulted concerning each situation.[78]

---

77. Tractate *Yoma* 81a, and *Sukkah* 28b; *Rambam, Hilkhoth Shevithath Asor* 1:4; *Sefer HaChinukh* 313 and 317; *Sdeh Chemed, Kellalim* 8:135.

78. Since Torah Law requires women to fast, only a potentially life-threatening situation exempts them. Sometimes, eating small amounts of food over a long period of time may remove the danger. Eating in this way, which only violates a Rabbinic prohibition, is to be preferred over eating normally, which violates a Torah prohibition.

The following selections from the *Shulchan Arukh* 617–618 represent a summary of general rules for pregnant women and those who have recently given birth.

1. In normal circumstances, pregnant women fast as usual.

2. A pregnant woman who is faint and feels that she must eat even after she is gently reminded that it is *Yom Kippur* may eat in small amounts until she regains her composure.

3. From the time labor begins until seventy-two hours after giving birth, a woman may not fast.

4. From seventy-two hours after giving birth until the end of seven days (one hundred and forty eight hours), a woman may fast if she feels strong enough and her doctor does not object.

5. If more than seven days have passed, a woman is required to fast unless she is unable due to some special problem.

No distinction is made between a normal birth and a miscarriage. A miscarriage that occurs more than forty days after conception gives a woman the status of one who has recently given birth.

The seventy-two hours and the seven days are calculated from the moment of birth. Thus, the status of a woman may change during *Yom Kippur*. For example, if the seventy-two hours end in the middle of *Yom Kippur*, she may eat before that time but not afterwards.

42. Children under the age of nine should not be allowed to fast on *Yom Kippur*. Children who have a strong constitution may begin fasting "hours" when they are nine years old; that is, they may eat breakfast later than usual or lengthen the time between meals. Weaker children may not fast "hours" until they are ten. Strong, healthy children over the age of eleven may fast the entire day, but no child under *bar* or *bath mitzvah* age should be coerced into fasting.[79]

43. Although people should refrain from handling food on *Yom Kippur*,[80] they may feed children.[81] Children may even

---

6. In normal circumstances, nursing women are obligated to fast.

7. A nursing woman is forbidden to fast if it will endanger her baby's life.

Shemirath Shabbath KeHilkhethah 39:13 rules that a woman who states that she does not need to eat and whose doctor does not object to her fasting is permitted to fast even within seventy-two hours of giving birth. It further states (*Ibid.*, note 32), that a pregnant woman who has a history of miscarrying and whose doctor fears that fasting may cause her to miscarry again is obligated to eat in small amounts.

The preceding is only a summary of guidelines. Specific situations must be clarified with a competent halakhic authority.

79. *Shulchan Arukh* and *Remah* 616:2; *Mishnah Berurah* 616:4 and 616:9; *Biur Halakhah*, beginning *B'na'ar*. The *Mishnah Berurah* explains that today most children, including those within a year of *bar* or *bath mitzvah*, are considered weak unless it is certain that they are strong enough to withstand the fast. The *Mishnah Berurah* 616:11 also rules that Torah Law does not require fasting for a boy or girl who has reached *bar* or *bath mitzvah* age on *Yom Kippur*, but has not attained physical maturity. (See Chapter 11, note 1, and Chapter 15, note 174.) They may eat if they feel weak. See also *Chatham Sofer, Orach Chayim*, No. 172, and *Iggeroth Moshe, Orach Chayim*, Vol. 1, No. 176.

80. *Kaf HaChayim* 603:55.

81. *Remah* 612:10, citing the *Terumoth HaDeshen*, No. 147. The *Mishnah Berurah* explains that unlike *Pessach*, when handling *chametz* is forbidden to safeguard against eating it (See *Shulchan Arukh* 446:3.), handling food on *Yom Kippur* is permitted. On *Pessach*, eating food is

be fed a holiday meal on *Yom Kippur.*[82]

A woman who serves food to children must be extremely careful not to taste any, even a tiny amount which she would immediately spit out.[83]

The Five Afflictions

44. Both men and women are obligated to "afflict their souls" on *Yom Kippur.* In addition to food and drink, bathing, wearing leather shoes, annointing oneself with fragrant oils, and engaging in sexual intercourse are forbidden.

When necessary, a woman who has given birth in the preceding thirty days, or a sick person, even when there is no danger to life, or someone who has a leg wound may wear leather shoes on *Yom Kippur.*[84]

---

generally permitted, so handling *chametz* may bring a person to eat it. The fact that people refrain from all food on *Yom Kippur*, together with the special reverence they have for the Day of Atonement, makes the possibility of their forgetting much less likely. The *Mishnah Berurah* explains that an adult may even handle food for a child who is able to take it by himself. A child should only be fed what is necessary for his or her well-being. See *Chanokh Le'na'ar*, Chapter 6, note 16.

82. *Orchoth Chayim*, 618:12. Children who eat bread on *Yom Kippur* are permitted to wash their hands. See *Levush Mordekhai, Tanina, Yoreh De'ah* 11:3, and *Responsa of Maharil Diskin, Kuntres Acharon*, No. 65.

The *Shulchan Arukh* 618:10 rules that one who eats on *Yom Kippur* should say *Ya'aleh v'yavo*, with the words *B' Yom HaKippurim ha'zeh*, in *Birkath HaMazon*. The *Mishnah Berurah* 618:29 adds that on *Shabbath, R'tzeh v'ha'chalitzeinu* should be said. Since some authorities do not require these additions, a person who forgets to include either of them does not repeat *Birkath HaMazon*.

Kiddush should not be recited by someone who eats on *Yom Kippur*, even if it falls on *Shabbath*. See the *Mishnah Berurah, Ibid.*

83. *Remah* 612:6, and the *Mishnah Berurah*.

84. *Shulchan Arukh* 614:3; *Mishnah Berurah* 614:10.

45. Leather shoes should not be put on a child, even one too young to understand that it is *Yom Kippur*. A child who puts on leather shoes should be reprimanded and instructed to change.[85]

Bathing or annointing children and infants with fragrant oils is forbidden. This includes asking a non-Jew to bathe an infant in cold water.[86]

46. A special dispensation is made for a bride so she will not be disagreeable to her husband; she may wash her face and annoint herself with fragrant oils during the first thirty days following the wedding.[87] Some authorities rule that she should not avail herself of this dispensation when her husband will remain in the synagogue the entire day and will not see her.[88]

Standing During Prayer

47. Some people stand during the entire *Yom Kippur* service. Women are not accustomed to do so.[89] Women should

---

85. *Shulchan Arukh* 616:1; *Mishnah Berurah* 616:2. It is forbidden to assist children of any age to do something forbidden. Feeding children on *Yom Kippur* is permitted only because it is indispensable for their well-being. Refraining from wearing leather shoes for a day will not impair a child's development; an adult may not place them on a child's feet.

86. *Mishnah Berurah* 616:3. Since it is unusual to bathe and apply fragrant oils to children every day, it is not crucial to their development.

87. *Shulchan Arukh* 613:10.

88. *Mishnah Berurah* 613:26. The *Kaf HaChayim* states that this depends on the custom in her community.

89. *Shulchan Arukh* 619:5. The *Mishnah Berurah* 619:13 explains the reason for standing the entire day is to express the idea that on *Yom Kippur* the Jewish people are like angels. The *Sha'ar HaTziyun* points out that women are not included in this comparison. The basis for this distinction is the *Yalkut Shimoni* on *Mishley* 21:22: "'A wise man scales the city of the mighty (*ir giborim*).' It is written *g'varim* (men). R.

stand during the recitation of confession.[90] A woman who feels weak should at least stand for the words, "but we and our forefathers have sinned."[91]

Ne'ilah and the Conclusion of the Fast

48. All authorities obligate women to recite *Ne'ilah*, the concluding *Shemoneh Esrey* of *Yom Kippur*.[92]

49. A woman who finds it difficult to wait for her husband to return home is permitted to recite *Havdalah* after the fast and eat immediately.[93] If possible, she should wait for his arrival, since some authorities rule that women do not recite *Havdalah* at the conclusion of *Yom Kippur*.[94]

Yehoshua said in the name of R. Acha, '*G'varim* — for all of them[the angels] are male, and there are no females among them.'"

Expanding on this theme, many authorities maintain that the custom to recite the phrase *Barukh shem k'vod malkhutho l'olam va'ed* aloud during *Kriath Shemah* is not practiced by women. The custom is based on a *Midrash* which explains that the angels praise God with the phrase *Barukh shem*. See the *Mishnah Berurah* 619:8.

90. *Sefer HaChinukh* 364; *Sha'arey Teshuvah* of Rabbenu Yona, *Sha'ar Revi'i* 17; *Shulchan Arukh* 607:3.

91. This is the essence of confession. See Tractate *Yoma* 87b.

92. *Yabia Omer*, Vol. 2, *Orach Chayim*, No. 6. No other prayer at any other time of the year begs God for mercy as much as *Ne'ilah*. See note 45.

93. *Shevet HaLevi, Orach Chayim*, Vol. 4, No. 54; *She'arim Metzuyanim BeHalakhah*, commentary on the *Kitzur Shulchan Arukh* 133:27.

94. *Mateh Ephrayim* 624:7. Those authorities who obligate women to recite *Havdalah* on Saturday night reason that *Havdalah* is a *mitzvah* related to *Shabbath*, in all of whose *mitzvoth* women are obligated. *Yom Kippur* is not a *Shabbath*.

CHAPTER 20
Sukkoth

The Sukkah

1. *Sukkah* is a time-bound *mitzvah* from which women are exempt.[1] Ashkenazic women recite the blessing *Ley'shev ba'sukkah* (To dwell in the *sukkah*),[2] but Sephardic women do

---

1. *Shulchan Arukh* 640:1; *Elef LaMateh*, commentary on the *Mateh Ephrayim* 625:59.

   Torah Lishmah, No. 172, maintains that a woman who fulfills the *mitzvah* for three consecutive years is considered to have taken a vow. If she wishes to discontinue this practice, the vow must be annulled. The same is true of a woman who fulfills the *mitzvah* of *Lulav* for three consecutive years. A verbal declaration to fulfill these *mitzvoth* is also considered a vow.

2. *Mishnah Berurah* 640:1, based on the view of Rabbenu Tam, which permits women to recite blessings when they voluntarily fulfill time-bound *mitzvoth*. See the Introduction, paragraph 8. Because Ashkenazic women recite the blessing voluntarily, they cannot *motzie* men, who are obligated to fulfill the *mitzvah*.

not.[3] A man may not recite the blessing for a woman unless he is reciting it for himself at that time.[4]

Some authorities maintain that a man's wife and family must dwell with him in the *sukkah* for him to fulfill the *mitzvah* fully.[5]

2. It is preferable that a woman not build a *sukkah* for her family,[6] but if she builds one according to the requirements of

---

3. This is based on the view of the *Beith Yosef* and the *Rambam*, which forbids women to recite blessings over time-bound *mitzvoth*.

4. Since the woman is not obligated to fulfill the *mitzvah*, *arvuth* does not apply. See Chapter 15, note 161.

5. *Kaf HaChayim* 640:5: "It is a *mitzvah* for every Jew to seat his wife and family with him in the *sukkah* so that they will also be in the protective shadow of the Faithful One and purify their souls. He should tell them about God's kindness to His people Israel... so that His love and fear will be with them, and they will cease from sin."

  Another reason for this practice is the dictum of *Chazal*, "You shall dwell [in the *sukkah*] the way you live [in your home]." Just as a man lives at home with his wife and family, so should he dwell in the *sukkah*.

  Sefer Minhagey Chatham Sofer 8:11 reports, "All [the *Chatham Sofer*'s] sons, daughters, sons-in-law and daughters-in-law ate with him in the *sukkah* the entire holiday."

6. The *Biur Halakhah* 14, beginning *Le'hatzrikh*, cites the *Magen Avraham* in the name of *Rabbenu Tam*, who explains that a person who is not obligated in a *mitzvah* should not prepare the object with which the *mitzvah* is performed. For this reason, Rabbenu Tam disqualifies women from attaching *tzitzith* threads to a four-cornered garment. The *Magen Avraham* adds that Rabbenu Tam would also not permit women to build a *sukkah*.

  The *Biur Halakhah* notes that most authorities offer a different reason for disqualifying women from attaching *tzitzith* threads to a four-cornered garment, one which does not disqualify them from building a *sukkah*. (See Chapter 14, note 48.) The *Biur Halakhah* concludes that although it is preferable to take the *Magen Avraham*'s view into account, if a woman does build a *sukkah* the majority view is to be followed, and it may be used.

the law, it may be used without hesitation.[7]

A husband who is incapable of building a *sukkah* should not hesitate to ask his wife to build one for him.[8]

3. A woman who builds a *sukkah* for her own personal use is forbidden to use it or its decorations during the holiday for any purpose other than the *mitzvah*. It is questionable whether a man is also prohibited from deriving personal benefit from it.[9]

4. A person fulfills the *mitzvah* by dwelling in the *sukkah* in the same manner as he dwells in his house. This includes eating, sleeping and other activities normally carried out there. Some authorities go so far as to maintain that if there is not a private area in the *sukkah* where a man can sleep with his wife, he is not required to sleep in the *sukkah* at all. In practice, although it is best for a man's wife to sleep with him in the

---

Dov Eisenberg, in *Guide for the Jewish Woman and Girl*, cites a ruling of HaGaon Rav Moshe Stern: A woman should not put the *skhakh* (leaves or evergreens that make up the roof of the *sukkah*) in place. If her husband is pressed for time, he may designate her his agent to place the *skhakh* for him. The same is true of a father and daughter.

7. See the *Shulchan Arukh* 635:1, and the *Mishnah Berurah*.

8. *Chokhmath Shlomoh, Orach Chayim*, No. 14.

9. An object which is designated for a *mitzvah* may not be put to any other use for the duration of the *mitzvah*. This principle, known as *muktzeh machmath mitzvah*, applies to the *sukkah* and its decorations, both of which have been set aside for a *mitzvah*. *Hithoreruth Teshuvah*, Vol. 1, No. 48, rules that a woman who wishes to fulfill the *mitzvah*, and builds her own *sukkah* for this purpose, may also not use her *sukkah* for any other purpose. The author is uncertain whether her designating the *sukkah* for the fulfillment of a voluntary *mitzvah* makes it *muktzeh machmath mitzvah* for a man, for whom the *mitzvah* is obligatory.

sukkah, he is not exempt from sleeping there even if she does not.[10]

5. Boys over five years old should be trained to fulfill the *mitzvah* of *Sukkah*. Some authorities maintain that a mother is responsible for *chinukh* in the father's absence.[11] She must make sure that her son does not eat outside the *sukkah*.[12]

A parent or stranger is forbidden to feed a child or instruct him to eat amounts of food outside the *sukkah* that must be eaten in the *sukkah*.[13]

If a *sukkah* is cold, and a child is uncomfortable eating there, he may eat in the house.[14]

---

10. *Remah* 639:2; *Mishnah Berurah* 639:18. Also see the *Torah Temimah's* commentary on *VaYikra* 23, par. 169.

11. *Shulchan Arukh* 640:2; *Mishnah Berurah* 640:4–5. Five is the age of *chinukh* for *Sukkah* because at that age a child is no longer completely dependent on his mother.

12. The *mitzvah* requires that a meal consisting of at least a *ke'betzah* of bread (approximately 45 grams) be eaten in the *sukkah*. Some authorities rule that cooked or baked grain products should also be eaten in the *sukkah*. The *Mishnah Berurah* 639:12 deems it proper to eat any meal, even one consisting entirely of meat, fish, or cheese in the *sukkah*. A person only recites the blessing *Ley'shev ba'sukkah* when eating a *ke'betzah* of bread or a volume of grain products which that person considers to be a meal.

13. *Mishnah Berurah* 640:4–5, citing the *Eliyahu Rabbah* and *Bikurey Yaacov*.

Once a boy reaches the age of *chinukh* (See note 11), feeding him outside the *sukkah* is tantamount to feeding him forbidden food. It is forbidden for any Jew to feed or instruct a child to eat such food. See note 12 for the amounts and kinds of food that may not be eaten outside the *sukkah*.

If a child begins eating outside the *sukkah*, his father is obligated to stop him and instruct him to eat there. This is based on the father's special responsibility to train his child in *mitzvah* observance. An outsider has no such responsibility. See Chapter 10, note 30.

14. *Orukh HaShulchan* 640:2. This applies even if it is not cold enough to exempt an adult from eating there.

Candle-lighting

6. *Shabbath* and *Yom Tov* candles should be lit in the *sukkah*.[15] Women who light candles in the *sukkah* and then transfer them to the house are not acting properly.[16]

7. If the candles might blow out, or the *sukkah* is very small and there is a possibility of fire, the candles should be left in the house on a window sill that faces the *sukkah*. Another method is to purchase a glass box in which to place the candles inside the *sukkah*.[17]

Kiddush

8. The *mitzvah* of *Kiddush* may only be fulfilled where a person eats. Thus a woman who hears *Kiddush* in the *sukkah* must be sure to eat something there. If she is unable to eat there, she may remain in the house, listen to someone recite *Kiddush* in the *sukkah*, and eat inside the house.[18] A woman may answer *amein* to the blessing *Ley'shev ba'sukkah* even if she eats in the house.[19]

Utensils in the Sukkah

9. All serving utensils normally used at the dining table may be brought into the *sukkah*. Pots should not be brought into the *sukkah*, even if their contents will be transferred directly to plates.[20]

---

15. *Shulchan Arukh* 639:1.
16. *Mishnah Berurah* 263:48.
17. *Mishnah Berurah* 639:8.
18. See the *Shulchan Arukh* 273:6, and the *Mishnah Berurah*.
19. *Iggeroth Moshe, Orach Chayim*, Vol. 4, No. 21:9.
20. *Shulchan Arukh* 639:1; *Mishnah Berurah* 639:5-6. Bringing pots into

It is not advisable to recite the blessing *Ley'shev ba'sukkah* when there are pots in the sukkah.[21]

The Four Species

10. Women are exempt from the *mitzvah* of *Lulav*.[22] Ashkenazic women may recite the blessing over the *Lulav*.[23] Some authorities maintain that women have accepted this *mitzvah* as an obligation.[24]

---

the *sukkah* is considered degrading to the *mitzvah*.

The *Mishnah Berurah* cites authorities who rule leniently in cases where the food is served directly from the pot, but he indicates that it is preferable to act stringently.

21. The *Mishnah Berurah* 639:6 rules that bringing pots into the *sukkah* does not invalidate it. In the *Sha'ar HaTziyun* 639:18, he cites other authorities who rule that the *sukkah* does become invalid according to Rabbinic Law while the pots are there. He therefore advises against reciting the blessing until they are removed.

22. *Remah* 658:9; *Mishnah Berurah* 654:1. The *mitzvah* of *Lulav* is fulfilled by taking a *lulav* (date palm stalk), three *hadassim* (myrtle branches), and two *aravoth* (willow branches), which are bound together in a particular way in the right hand (for a right-handed person), and an *ethrog* in the left hand, then holding them together. Although all four species are needed for the *mitzvah*, it is commonly referred to as the *mitzvah* of *Lulav* after the largest of the four. This *mitzvah* is time-bound thus women are exempt.

Although they are exempt, women may not recite the blessing over a set of four species that does not conform to the requirements of the law. See *Bikurey Yaacov* 657:5.

23. *Mishnah Berurah* 654:1 and 658:41, based on the view of Rabbenu Tam permitting women to recite blessings over time-bound *mitzvoth*. Also see the *Shulchan Arukh* and *Remah* 589:6; *Taz* 658:6; *Magen Avraham* 658:11.

24. *Responsa of Rabbi Akiva Eiger, Hashmatoth* (additions) to *responsum* No. 1: "Most women act strictly. They are diligent and careful to fulfill time-bound *mitzvoth* such as *Shofar* and *Lulav*. These are considered obligatory for them."

Some Sephardic authorities rule that women should not recite the blessing,[25] while others maintain that they may.[26]

In communities where funds are collected to purchase sets of the four species for communal use, women are exempt from contributing. An unmarried woman who wishes to recite the blessing over the communal four species is required to contribute towards their purchase. See the *Mishnah Berurah* 658:41 and *Sha'ar HaTziyun* 658:41.

25. *Nechpah B'Kesef* (written by HaGaon R. Yona Navon, the teacher of the *Chida*), Vol. 1, p. 181; *Birkey Yosef* 654:2, in accord with the view of the *Beith Yosef*. The general Sephardic practice is for women to refrain from blessings over time-bound *mitzvoth*. See further in *Ye'chaveh Da'ath*, Vol. 1, Nos. 88–89 and *Yabia Omer*, Vol. 1, *Orach Chayim*, Nos. 40–42, and Vol. 5, *Orach Chayim*, No. 43.

26. The *Chida*, in *Birkey Yosef, Ibid.*, and in *Yosef Ometz*, No. 82, cites Sephardic authorities who except *Lulav* and *Shofar* from the general rule. (See Chapter 19, paragraph 10.) In *Birkey Yosef*, the *Chida* writes, "Afterwards, a notebook of Rabbenu Yaacov of Marvish came into my hands. In it was a list of questions he asked from Heaven and the answers that were revealed to him. It is written there: 'Everything Sarah says to you, hearken to her voice' (*Bereshith* 21:12). There is a hint [for allowing women to recite the blessing] in the similarity of the word *lulav* (date palm) to the word *lev* (heart), denoting that [one who takes the *lulav*] has only one heart for his Father in Heaven. [Since this idea applies to women as well] they may recite the blessing."

In *Yosef Ometz*, the *Chida* states, "After seeing the answer revealed to Rabbenu Yaacov, I began to instruct women to recite the blessing, in accord with the ancient practice of women in the Holy City. Although our Master [the *Beith Yosef*] rules that they should not recite it, I am convinced that if his holy eyes had seen the words of Rabbenu Yaacov, he too would have ruled differently."

The *Kaf HaChayim* 589:23 also reports the ancient custom in Jerusalem for Sephardic women to recite the blessing over the *lulav*. *Rav Pe'alim*, Vol. 1, *Kuntres Sod Yesharim* 2, reports that this was also the practice in Iraq.

In fact, *Tzitz Eliezer*, Vol. 9, No. 2, concludes that Sephardic women may recite blessings over all time-bound *mitzvoth*: "The custom of reciting blessings over time-bound *mitzvoth* is in accordance with the will of the wise men, even among our Sephardic brothers. This is

11. Women who intend to recite the blessing over the *lulav* customarily delay eating until after performing the *mitzvah* unless they feel weak.[27]

12. Some authorities rule that women should hold the *lulav* without waving it.[28]

13. A woman should remove any rings from her fingers before taking the *lulav*.[29]

14. Some authorities rule that on *Yom Tov* it is forbidden to carry a *lulav* to a woman through an area which has no *eiruv*.[30] Others are lenient.[31]

15. A woman may handle a *lulav* on *Yom Tov*. It is not considered *muktzeh*, even for a person who does not recite the

especially true in regard to the *mitzvah* of *Lulav*. One should not protest against those who act this way, but should encourage and strengthen them." This is also the conclusion of *Sdeh Chemed, Ma'arekheth Mem*, No. 136.

At the opposite extreme, the *Yeshuoth Yaacov, Orach Chayim* 17:1, reports that the *Chacham Tzvi* even protested against Ashkenazic women reciting blessings over time-bound *mitzvoth*. See the latter's *responsum*, No. 4:8, in his additional *responsa*.

In *Otzar Chayim, Minhagey Zanz, Perek Chag HaSukkoth*, par. 258, it is reported that HaGaon Rav Chayim of Tzanz was particular that women not recite the blessing over the *lulav*. In fact, he was a grandson of the *Chacham Tzvi*. In practice, however, the general Ashkenazic custom is for women to recite the blessing.

27. *Eshel Avraham* (Butchach) 589.
28. *Rav Pe'alim*, Vol. 1, *Kuntres Sod Yesharim* 12, based on the *Ari*.
29. *Remah* 651:7, and *Mishnah Berurah*. There should be no *chatzitzah* between the hands and the *lulav*.
30. *Sha'agath Aryeh*, No. 24, cited by the *Sha'arey Teshuvah* 589. See Chapter 19, notes 27–28.
31. *Iggeroth Moshe, Orach Chayim*, Vol. 3, No. 94; *Mishneh Halakhoth*, Vol. 6, No. 116.

blessing.[32]

16. Women are advised not to bind the *hadassim* (myrtle) and *aravoth* (willow) to the *lulav* unless their husbands do not have time to do it.[33]

A woman may tie the knots that are customarily made along the length of the *lulav*.[34]

17. On the first day of *Sukkoth* (the first two days outside *Eretz Yisrael*), the four species must belong to the person performing the *mitzvah*.[35] A married woman who wishes to recite the blessing over her husband's *lulav* must acquire it from him. Her husband should state that he is giving it to her, and she must intend to acquire it. After fulfilling the *mitzvah*, she must give it back to him.[36]

---

32. *Shulchan Arukh* 654:1. Since it is used by men, the *lulav* may be handled by everyone.

33. *Remah* 649:1; *Magen Avraham* 649:1; *Mishnah Berurah* 649:14; *Sha'ar HaTziyun* 649:15. Also see *Bikurey Yaacov* 649:14 and 635:2. This is based on Rabbenu Tam's view cited in note 6.

34. Binding the *aravoth* and *hadassim* to the *lulav* is essential to the *mitzvah*. Tying the knots is not.

35. Tractate *Sukkah* 27b expounds on the verse, "And you shall take for *yourselves* on the first day" (*VaYikra* 23:40), that on the first day of *Sukkoth* the four species must belong to the person performing the *mitzvah*. The *Mishnah Berurah* 558:23 adds that outside *Eretz Yisrael*, where *Yom Tov* is observed for two days, this requirement applies on both days.

36. *Mishnah Berurah* 549:15. Jewish Law views a gift which is given on the condition that it be returned as a full legal transfer. When a person gives his *lulav* to someone to fulfill the *mitzvah*, it is assumed that it is being "given away" on condition that it be returned. The transfer is only valid if the *lulav* is returned; if the *lulav* is not returned, the recipient never owned it and the performance of the *mitzvah* was invalid. The *Mishnah Berurah* instructs the "giver" to inform the "receiver" that the *lulav* is being given on the condition that it be returned.

The same procedure should be followed when a girl above *bath mitzvah* age wishes to recite the blessing over her father's *lulav*.

18. A man who has not fulfilled the *mitzvah* should not give his *lulav* to a minor.[37] Outside of *Eretz Yisrael*, a man should not give his *lulav* to a minor on the first day of *Sukkoth*, even after he has fulfilled the *mitzvah*.[38]

19. If a woman's husband does not have a *lulav*, or if he is not at home, another man may give her his *lulav* with these words: "Acquire this *lulav* on condition that it be returned and on condition that your husband has no rights in it."[39]

Nevertheless, it is considered immodest for a man to give his *lulav* to any woman other than his wife, mother, daughter, or sister. This is especially true if the recipient is an unmarried woman.[40]

---

37. *Shulchan Arukh* 558:6. Although minors can acquire objects, they are deemed halakhically incapable of transferring possession to another party. If a man gives his *lulav* to a minor before fulfilling the *mitzvah*, he will be unable to reacquire it when he himself wants to fulfill the *mitzvah*. The *Mishnah Berurah* advises an adult to loan his *lulav* to a minor. Although the minor is not fulfilling the *mitzvah* in accordance with all its details, since he performs the *mitzvah* with a kosher *lulav*, the obligation of *chinukh* is satisfied. This is certainly true of a girl who is a minor since even when she grows up she will not be obligated in the *mitzvah*.

38. *Mishnah Berurah* 558:23. The man needs to reacquire the *lulav* to fulfill the *mitzvah* on the second day of *Yom Tov*.

The *Biur Halakhah* 558, beginning *MiKodem*, advises against giving the *lulav* away to a minor even after fulfilling the *mitzvah* on the second day of *Yom Tov*. Another adult may ask to use it later in the day, and he will be unable to acquire it from the minor.

39. *Bikurey Yaacov* 657:5. When a woman acquires on object, it legally belongs to her husband unless the giver specifically excludes him from ownership.

40. *Mo'ed LeKol Chai*, No. 23:40. *Yafeh LeLev*, Vol. 2, No. 658, explains

20. In his absence, a woman should not give away her husband's *lulav*.[41]

21. The requirement to own the *lulav* only applies on the first day of *Sukkoth* (the first two days outside *Eretz Yisrael*).[42] On the other days, a woman may borrow another person's *lulav* and recite the blessing over it even without the owner's knowledge.[43]

---

that when a man gives a gift to an unmarried woman, a suspicion may arise that he has betrothed her.

If there is a female guest in the house for *Yom Tov*, the host should give his *lulav* to his wife who may then give it to the guest on condition that it be returned.

41. *Mishnah Berurah* 658:8; *Sha'ar HaTziyun* 658:11. See note 43. Although we assume that a person does not mind if someone borrows his possessions to fulfill a *mitzvah*, there is no assumption that the owner would not mind if someone *acquires* his *lulav* to fulfill a *mitzvah*. Since the *lulav* must be owned by the person fulfilling the *mitzvah* on the first day, a woman does not have authority to give away her husband's possessions without his knowledge.

42. *Mishnah Berurah* 558:23.

43. *Iggeroth Moshe, Orach Chayim*, Vol. 2, No. 106; *Hithoreruth Teshuvah*, Vol. 1, No. 177, based on the *Remah* 649:5 and *Mishnah Berurah* 649:33.

Using someone's *lulav* without permission does not constitute theft: "A person is pleased when someone uses his possessions to carry out a *mitzvah*." This rule only applies when the borrowed object will not be damaged in any way.

The *Mishnah Berurah* 649:34 limits the rule:

a) If the borrower knows that the owner is particular that people not take his *lulav*, it is forbidden.

b) If the owner is nearby, his permission should be sought.

c) The borrowed *lulav* may not be given to a third party.

d) It should not be taken on a regular basis without asking permission.

e) It may only be used where it is borrowed, not in any other location.

22. On *Yom Tov*, a woman may return a *lulav* to the water in which it was placed before *Yom Tov*. When necessary, water may be added on *Yom Tov*, but not changed. Some authorities maintain that if a person forgot to place a *lulav* in water before *Yom Tov*, she may place it in water for the first time on *Yom Tov* itself.[44]

Hadassim with buds that are liable to open may not be placed in or returned to water on *Yom Tov*.[45]

Hoshanah Rabbah and Simchath Torah

23. Women may recite the *tikkun* of the night of *Hoshanah Rabbah*.[46] It is customary to provide them with aravah branches for the beating of the *aravoth*.[47]

24. A woman who normally recites *She'he'che'yanu* when she lights *Yom Tov* candles also recites it when lighting candles for *Shemini Atzereth*.[48]

25. One must be on guard to observe all the requirements of modest behavior during the dancing on *Simchath Torah*. A proper *mechitzah* (partition) should be maintained between the

---

44. *Shulchan Arukh* 654:1.
45. See the *Remah* 336:1 and the *Mishnah Berurah* 336:54.
46. The *Ben Ish Chai, Shanah Rishonah, Parshath VaYishlach* 6, and *Rav Pe'alim*, Vol. 1, *Kuntres Sod Yesharim*, No. 9, explain that the *tikkun* recited on the night of *Hoshanah Rabbah* helps to improve a person's final seal of judgement. Women can benefit from reciting it as much as men can. See Chapter 24, paragraph 6, regarding the *tikkun* recited on the night of *Shavuoth*.
47. Special prayers for rain are recited on *Hoshanah Rabbah*. At their conclusion, five *aravah* branches are taken and beaten on the floor.
48. *Shulchan Arukh* 668:1; *Mishnah Berurah* 661:8. *Shemini Atzereth* is a separate holiday with its own *She'he'che'yanu*.

men's and women's sections of the synagogue.[49] In this way, the joy and honor of our holy Torah will be properly expressed.

---

49. See Chapter 2, paragraph 46.

CHAPTER 21
Chanukah

Kindling Chanukah Lights

1. Both men and women are obligated to kindle *Chanukah* lights.[1] It is customary for married women to fulfill the

---

1. *Shulchan Arukh* 675:3, based on Tractate *Shabbath* 23a, which quotes Rabbi Yehoshua ben Levi: "Women are obligated in the *mitzvah* of kindling *Chanukah* lights, for they were also included in the miracle."

Rashi explains that Rabbi Yehoshua ben Levi is alluding to the decree imposed by the Greeks forcing every virgin to submit to the Greek governor before her marriage. The miraculous victory of the Maccabees delivered young women from this fate.

A different interpretation is cited in the *Beith Yosef* 675 in the name of the *Ran*: Women are obligated to commemorate the miracle of *Chanukah* because a woman was instrumental in bringing about salvation from Greek oppression. When Yehudith, the daughter of Yochanan the High Priest, was called to the tyrannical governor, she fed him cheese dishes and these made him drowsy. Then she offered him wine, inducing a drunken stupor. After he fell asleep, she cut off his head and brought it up to Jerusalem. When the Greek army saw their leader dead, they fled in disarray. (The *Kaf HaChayim* 675:17

mitzvah through their husbands.[2] Although the Ashkenazic custom is that each member of the family kindles lights, single girls do not generally kindle them. They fulfill the *mitzvah* by standing near their fathers when they light and listening to them recite the blessings.[3]

---

and the *Ben Ish Chai, Shanah Rishonah, Parshath VaYeshev* 24, cite opinions that although it actually occurred at a different time, this event is commemorated during *Chanukah* because it did occur under Greek oppression.)

See also Tractate *Pesachim* 108b, with the commentaries of the *Rashbam* and *Tosafoth*. Also see note 35.

2. *Mishnah Berurah* 675:9, citing *Olath Shmuel*, No. 108. An analysis of the unique structure of the *mitzvah* of *Chanukah* will clarify why married women do not kindle the lights.

Tractate *Shabbath* 21b teaches, "The [basic] *mitzvah* of *Chanukah* is [fulfilled] by *one* member of the household lighting one candle [each night on behalf of the entire household]. If they wish to beautify the *mitzvah* (*mihadrin*), *each* individual in the household should light one candle each night. If they wish to beautify the *mitzvah* in the best possible way (*mihadrin min ha'mihadrin*), according to *Beith Shamai*, they should light in descending order (eight lights the first night, seven the second, and so on); according to *Beith Hillel* they should light in ascending order (one light the first night, two the second, and so on)."

Although the law follows *Beith Hillel*, there is a controversy over the meaning of their words. The *Shulchan Arukh* 675:2 follows *Tosafoth*'s interpretation: *Beith Hillel*'s procedure should be viewed as an addition to the basic *mitzvah*, i.e., *mihadrin min ha'mihadrin* is fulfilled by *one* person lighting on behalf of the entire household in ascending order. The *Remah, Ibid.*, following the interpretation of the *Rif* and the *Rambam*, attaches *mihadrin min ha'mihadrin* to *mihadrin*, i.e., *each* member of the household should light his own *menorah* in ascending order. The Sephardic custom follows the view of the *Shulchan Arukh*, the Ashkenazic custom the *Remah*.

In Ashkenazic families every member of the household except the wife lights his own *menorah*. This accords with the concept *ishto k'gufo*. (One's wife is as one's self.) When her husband lights, she is also lighting and fulfilling the *mitzvah mihadrin min ha'mihadrin*.

3. See the novellae of the *Chatham Sofer* on Tractate *Shabbath* 21b,

A woman may kindle her own *menorah*. If she is Ashkenazic, she may recite the blessings, but she should have intention not to fulfill the *mitzvah* through her father or husband.[4] A Sephardic woman may not recite the blessings unless her father does not light.[5]

2. The master of the house should gather together his

---

where he explains that although a daughter and her father are not considered one (so she does not fulfill *mihadrin min ha'mihadrin* when her father lights), it is not customary for her to light: "We have a tradition from our forefathers, from the days when they would kindle *Chanukah* lights outside, that single girls do not light. They refrained because it was unseemly for them to go out in public and stand among the men at the entrances to houses. They stood at a distance to hear the blessings... We also follow this custom...and single women do not light [even though today we light indoors]."

Mishmereth Shalom offers another reason why single girls do not fulfill *mihadrin min ha'mihadrin* (according to the Ashkenazic custom). Since their mothers fulfill *mihadrin min ha'mihadrin* through their husbands' lighting, their mothers have no reason to light for themselves. Single girls forgo the extra beautification of the *mitzvah* to avoid slighting a parent since it might appear disrespectful for them to light when their mothers do not. According to this view, a girl whose mother is a widow or a divorcee and lights her own *menorah* should also light.

4. The *Mishnah Berurah* 675:9, citing *Olath Shmuel*, states that even a married woman who wishes to light may do so and recite the blessings. Since women generally do not light (they are assumed to fulfill the *mitzvah* through a husband or father), one who wishes to light must specifically intend not to fulfill the *mitzvah* through any other person.

5. This is based on a decision of HaGaon Rav Ben Zion Abba Shaul, who cites the ruling of the *Ben Ish Chai, Shanah Rishonah, Parshath VaYeshev* 9 — even a single man should not light his own *menorah*, but rely on his father in accordance with Sephardic custom. This would also be the case with respect to women. She should certainly not recite the blessings if she does light.

whole family — wife, sons and daughters[6] — before kindling the lights, especially if he does it indoors.[7]

3. According to the law, a woman may kindle *Chanukah* lights and recite the blessings on behalf of her husband, other members of her family, or other men.[8]

---

6. *Mishnah Berurah* 672:10, in order to publicize the miracle. The *Magen Avraham* stresses the importance of the family gathering together when they kindle the lights late and there are no longer passersby on the street to see them. But the *Chaye Adam* 154:20 indicates that the family should gather together even when they light on time.

7. When the lights are kindled indoors, the miracle is primarily publicized to those inside. *Chovath HaDar*, citing the *Bach*, offers an additional reason: In addition to the *mitzvah* of lighting, which can be performed by one person for the whole family, there is also a *mitzvah* to *see* the *Chanukah* lights and recite a blessing over them. Each member of the family fulfills this *mitzvah* by being present when the lights are kindled and by listening to the head of the household recite the blessings. See note 8 for a detailed discussion.

8. *Shulchan Arukh* 675:3, and *Mishnah Berurah*. In his commentary on Tractate *Shabbath*, the *Me'iri* explains, "It follows [from the fact that a woman is obligated in the *mitzvah* of *Chanukah*] that she may light the *menorah* and *motzie* others, just as anyone obligated in a *mitzvah* may perform it on behalf of others." Also see the *Ohr Zarua* 324:20 and the *Kol Bo*, Laws of *Chanukah*, No. 44. The *Bach* 676 explains that the opposite is also true — a man may perform the *mitzvah* on behalf of a woman.

The *Mishnah Berurah* 677:9 emphasizes that when one person who has already fulfilled the *mitzvah* lights the *menorah* for another, the other person must be present to hear the blessings. Commentators are baffled by the *Mishnah Berurah*'s ruling because there is usually no need for the person for whom the *mitzvah* is being performed to be present. For example, a woman discharges the obligation of the other members of her family to light *Shabbath* candles, whether or not they are present when she lights. An agent appointed to search a house for *chametz* recites the blessing in the absence of the owner. Why then does the *Mishnah Berurah* insist that the second person be present?

Chazal, however, discourage a man from allowing his wife to perform *mitzvoth* and recite blessings on his behalf when he is capable of doing so himself.[9]

In *Mikra'ey Kodesh, Chanukah V'Purim*, No. 23, HaGaon Rav Tzvi Pessach Frank explains that the *mitzvah* of lighting the *menorah* and its accompanying blessing, *LeHadlik ner shel Chanukah*, can be carried out for someone *in absentia*. The *Mishnah Berurah* only insists that the person be present for the blessing *She'asah nissim la'avotheinu* to be recited on his behalf. This insistence is based on a ruling of the *Bach*.

The *Shulchan Arukh* 676:3 rules that a person who has not kindled *Chanukah* lights, who will not be able to kindle them, and for whom they are not being kindled at home, should recite the blessing *She'asah nissim* when he sees *Chanukah* lights. The *Bach* agrees with the dissenting view of Rabbenu Yerucham, that even if someone *is* lighting for him at home he should recite the blessing *She'asah nissim* when he sees *Chanukah* lights. The *Bach* explains that there are two aspects to the *mitzvah* of *Chanukah*: lighting to publicize the miracle, and personally giving praise to God when seeing the lights. The *mitzvah* of lighting may be performed by an agent, but not the *mitzvah* of praising God for the miracle, because it is a personal *mitzvah*. The *Bach* explains that the blessing *She'asah nissim* expresses this personal aspect of the *mitzvah*. One must either recite it oneself, or listen to it being recited, in keeping with the principle *shomey'ah k'oneh* (hearing is like responding). Because in a situation of doubt a blessing is not recited, in practice we follow the view of the *Shulchan Arukh*. A person who is away from home does not recite the blessing *She'asah nissim* when someone at home is lighting for him.

Thus, concludes HaGaon Rav Frank, it is now clear why the *Mishnah Berurah* requires a person to be present when someone who has already fulfilled the *mitzvah* lights for him. Since the *Bach* maintains that the blessing *She'asah nissim* relates to the personal aspect of the *mitzvah*, it must be heard or recited by the person obligated. When that person is not present, the *Bach* considers the blessing to be said in vain.

An alternate explanation of the *Mishnah Berurah* is found in *Iggeroth Moshe, Orach Chayim*, Vol. 1, No. 190. See also *Ner Ish U'Beitho*, par. 4.

9. Tractate *Berakhoth* 20b, cited in the *Biur Halakhah* 675, beginning

4. If a husband plans to come home after the preferred time for lighting, and he gives his wife permission to light for him, she should light on time rather than wait for him.[10] Some authorities maintain it is preferable that she does wait for him to come home and light.[11]

5. A woman whose husband will not return home that night is obligated to light and recite the blessings.[12]

6. A single girl who is away from home during the day and will not return home in time for lighting does not need to light where she is.[13] Even though she is absent, her obligation is fulfilled when her family lights. She should listen to someone who is lighting recite the blessings in order to

---

Ishah madleketh. See Chapter 15, paragraph 64.

10. In *Eretz Yisrael*, most people follow the view that *Chanukah* lights should be kindled at sunset. Many communities outside *Eretz Yisrael* follow the opposing view; they kindle them approximately one half-hour after sunset.

HaGaon Rav Shlomo Zalman Auerbach has written to me, "Family harmony may be upset if a woman lights on time without her husband's permission. It is preferable for her to wait for him. If he knows in advance that he will come home late, he should give her permission to light on time."

Chovath HaDar cites authorities who rule it is better to appoint an agent to light on time than to light late. *Ye'chaveh Da'ath*, Vol. 3, No. 51, reaches a similar conclusion: "When a man plans to come home late, it is proper for him to appoint his wife to light at the proper time."

11. HaGaon Rav Shmuel Wossner, in a letter printed in *Chovath HaDar*, p. 127, expresses a preference for a man lighting late instead of appointing someone to light for him on time. Also see *Shevet HaLevi*, Vol. 4, No. 66.

12. *Mishnah Berurah* 675:9. *Chovath HaDar*, Chapter 1, note 39, points out that if she is unable to light, it is better to appoint a member of the family rather than a stranger to light in her place.

13. See the *Mishnah Berurah* 677:12.

participate in the *mitzvah* of publicizing the miracle.[14]

7. A permanent boarder is considered to be part of the family with which she boards.[15] If a boarder does not take all her meals with the family, or if someone is a guest on one of the nights of *Chanukah*, she should either purchase a small portion of the host's oil,[16] or formally accept some as a gift.[17] She should also be present when the lights are kindled and listen to the blessings.[18]

---

14. See paragraph 11. She should listen to someone else's blessings in order to accommodate the *Bach*'s view cited in note 8. See the *Mishnah Berurah* 677:14 and the *Sha'ar HaTziyun* 677:21.

15. *Mishnah Berurah* 677:1.

16. *Ibid.* Even if she frequently dines there, she is not considered a "permanent boarder".

17. *Mishnah Berurah* 677:4, and *Sha'ar HaTziyun* 677:9, citing the *Magen Avraham* and the *Rashba*. The gift must be a legal acquisition, either through the symbolic handing over of a handkerchief or lifting up the oil. It is not sufficient merely to say, "I give it to you as a gift". See *Az Nid'biru*, Vol. 2, Nos. 67–68.

According to the *Bach* and the *Magen Avraham*, the host should add a little more oil than usual to the *menorah* to clearly indicate that his guest has acquired a portion. Otherwise, she may be suspected of not fulfilling the *mitzvah*. The *Pri Chadash* fails to see how adding oil to the *menorah* removes suspicion. He argues that there is no concern for suspicion, and extra oil need not be added.

Although the *Mishnah Berurah* 677:1 and 677:3 advises guests to light their own *menorah*s in order to comply with *mihadrin min ha'mihadrin*, it appears that this only applies to men. Since women generally do not fulfill *mihadrin min ha'mihadrin* (See note 3.), it is better for a female guest to acquire a portion of the oil.

18. *Mishnah Berurah* 677:16. The host should intend to *motzie* his guest, and she should intend to fulfill her obligation through his recitation. If she does not hear the blessings, she is required to recite the blessing *She'asah nissim* when she sees *Chanukah* lights herself. This is true even according to authorities who disagree with the *Bach* (See note 8.) because no one lights for her. See the *Shulchan Arukh* 676:3. On the first night of *Chanukah*, she should also recite *She'he'che'yanu*.

8. When women are living together in a dormitory or an apartment, each one should contribute to the cost of oil. One of them may then light for everyone.[19] They may not fulfill their obligation at someone else's house, even if they contribute to the cost of oil there.[20]

9. A woman who sleeps away from home one of the nights of *Chanukah* alone in an apartment should light there even if her family intends to light for her.[21] If she lights before her family does, she may recite the blessings. Otherwise, she should try to go somewhere and listen to someone else recite them.[22]

A guest should contribute to the cost of her host's oil even if her family intends to light for her.[23]

Lighting When a Husband Is Away from Home

10. When a woman lights for her husband who is away from home on the first night of *Chanukah*, he is considered to have lit. If he lights at home on the second night he should, therefore, not recite *She'he'che'yanu.*[24]

According to HaGaon Rav Shlomo HaCohen of Vilna, cited in *Sdeh Chemed, Ma'arekheth Chanukah*, the blessing on seeing the lights may be recited only if they have not been burning for more than a half-hour. Since the *mitzvah* only requires that they burn for a half-hour, after that time they are not considered to be "*Chanukah* lights".

19. The other women should stand near her and listen to the blessings. See notes 8 and 18.
20. Contributing to the cost of a host's oil is only effective if a guest is staying overnight.
21. *Mishnah Berurah* 677:7. Since people do not know that her family is lighting for her, she will be suspected of not fulfilling the *mitzvah*.
22. *Mishnah Berurah* 677:16.
23. *Mishnah Berurah* 677:7.
24. *Mishnah Berurah, Ibid.*, citing the *Magen Avraham*.

11. When a woman lights for a husband who is away from home, he need not contribute to the cost of his host's oil. If he wishes to light, he should listen to his host recite the blessings or light before his wife does and recite the blessings.[25]

Some authorities maintain that a man who is uncertain whether his wife is lighting for him should light himself and recite the blessings.[26]

Shabbath and Chanukah Lights

12. A person who cannot afford to purchase both *Shabbath* and *Chanukah* candles should purchase *Shabbath* candles.[27]

---

25. Since he has fulfilled the *mitzvah* through his wife, if he lights after she does, he may no longer recite the blessings. See paragraph 9.

    Mishneh Halakhoth, Vol. 6, No. 119, points out that even when a husband is in a different time zone he fulfills the *mitzvah* through his wife.

26. *Mishnah Berurah* 677:2, citing the *Taz*. The *Mishnah Berurah* adds that according to this view he is required to light even if he comes home and discovers his wife has already lit for him. Since he was uncertain whether his wife would light for him, he did not intend to fulfill the *mitzvah* through her. The *Magen Avraham*, however, rules that he should not recite the blessings.

    The *Sha'ar HaTziyun* 677:4 cites the view of the *Terumoth HaDeshen*: As long as he knows his wife is familiar with the laws concerning a husband away from home, he may assume that she lit for him, and he is not obligated to light on his return.

    Divrey Shalom, Vol. 4, *Piskey Halakhoth* 89–90, rules that a woman who is in the hospital during *Chanukah* may light there. If she fears the hospital workers will extinguish the lights before a half-hour has elapsed, she should not recite the blessings. Alternatively, she may also rely on her husband lighting at home.

27. *Shulchan Arukh* 678:1. One of the purposes of the *mitzvah* of *Shabbath* candle-lighting is to foster family harmony. (See Chapter 15, note 36.) Family harmony is so important that it overrides the *mitzvah* of *Chanukah*.

    The *Mishnah Berurah* cites the view of the *Magen Avraham*: "Today, when they are kindled indoors, *Chanukah* lights take

In this situation, it is acceptable to light only one candle for *Shabbath*.[28]

The purchase of candles for *Chanukah* takes precedence over the purchase of wine for *Kiddush* and *Havdalah*.[29] The purchase of bread for the *Shabbath* meals, however, takes precedence over the purchase of *Shabbath* candles.[30]

13. On Friday afternoon, *Chanukah* lights are kindled before *Shabbath* lights.[31] A woman who lights her own *menorah* may not do so after she has lit *Shabbath* candles.[32] She should ask a neighbor who has not accepted *Shabbath* yet to light for her. The neighbor should recite the blessing *LeHadlik ner shel Chanukah*, and she should recite the

---

precedence over *Shabbath* candles because they themselves illuminate the house." But most authorities do not distinguish between Talmudic days and today; even if electric lights illuminate the house, *Shabbath* candles take precedence.

28. *Magen Avraham* and *Pri Megadim*, cited in the *Mishnah Berurah* 678:2. Although the *Shulchan Arukh* 263 states it is proper to light a minimum of two *Shabbath* candles, in an emergency one is sufficient. Whatever money remains should be used to purchase *Chanukah* lights.

29. *Shulchan Arukh* 678:1. "Publicizing the miracle" overrides the *mitzvoth* of *Kiddush* and *Havdalah*. The Torah obligation to make *Kiddush* may be fulfilled with words in praise of *Shabbath*. (See Chapter 15, note 174.) The Rabbinic obligation to recite *Kiddush* over wine may, if necessary, be performed over bread.

30. *Mishnah Berurah* 678:4.

31. *Shulchan Arukh* 679. A woman accepts *Shabbath* when she lights *Shabbath* candles. See Chapter 15, paragraph 25.

   The *Sha'ar HaTziyun* 679:2 points out that a man who lives alone and lights *Shabbath* candles every week is also assumed to accept *Shabbath* when he lights. A man who does not usually light *Shabbath* candles is not assumed to accept *Shabbath* when he lights. If he lights *Shabbath* candles in his wife's absence before the *menorah*, he may light the *menorah* afterwards. See the *Mishnah Berurah* 679:1.

32. *Magen Avraham*, cited in the *Mishnah Berurah* 679:1.

blessing *She'asah nissim* (and *She'he'che'yanu* on the first night).[33]

Working while the Lights Are Burning

14. Since a woman was instrumental in bringing about the miracle of *Chanukah*,[34] it is customary for women not to work during the first half hour the lights burn. They are cautioned not to take this custom lightly.[35] All forms of work are permitted during the rest of the holiday.[36]

---

33. *Pri Megadim*, cited in the *Mishnah Berurah, Ibid.*
34. See note 1. Concerning the role women played in the *Chanukah* miracle, another tradition attributes the beginning of the rebellion against the Greeks to the heroic actions of a woman. After secretly circumcising her son, she climbed with him in her arms to the top of the wall surrounding Jerusalem and hurled herself to the ground. She called to her brethren, who were afraid to stand up to the Greek oppressors, "If you do not fight against your enemies, you will all be destroyed." The powerful impression made by her sacrifice helped arouse Matithyahu and his sons to gather all men of faith and march out to destroy the enemies of God.
35. *Shulchan Arukh* 670:1. The *Mishnah Berurah* 670:4 cites the Vilna Gaon's view that the purpose of this custom is to emphasize the prohibition against deriving benefit from the *Chanukah* lights.
    Mo'ed LeKol Chai, No. 27:65, and the *Ben Ish Chai, Shanah Rishonah, Parshath VaYeshev* 27, limit the application of this custom to time-consuming work such as sewing, laundering and so forth.
    Rivevoth Ephrayim, Vol. 1, No. 426, cites different opinions whether there is a distinction between hand-work and machine-work. According to those who make such a distinction, laundering clothes in a washing machine would be permitted. The author then discusses whether cooking is permitted, and cites the ruling of HaGaon Rav Yisrael Yaacov Fisher of Jerusalem that it is not. The *Eliyahu Rabbah*, cited in the *Mishnah Berurah* 670:2, quotes the *Maharil* that in some communities men also refrain from work during the first half hour. See also *Sefer Chassidim* 121.
36. *Shulchan Arukh* 670:1. *Chanukah* was established for the purpose of giving praise and thanksgiving to God. It was not vested with the full

Women do not customarily eat until after their husbands light.[37]

Hallel

15. There is a debate whether women are obligated to recite *Hallel* on *Chanukah*.[38] Some maintain that it is sufficient to recite one Psalm containing words of praise and thanksgiving to God.[39] Ashkenazic women may recite *Hallel* with its blessings.[40]

---

status of a holiday on which work is forbidden. The *Mishnah Berurah* 670:5, citing the *Shiltey HaGiborim*, rules that one must object to any community adopting a custom to refrain from work the entire day.

37. See *Be'tzeyl HaChokhmah*, Vol. 4, No. 58.

38. *Torath Raphael, Orach Chayim*, No. 75, infers that according to *Tosafoth*, Tractate *Sukkah* 38a, women are obligated to recite *Hallel* on *Chanukah*. *Tosafoth* rules that women are required to recite *Hallel* at the *Pessach Seder* to commemorate the miracle in which "they were also included". For the same reason, *Tosafoth* would also obligate women to recite *Hallel* on *Chanukah*.

The *Rambam, Hilkhoth Chanukah*, Chapter 3, appears to exempt women from *Hallel* on *Chanukah*. *Beith She'arim, Orach Chayim*, No. 359, explains his view: The *Rambam* considers the *mitzvah* to commemorate a miracle through the recitation of *Hallel* a Torah obligation; *Chazal* only formulated the wording. *Tosafoth*, on Tractate *Pesachim* 108b, maintains that the principle "they, too, were included in the miracle" only obligates women in Rabbinic time-bound *mitzvoth*. According to this view, women are exempt from the *Torah mitzvah* to praise God for a miracle. See *Marchesheth*, Vol. 1, No. 22, *Moa'dim U'Zmanim*, Vol. 1, No. 91, and *Machazeh Eliyahu*, No. 22, for further discussion.

39. See *Sdeh Chemed, Ma'arekheth Chanukah* 9:2, citing HaGaon Rav Shlomo of Vilna. An additional reason for exempting women from *Hallel* on *Chanukah* is brought in *Sdeh Chemed*: *Hallel* commemorates the military victory over the Greeks. Women do not wage war.

40. *Yeshuoth Yaacov, Orach Chayim* 602:2, based on the view of Rabbenu Tam, which permits women to recite blessings when they

Chanukah Foods

16. Milk and cheese dishes are customarily served during *Chanukah*.[41]

17. Some authorities maintain that there is a *mitzvah* to celebrate *Chanukah* with a festive meal,[42] but it is only invested with the status of a *se'udath mitzvah* if there are words or songs of praise and thanksgiving to God at the meal.[43]

---

voluntarily fulfill time-bound *mitzvoth*.

Sephardic women should consider the words of *Ye'chaveh Da'ath*, Vol. 1, No. 78: "It is clear that Sephardic women are not permitted to recite the blessing over *Hallel* on *Chanukah* because they have accepted the ruling of the *Beith Yosef* 589, which forbids women to recite blessings over the voluntary fulfillment of *mitzvoth*. They may recite *Hallel* on *Chanukah* without its blessings if they wish."

41. *Kol Bo* and the *Ran*, cited by the *Remah* 670:2, based on the tradition that Yehudith served cheese and milk to the Greek governor. See note 1.

42. *Remah, Ibid.* As an additional reason for holding a festive meal during these days, the *Mishnah Berurah* cites the *Midrash*, which relates that the Tabernacle in the desert was completed on the 25th day of *Kislev*. God postponed the actual inauguration until *Nissan*, the month in which Yitzchak was born. He "repaid" the 25th of *Kislev* with a new inauguration of the Temple in the days of the Chashmonaim. (See the *Yalkut* on *Melakhim*, *Remez* 184.) See also the *Rambam*, *Hilkhoth Ta'anith* 3:3, and *Tosafoth* on Tractate *Ta'anith* 18b, beginning *Halakhah*.

43. The *Remah* states, "If songs of praise are sung at the meal, it is considered a *se'udath mitzvah*." The *Pri Megadim, Eshel Avraham* 670:4, comments that singing songs of praise to God invests a meal with the status of a *se'udath mitzvah* only during *Chanukah*, because *Chanukah* was established to praise God for the miracle. At other times of the year, praises do not by themselves invest a meal with the status of a *se'udath mitzvah*.

CHAPTER 22
Purim

Parshath Zakhor

1. The section of the Torah which discusses the *mitzvah* to "Remember (*zakhor*) what *Amalek* did to you when you left Egypt" is read in the synagogue on the *Shabbath* before *Purim*. Although some authorities rule that women are exempt from hearing it,[1] many others rule that they are obligated.[2] Some of

---

1. This special reading consists of the last three verses of *Parshath Ki Thetze (Devarim* 25:17–19). It is one of the four special *maftirs* read during the month of *Adar*. (The *maftir* is the last person called up to the Torah on *Shabbath*; he also reads a selection from the Prophets.) The other special *maftirs* are *Parshath Shekalim, Parshath Parah*, and *Parshath HaChodesh*.

 There are two aspects to the *mitzvah* of *Zakhor*: the cognitive act of remembering Amalek's great wickedness, and the physical act of destroying the Amalekite nation by participating in the war against it.

 In reference to the latter, the *Sefer HaChinukh* 603 states, "This *mitzvah* is practiced in all places and at all times by males, for they are obligated to wage war and wreak vengence on the enemy. Women are

these authorities are very particular that women hear it.[3] It is,

---

not." The *Sefer HaChinukh* indicates that women are exempt from both aspects of the *mitzvah*, recalling Amalek's actions by listening to *Parshath Zakhor* and participating in the war.

In the same vein, the author of *Torath Chesed* (Lublin), *Orach Chayim*, No. 37, remarks that he never heard of women attending synagogue services on *Shabbath Zakhor*. He concludes, "We should leave Jews to their traditional customs."

The *Kaf HaChayim* 685:30 suggests that the Torah requirement to "remember Amalek" is fulfilled simply by remembering. The *mitzvah* to hear *Parshath Zakhor* read from the Torah is a time-bound Rabbinic requirement. Even if women are required to remember the acts of Amalek they are not required to attend the synagogue on the *Shabbath* before *Purim* (a specific time) for the reading.

In *Sefer Ta'amah D'Kra*, HaGaon Rav Chayim Kanievsky reports that the Chazon Ish also exempted women from hearing *Parshath Zakhor*.

2. *Minchath Chinukh* 603; *Chatham Sofer*, novellae on Tractate *Megillah* 23b; *Tzitz HaKodesh*, No. 51. This also appears to be the opinion of the *Rambam, Sefer HaMitzvoth, Mitzvath Aseh* 189.

The *Minchath Chinukh* brings forward a number of arguments to refute the *Sefer HaChinukh*'s exempting women from *Parshath Zakhor*. Assuming that Torah Law itself obligates people to hear *Parshath Zakhor* once a year (contrary to the *Kaf HaChayim*'s view cited in the preceding note), the Torah obviously does not demand that *Parshath Zakhor* be read on the *Shabbath* before *Purim*! The Torah requirement may be fulfilled any time; hearing *Parshath Zakhor* is thus a non-time-bound *mitzvah*. *Chazal* cannot transform a non-time-bound Torah *mitzvah* into a time-bound one by fixing the *Shabbath* before *Purim* as the time to read *Parshath Zakhor*. Moreover, the Torah states, "You shall not forget" (*Devarim* 25:19), implying that anyone who fails to perform this *mitzvah* also transgresses a negative commandment.

The *Minchath Chinukh* raises two objections to the *Sefer HaChinukh*'s argument that it is not the way of women to wage war: What proof do we have that the *mitzvah* "to remember" is linked with the *mitzvah* to wage war? "Perhaps, even in Messianic days, when the nation of Amalek will be totally obliterated, there will still be a *mitzvah* to remember[their actions]." Furthermore, the *Mishnah*, Tractate *Sotah*, Chapter 8, states, "When a *milchemeth mitzvah* (an obligatory war) is

therefore, customary for women to attend synagogue services

---

waged, even a groom from his wedding room and a bride from her canopy [are required to go out and assist in the war effort].'' This implies that women must also participate in waging war against Amalek.

In defense of the *Sefer HaChinukh*, we must assume that remembering and waging war are linked. We "remember" so as not to forget to wage war against Amalek. If women are exempt from participating in the war, they are also exempt from remembering.

The *Minchath Chinukh*'s contention that women are obligated to participate in the war against Amalek is rejected by other authorities.

The *Radvaz*, in his commentary on the *Rambam, Hilkhoth Melakhim* 7:4 states, "Is it the way of women to wage war?... Yet, we have been taught, 'The bride goes out from her canopy.' But[the explanation of the *Mishnah* in *Sotah* is] once the groom leaves his wedding room [to go and fight] his bride is forced to leave her canopy. She does not celebrate the day of her *chupah*."

The *Ra'Shash*, in his novellae on Tractate *Sotah*, offers another possibility: "Perhaps they only go out to cook and bake for the men at the front [but do not actually participate in the fighting]. The same view is also expressed by the *Tifereth Yisrael* in his commentary on the *Mishnah*.

Zekher Simchah, No. 75, cites another interpretation in the name of HaGaon Rav Yaacov Etlinger. Women were only required to participate in wars to conquer the Land of Israel during the days of Joshua. Since those wars were carried out pursuant to the *mitzvah* to conquer *Eretz Yisrael* in order to dwell in it (a *mitzvah* which may be carried out at all times), they had a non-time-bound character. The war against Amalek, however, does not involve the conquest of the Land of Israel; Amalek is not counted among the seven nations who lived in *Eretz Yisrael*. Since this *mitzvah* is only fulfilled at certain times, women are exempt.

Expanding on this theme, *Marchesheth*, Vol. 1, No. 22, cites *Rashi*'s commentary on Tractate *Megillah* 3a: The *mitzvah* of waging war is not practiced at night. (The author explains that the *mitzvah* to wage war has the character of judgement, and a court does not sit in judgement at night.) Waging war is a time-bound *mitzvah*, and women are exempt.

3. *Binyan Tziyon* (*Chadashoth*), No. 8, reports that HaGaon Rav Nathan Adler insisted that even his Jewish maid attend synagogue services to

to hear *Parshath Zakhor*.[4]

The Fast of Esther

2. According to some authorities, pregnant and nursing women need not fast on *Ta'anith Esther* (The Fast of Esther), even if the fast would not cause any hardship. The fast need not be made up at a later date.[5]

---

hear *Parshath Zakhor*. The author of *Binyan Tziyon*, HaGaon Rav Yaacov Etlinger, writes that he also follows this practice. HaGaon Rav Moshe Feinstein also rules that women should go to the synagogue to hear *Parshath Zakhor*.

Women are certainly exempt from hearing the other three *maftirs* read during the month of *Adar*. See *Mo'adim U'Zmanim*, Vol. 2, No. 168, and *Biur HaGra* on the *Shulchan Arukh* 685:7.

4. *Ye'chaveh Da'ath*, Vol. 1, No. 84, rules that women should attend the synagogue to hear *Parshath Zakhor* in order to satisfy the different views cited in the preceding notes. In many places, it is customary to schedule a reading of *Parshath Zakhor* on *Shabbath* afternoon for all the women who could not attend in the morning. Although the *Kaf HaChayim* exempts women from hearing the reading from a *Sefer Torah* (See note 1.), he still reminds them, "If they come they receive reward, for even a person who is not obligated in a *mitzvah* receives reward for voluntarily fulfilling it."

A *minyan* of ten men must be present at a special reading of the *Torah* for women, for the Torah may only be read in the presence of a *minyan*. *Torath Chesed, Ibid.*, and *Binyan Tziyon (Chadashoth)*, No. 10, rule that even those who obligate women to hear *Parshath Zakhor* do not count them for the *minyan*. This is also the ruling of HaGaon Rav Yosef Sholom Eliashiv.

5. The *Remah* 286:2 states, "This fast is not as stringent [as other fasts]. Therefore, pregnant or nursing women, or sick people, may be lenient. Even people who have an eye ache should not fast if they are in pain, but they should make up the omitted fast later." The *Mishnah Berurah* 286:4 cites *Yeshuoth Yaacov* who interprets the phrase "if they are in pain" as referring only to people who have an eye ache, not to pregnant and nursing women. These are exempt from the fast even if they are not in pain. The *Mishnah Berurah* 286:5 explains that

Others rule they should fast if it does not entail hardship, and a woman who finds it difficult to fast should make up the omitted fast on another day.[6] A woman should follow the prevailing custom of her community.

3. All authorities agree that a woman who gives birth during the thirty days preceding *Ta'anith Esther* is exempt from fasting.[7]

Commemorating Machatzith HaShekel

4. Before *Purim*, it is customary to donate three coins to charity. Each coin should be one-half of the basic unit of the local currency, i.e., three half-dollars (in the United States). This donation commemorates the *mitzvah* of *Machatzith HaShekel*, the annual half-*shekel* that was donated to the *Beith HaMikdash* for the purchase of communal sacrifices.[8] Some authorities exempt women from this donation,[9] others obligate

---

according to *Yeshuoth Yaacov*, the concluding statement, "but they should make up for the omitted fast later", also refers only to sick people.

6. The *Mishnah Berurah, Ibid.*, cites the *Eliyahu Rabbah*'s interpretation of the *Remah*'s phrase, "if they are in pain", that it also refers to pregnant and nursing women. Accordingly, they should fast if it is not painful and make up an omitted fast later.

7. *Mishnah Berurah, Ibid.*

8. In the days of the *Beith HaMikdash*, every male Jew over the age of twenty was required to donate half a *shekel* toward the cost of the communal sacrifices offered during the year. Communal sacrifices offered after the first of *Nissan* had to be purchased with new *shekalim* so their collection began during the month of *Adar*, which precedes *Nissan*. The custom to commemorate *Machatzith HaShekel* by donating three coins to charity at *Purim* is cited by the *Remah* 694:1, who explains that since the word *terumah* (donation) is repeated three times in the verses describing *Machatzith HaShekel* (*Shemoth* 30:11–16), it is customary to give three "half-*shekels*".

9. *Magen Avraham* 694:3. Women were exempt from *Machatzith HaShekel*

them.[10] A pregnant woman makes the donation on behalf of her unborn child.[11]

The Megillah

5. Women are obligated to hear *Megillath Esther* (The Scroll of Esther) *Purim* night and *Purim* day.[12]

6. A person should try to hear the *Megillah* read in the

---

when it was in force, so they are certainly exempt from its commemoration. This also appears to be the conclusion of the *Mishnah Berurah* and the *Orukh HaShulchan*.

The *Remah* rules that only males older than twenty are obligated to donate, but the *Mishnah Berurah* 694:5 cites the *Tosafoth Yom Tov*, who rules that every male older than thirteen should donate. The *Mishnah Berurah* adds that a father should donate on behalf of each of his minor children and a pregnant woman on behalf of her unborn child.

10. *Hagahoth Maimoni*, cited in the *Magen Avraham, Ibid.* The *Kaf HaChayim* 694:27 states, "Since it is written with respect to *shekalim*, 'to atone for your souls' (*Shemoth* 30:16), a donation should also be made for women and children. We also find that although *Machatzith HaShekel* was not collected from women, they could voluntarily donate it, and this is certainly true today when the money goes to charity."

It is reported in *Minhagey Admor*, printed in the back of the *Shulchan Arukh HaRav*, Vol. 3–4, that the *Ba'al HaTanya* donated *Machatzith HaShekel* for the Rebbetzin and young children in his family.

11. *Mishnah Berurah* 694:5.

12. *Shulchan Arukh* 689:1, based on Tractate *Megillah* 4a: "Women are obligated to hear the *Megillah*, for they were also included in the miracle." In the Introduction, paragraph 5 and note 9, two reasons are given: A woman was instrumental in bringing about the miracle; women were also included in Haman's evil decree and miraculously saved.

Although the *Shulchan Arukh* does not distinguish between men's and women's obligations, see note 15.

presence of ten people.[13] It is questionable whether men and women may be counted together to form this group.[14]

7. A woman may not read the *Megillah* for a man[15] unless he

---

13. *Shulchan Arukh* 690:18.

14. *Remah, Ibid.*, citing the *Hagahoth Ashri*. It is preferable to hear the *Megillah* read in the presence of ten people for the purpose of publicizing the miracle. Since women were also included in the miracle, it would seem that they may be counted to give public expression to its commemoration. The *Hagahoth Ashri* raises a question on the grounds of a possible lack of propriety. The same concern is the basis of a ruling regarding *Birkath HaMazon*: Although three women may combine to form a *zimun*, two men and a woman may not. (See Chapter 3, paragraph 18.) Nevertheless, the *Chazon Ish, Orach Chayim* 155:2, citing the *Ohr Zarua*, maintains that women may join with men for a public reading.

It appears that the *Remah* is questioning the ability of women to *join* with men for a public reading. When the *Megillah* is read before ten women, it is certainly a public reading, which fulfills *pirsumey nisa* (publicizing the miracle). See *Salmath Chayim*, Vol. 1, No. 101, and *Mikra'ey Kodesh, Purim*, No. 35.

A woman who is unable to attend a public reading of the *Megillah* may read it privately with its blessings. See the *Remah* 690:18.

15. *Shulchan Arukh* 689:2. A number of reasons are put forward for this ruling. The *Kol Bo*, No. 45, includes it under the prohibition against a man listening to a woman's voice. In his view, chanting the *Megillah* is like singing.

The *Magen Avraham* 689:5 compares it to reading the Torah. Women are disqualified from reading the Torah for a congregation because it is considered disrespectful for them to read before men. To avoid exceptions to the rule, they also refrain from reading for men in private.

In his glosses on the *Shulchan Arukh*, the Vilna Gaon traces this ruling to the opinion of the *Ba'al Halakhoth Gedoloth* (*B'hag*), who distinguishes the obligation of men from that of women in *Megillah*. A man is obligated to *read* the *Megillah*. His listening to the *Megillah* with intention to fulfill the *mitzvah* is considered like reading it; this is an application of *shomey'ah k'oneh* (hearing is like reciting). A woman is not obligated to *read* the *Megillah*, only to *hear* it, thus fulfilling the

does not know how to read it and there is no other man available who can read it for him.[16]

8. A woman may read the *Megillah* for another woman,[17] but she should not read it for a group of women.[18]

---

mitzvah without recourse to *shomey'ah k'oneh*. Since a man's obligation in this *mitzvah* is more extensive than a woman's, she cannot *motzie* him.

Marchesheth, Vol. 1, No. 22, offers a rationale for the distinction the *B'hag* draws between men and women. The *mitzvah* of *Megillah* consists of two parts. *Reading* the *Megillah* reminds one of Amalek's actions (Haman was a descendant of Amalek), making it an extension of the *mitzvah* of *Zakhor*. (See note 1.) Being present and *listening* to the reading also fulfills the requirement to publicize the miracle (*pirsumey nisa*). Apparently, the *B'hag* concurs with the *Sefer HaChinukh* (See note 2.), who exempts women from *Zakhor*. Women are, therefore, only included in the *pirsumey nisa* aspect of the *mitzvah*, which can be fulfilled simply by being present and listening.

Emek Brakhah, *K'riath HaMegillah*, par. 3, argues that the *B'hag*'s distinction only applies on *Purim* night. Citing Tractate *Megillah* 14a, the author shows that the *Megillah* is read on *Purim* morning in lieu of *Hallel*. (In fact, the *Mei'ri* rules that someone who does not have a *Megillah* should recite *Hallel*.) He cites *Tosafoth*, *Sukkah* 38a, which obligates women to read *Hallel* at the *Pessach Seder* because it commemorates the miracle of the Exodus from Egypt. By the same token, women should be required to *read Hallel* on *Purim* to commemorate that miracle, so they are required to *read* the *Megillah* in its place. According to *Emek Brakhah*, the *B'hag* would concede that a woman may read the *Megillah* for a man on *Purim* morning. For further discussion, see *Machazeh Eliyahu*, No. 22.

16. *Kaf HaChayim* 689:16. If he later finds a man who knows how to read the *Megillah*, he should ask him to read it without the blessings. See also *Ben Ish Chai, Shanah Rishonah, Parshath TeTzaveh* 2.

17. *Mishnah Berurah* 689:7. The *Biur Halakhah* 689, beginning *V'Nashim*, questions whether a woman who has already fulfilled the *mitzvah* may read for another woman. The question has its source in the issue whether *arvuth* (mutual responsibility) applies to women. (This issue is discussed at length in Chapter 15, notes 162 and 176.) But see the *Mishnah Berurah* 271:5, which concludes that it does apply.

18. The *Sha'ar HaTziyun* 689:15 cites the *Korban Nethanel*, who infers

9. Eating or drinking is forbidden before hearing the *Megillah*. A woman who does not attend the reading in the synagogue, and who finds it difficult to wait for someone to come read for her, may take a small amount of food or drink. This is true *Purim* night and *Purim* day.[19]

A woman may eat and drink normally if she might otherwise become ill. She should ask someone to remind her to hear the *Megillah*.[20]

When necessary, the *Megillah* may be read before nightfall for a sick woman or for a woman who has recently given birth.[21]

10. Young girls should be trained to hear the *Megillah*.[22] It is proper to bring them to the synagogue for the public reading, but only if they will not disturb the congregation.[23]

11. If children will cause a disturbance in the synagogue,[24] it

------

from *Tosafoth*, Tractate *Sukkah* 38a, that it is improper for a woman to read the *Megillah* for a group of women. But see *Halikhoth Beythah*, p. 71, which cites HaGaon Rav Shlomo Zalman Auerbach's objection to the *Korban Nethanel*'s inference. HaGaon Rav Auerbach finds nothing wrong with a woman reading the *Megillah* for other women.

19. *Remah* 692:4; *Mishnah Berurah* 692:14. Anything less than a *ke'betzah* of bread (approximately 45 grams) or a *revi'ith* of drink is considered a small amount.

20. *Mishnah Berurah* 692:16, *Sha'ar HaTziyun* 692:29.

21. *Mishnah Berurah* 692:14.

22. *Mishnah Berurah* 689:3.

23. *Shulchan Arukh* 689:1 and 689:6; *Mishnah Berurah* 689:16.

The *Mishnah Berurah* cites the *Levush*, who explains that one reason for the entire congregation reading aloud the "four verses of redemption" — *Ish Yehudi* (2:5), *U'Mordekhai yatza* (8:15), *LaYehudim* (8:16), and *Ki Mordekhai HaYehudi* (10:3) — is to maintain children's attention. The *Kaf HaChayim* 690:106 emphasizes this reason: "When they (children) observe this, they will inquire about it. To satisfy their curiosity, they should be told about God's greatness, and they will rejoice and learn to fear Him."

24. The *Remah* 689:6 recommends bringing children to the synagogue.

is best to hear the reading of the *Megillah* privately at home since it may be impossible to hear every word in the synagogue.[25]

12. Women should make every effort to attend public readings of the *Megillah*, even when this entails leaving a child below *bar* or *bath mitzvah* age at home to care for younger children. The child should hear the *Megillah* read privately.[26]

Reading for a Woman

13. Rather than read the *Megillah* for herself, a woman

The *Chaye Adam* 155:7 writes, "Even if ten people can be gathered at home, attending a public reading in the synagogue is a special *mitzvah*. [A man should bring] his wife and children to hear the reading with the community."

The *Mishnah Berurah* 689:18 laments today's decorum: "Now, due to the multitude of our sins, this [custom] has become twisted. Besides the fact that children do not listen to the reading, they confuse and disturb the adults so they, too, cannot hear. They only come [to the synagogue] to bang [when hearing the name of] Haman. A father does not fulfill the *mitzvah* of educating his children [when they behave in this way]. From the point of view of *chinukh*, every father should stand near his small children and supervise them, making sure they listen to the reading. When the name of Haman is read, they may bang as much as they want. But this should not be the main purpose of bringing them to the synagogue."

25. The *Mishnah Berurah* 689:1, citing the *Pri Megadim*, wonders how women fulfill the *mitzvah* in the synagogue: "It is impossible for them to hear the reading properly." The *Orukh HaShulchan* 690:23 states, "When the youngsters are banging [at the mention of] Haman, their mouths are filled with laughter... If it is impossible to stop them, it is better to read at home with ten people even though there is a larger group in the synagogue, since the great confusion makes it impossible to hear properly. This is especially true for women."

26. *Chelkath Ya'acov*, Vol. 3, No. 144. Also see *Mishneh Halakhoth*, Vol. 4, No. 82.

should enlist someone to read it for her. If no one is available, she should read it for herself from a kosher *Megillah.*[27]

When a woman reads the *Megillah*, she recites the blessing *Lishmo'a mikra Megillah* (To hear the reading of the *Megillah*) instead of the usual *Al mikra Megillah* (On reading the *Megillah*). She should also say the blessings, *She'asah nissim la'avotheinu* and *She'he'che'yanu.*[28]

14. A man who reads the *Megillah* for a group of women is advised not to fulfill his obligation at the same time. He should either have read the *Megillah* in the synagogue or plan to hear it there later.[29]

---

27. *Mishnah Berurah* 689:8; *Sha'ar HaTziyun* 689:16. The *Magen Avraham* 689:6 cites the *Midrash HaNe'e'lam*, which states that a woman should not read the *Megillah*. The *Sha'ar HaTziyun* questions the authenticity of this source and concludes that if she cannot find someone to read it, she should certainly read it herself.

28. The reason for this change, explains the *Remah* 689:2, is the *B'hag's* view cited in note 15. His view — that women are only required to *hear* the *Megillah* not to *read* it — is reflected in the words of her blessing. Also see *Mo'adim U'Zmanim*, Vol. 2, No. 171.

   A number of authorities rule contrary to the *Remah*. In *Ma'asey Rav*, No. 237, the view of the Vilna Gaon is cited: "Women are obligated to read the *Megillah* and recite the same blessing men recite." This follows the Vilna Gaon's rejection of the *B'hag* in his glosses to the *Shulchan Arukh* 689. Also see *Yabia Omer*, Vol. 1, No. 44.

29. *Mishnah Berurah* 692:11. It is explained in note 14 that one should make every effort to fulfill the *mitzvah* through a public reading. Although it is questionable whether men and women may combine for a public reading, a reading before ten women is definitely considered "public". A man should therefore be allowed to fulfill his obligation when reading for ten women. We have not differentiated in the text between reading for a small group of women and for ten women, because this distinction is not explicitly made by the *Mishnah Berurah*.

15. When a man reads the *Megillah* for women, the blessing *Lish'mo'a mikra Megillah* is said together with *She'asah nissim* and *She'he'che'yanu*.[30] Each woman may recite the blessings herself,[31] or one woman may recite them for everyone.[32] In many communities it is customary for the reader to recite the blessings, even when one of the women is capable of reciting them.[33]

16. Although some authorities maintain that the concluding blessing, *HaRav eth riveinu*, is recited when ten women listen to the *Megillah*, the prevailing practice is to omit it.[34]

Mishlo'ach Manoth and Matanoth LaEvyonim

17. On *Purim*, women are obligated to give a monetary gift to at least two poor people (*matanoth la'evyonim*), and to send

---

30. *Ibid*. This form of the blessing is explained in note 28. A man who is unable to attend the synagogue and fulfills his obligation in a reading for women should recite the usual blessing, *Al mikra Megillah*.
   The *Magen Avraham* 690:1 advises people to stand while listening to the blessings. In *Mikra'ey Kodesh, Chanukah V'Purim* p. 142, HaGaon Rav Tzvi Pessach Frank justifies sitting. The *Megillah* itself may be heard while standing or sitting.
31. *Minchath Yitzchak*, Vol. 3, No. 54. The principle of *arvuth* allows the reader to recite the blessings for the listeners even when he himself is not fulfilling the *mitzvah* at that time. But see Chapter 15, note 172 — it is preferable for listeners who know the blessings to recite them themselves. *Minchath Yitzchak* therefore recommends that each woman recite her own blessings.
32. The *Mishnah Berurah* 692:10 does not indicate a preference for each woman reciting the blessings. The custom that one woman recites the blessings for everyone is cited in HaGaon Rav Y.M. Tikotzinski's *Luach Eretz Yisrael*.
33. *Mishnah Berurah* 692:10.
34. The blessing *HaRav eth riveinu* is only recited when the *Megillah* is read in public, which includes a situation where it is read before ten women.

a minimum of two items of food to at least one neighbor (*mishlo'ach manoth*).[35] A married woman should not rely on her husband to fulfill these *mitzvoth* for her.[36]

Children who have reached the age of *chinukh* should be trained to give *matanoth la'evyonim* and send *mishlo'ach manoth.*[37]

18. A husband should give his wife food and money to ensure that she is giving away what belongs to her.[38]

See note 14, *Yalkut Yosef*, p. 90, and HaGaon Rav Y. Cohen, in his notes on *Mikra'ey Kodesh, Chanukah V'Purim*, p. 144. *Sefer Purim M'Shulash* 2:8 cites authorities who rule to the contrary.

35. *Remah* 695:4; *Mishnah Berurah* 694:1 and 695:25.

The *Pri Chadash* challenges this ruling, citing the verse, "And sending gifts, a man to his friend" (*Esther* 9:22). But both the *Shevuth Yaacov*, Vol. 1, No. 41, and *She'ilath Ya'avetz*, Vol. 1, No. 120, note that the word *ish* (man) often denotes men *and* women in Scripture. See, for example, *Vayikra* 19:3, "A man shall fear his father and mother." Moreover, we find in the *Megillah*, "The Jews arose and accepted upon themselves and their seed [all the *mitzvoth* of Purim]." "Seed" denotes both men and women. Still, in his glosses to the *Shulchan Arukh* 695:4, the Vilna Gaon decides in favor of the *Pri Chadash*, and exempts women from *Mishlo'ach Manoth*. See also *Tosafoth Ma'asey Rav*, par. 240; *Sha'arey Teshuvah* 695:9; *Chatham Sofer, Orach Chayim*, No. 196.

36. The *Magen Avraham* 695:14 reports that women are not particular to send their own gifts: "Perhaps the *Remah* only refers to a widow [who lives alone, without a husband to send them on her behalf]... But [it is best that even a married woman] acts strictly and sends her own gift."

The *Orukh HaShulchan* 692:2 cites the principle that a man and his wife are considered as one and rules that they may fulfill the *mitzvah* jointly.

37. *Pri Megadim, Eshel Avraham* 695:14; *Orukh HaShulchan* 694:2. The Lubavitcher Rebbe writes in *Teshuvoth U'Biurim*, No. 131, "Every adult Jew and every child who has reached the age of *chinukh* should fulfill the *mitzvoth* of *Matanoth LaEvyonim* and *Mishlo'ach Manoth*.

38. This is based on a ruling of HaGaon Rav Shlomo Zalman Auerbach.

19. A woman should not send *mishlo'ach manoth* to a man or a man to a woman.[39] This restriction does not apply to *matanoth la'evyonim*.[40]

20. A woman who wishes to send a food parcel to a distinguished man, such as a Torah scholar or teacher, should send it to his wife, for whatever she acquires belongs to her husband.[41]

21. A person who receives many cakes from many different people and places them in one container should separate *Challah* from one of them without a blessing.[42]

The Purim Feast

22. Women are obligated to eat a festive meal on *Purim*,[43] but they are not included in the dictum of the Sages to become

---

39. *Remah* 695:4. A woman should not send *Mishlo'ach Manoth* to a man so as to avoid his sending her one in return. When a man sends a gift to an unmarried woman, a suspicion may be raised that he has betrothed her. Even if she is married, exchanging gifts is to be discouraged on the grounds of propriety. See *Sha'arey Teshuvah* 695:9 and *Shevuth Yaacov*, Vol. 1, No. 41.

40. *Remah*, *Ibid.* A person does not usually send monetary gifts to his fiancee. Also, *tzedakah* does not normally lead to impropriety.
    The *Orukh HaShulchan* 694:2 rules that someone who gives a monetary gift both to a man and his wife is not considered to have given to two individuals since a man and his wife are considered as one. To the contrary, the *Kaf HaChayim* 694:10 rules that a person fulfills the *mitzvah* of *Matanoth LaEvyonim* by giving one monetary gift to a man and another to his wife.

41. *Kaf HaChayim* 695:58.

42. See Chapter 13, note 20.

43. *Heikha'ley Shein T'litha'i*, No. 7–8.

so intoxicated that "one does not know the difference between blessed be Mordekhai and cursed be Haman".[44]

Costumes

23. In some communities women wear male garments, and men wear women's garments for the sake of merrymaking.[45] Many authorities wish to abolish this custom.[46] If only one garment of the opposite sex is worn, so that the true sex of the person is apparent, these authorities might agree that no objection need be made.[47]

In any case, it is forbidden for a woman to wear immodest clothing, such as women's pants, where men are present.[48]

---

44. *Mo'adim U'Zmanim*, Vol. 2, No. 190, citing the *Sha'ar HaTziyun* 199:6, explains that it is not the manner of women to drink wine. Also see *Rivevoth Ephrayim*, Vol. 1, No. 458.
45. *Remah* 696:8. *Mahari Mintz*, No. 16, cites a number of great Torah personalities who were aware of this practice and raised no objection.
46. *Remah, Ibid.*, and *Mishnah Berurah*, based on the *Taz, Yoreh De'ah* 182, in the name of the *Bach*. The *Bach* objects to this practice, both on *Purim* and at weddings. The *She'lah* also cautions people against it. Also see *Ba'er Heytev* 696:13; *Birkey Yosef* 696:13; *Kaf HaChayim* 696:57.
47. *Mishnah Berurah, Ibid.*, based on the *Pri Megadim*.
48. See Chapter 7, paragraph 1.

CHAPTER 23
Pessach

Searching for and Destroying Chametz

1. Children should not be sent to the synagogue with baked goods or other *chametz* products during the weeks preceding *Pessach*.[1]

2. On the night of the fourteenth of *Nissan*, all Jews are required to search their homes and all their belongings for

---

1. *Shulchan Arukh* 433:10; *Mishnah Berurah* 433:43. Tractate *Pesachim* 2a: "On the night of the fourteenth [of *Nissan*], we search for *chametz* by the light of a candle. All places where *chametz* is normally brought [during the year] need to be searched."

   Because *chametz* is brought into synagogues and study halls during the year, they must be searched by candle-light on the night before *Pessach*. The *Mishnah Berurah* adds, "Sextons who are not particular to search at night, but rely on the general cleaning done during the day, are not acting properly. They should be instructed to fulfill the law of the Sages in the proper way. A blessing is recited when searching the synagogue for *chametz*, but the *bitul* declaration is not said."

chametz. Although the *mitzvah* of *Bedikath Chametz* (Searching for Leaven) is fulfilled on the night of the fourteenth, a person may lighten the burden of searching every nook and cranny by "pre-searching" part of the house. This may be done during the weeks before *Pessach*, after cupboards, shelves, closets, and other places where *chametz* may have been left have been cleaned out. Before their contents are returned, these places should be searched, at night by candlelight, during the day by sunlight, if the area is well lit. A blessing is not recited.[2] A part of the house should be left for searching at the time prescribed by *Chazal* for fulfillment of the *mitzvah*.[3]

3. All rooms in the house must be swept and cleaned thoroughly before searching for *chametz*.[4] One should remember to clean under heavy furniture such as beds, tables, and sofas.[5]

4. A man may designate a woman his agent to search for *chametz* on his behalf. Similarly, a man may rely on his wife or daughter to search.

Some authorities rule that it is preferable for an adult male

---

2. Searching in advance is suggested by the *Chok Yaacov* 433:1 and the *Shulchan Arukh HaRav* 433:7. When these places are searched in advance, and care is exercised not to place *chametz* in them afterwards, there is no need to search them again on the night of *bedikath chametz*; they are no longer "places where *chametz* is brought". This suggestion is especially helpful for cupboards, closets, clothes and drawers, which are practically impossible to search thoroughly on the night of *bedikath chametz*.

   The blessing over the *mitzvah* is recited only on the night of the fourteenth of *Nissan*, the time prescribed by *Chazal*.

3. *Shulchan Arukh HaRav, Ibid.*

4. *Shulchan Arukh* 433:11; *Mishnah Berurah* 433:46.

5. *Mishnah Berurah* 433:24.

to carry out the search since it involves a great deal of time and effort.[6]

5. A woman whose husband is away on the night of *bedikath chametz* should search with the appropriate blessing. After completing the search, she should recite the *bitul* declaration, declaring all unfound *chametz* ownerless and like the dust of the earth. If possible, her husband should specifically designate her his agent to carry out the *mitzvah*.[7]

When necessary, a woman may designate an agent to search for *chametz* in place of her husband, but she should recite the *bitul* declaration.[8] When she recites it, she should say, "All leaven that is in my husband's possession, etc."[9]

---

6. *Mishnah Berurah* 432:8. Contrary to the *Mishnah Berurah*, the *Orukh HaShulchan* 437:7 states, "Nowadays, women search thoroughly, even for the smallest amount of *chametz*. They wash and scrub all parts of the house and are more particular [about cleaning] than men." The Vilna Gaon, in his glosses to the *Shulchan Arukh* 436:2, also indicates that women may be relied on to search for *chametz*.

7. *Remah* 436:2; *Shulchan Arukh* 434:4; *Sha'arey Teshuvah* 434:8.

The *Biur Halakhah* 434, beginning *She'ti'vateil ishto*, cites authorities who maintain that a woman may search on her husband's behalf without being designated his agent, in accord with the principle *ishto k'gufo*. (A man's wife is as himself.) But it is preferable to take into account other authorities who rule that he should designate her his agent.

The *Sha'arey Teshuvah* adds that a man's adult children who live at home may search for *chametz* on his behalf without being designated his agents. See also the *Shulchan Arukh* 436:2 and the *Sdeh Chemed, Ma'arekheth Chametz U'Matzah* 5:27.

8. *Sha'arey Teshuvah* 434:8; *Mishnah Berurah* 434:19, and *Biur Halakhah*. The *Mishnah Berurah* 434:15 refers to a dispute as to whether a man may designate an agent to recite the *bitul* declaration. In practice, this is only permitted when absolutely necessary. If his wife designates an agent, it is certainly recommended that she recite the *bitul* declaration. Also see *Ma'ada'ney Shmuel*, No. 112:52, citing *Mahari Assad*.

9. *Mishnah Berurah* 434:19.

6. After the search, the leftover *chametz* that is to be eaten or burned should be placed in a corner of the house.[10]

7. The word of a woman or a child with mature intelligence that a house has been searched and has no *chametz* in it is to be trusted.[11]

8. A woman is obligated to destroy all *chametz* in her possession, preferably by burning, before the beginning of the sixth hour on *Erev Pessach*.[12]

---

10. *Shulchan Arukh* 434:1, and *Mishnah Berurah*. The *Mishnah Berurah* adds, "Most people only put aside *chametz* which is found during the search. They are not particular with the rest of it and carry it from place to place. This is not proper, for [if they act this way] what does their search accomplish?" The *Mishnah Berurah* further cites the *Chaye Adam* who rules that the house must be searched again (without a blessing) if *chametz* was carried around the house after the original search.

11. *Shulchan Arukh* 437:4; *Mishnah Berurah* 434:7–8, 10, 16–18.

This refers to a guest who arrives before *Pessach* and does not know if the house has been searched for *chametz*. He may rely on the word of a woman or child with mature intelligence that the house has been searched. He may do so even if there was definitely *chametz* in the house.

The *Mishnah Berurah* points out that a woman and child are only to be relied on if they are queried before the beginning of the sixth hour on *Erev Pessach*, the time when deriving benefit from *chametz* becomes forbidden. The person who has come to stay in the house can still nullify any *chametz* that might remain. After the sixth hour, when *bitul* may no longer be said, he should search himself instead of relying on the word of a woman or child.

12. The exact time is listed in local *Pessach* bulletins distributed in all Jewish communities.

The *Pri Megadim*, Introduction to the Laws of *Pessach*, par. 7, rules that the *mitzvah* of destroying *chametz* is time-bound, and women are exempt. The *Sefer HaChinukh*, No. 9, *Sha'agath Aryeh*, No. 82, and *Avney Neizer*, No. 320, obligate women in this *mitzvah*.

A married woman whose husband is away from home should burn the *chametz* for him. If possible, her husband should specifically appoint her his agent to carry out this *mitzvah*. As above, when she recites the *bitul* declaration in the morning, she should say, "All leaven that is in my husband's possession." Her husband should also recite the *bitul* declaration wherever he is.[13]

Women Who Live Together

9. Women who live together in a dormitory or rented apartment, and who plan to be away between the fourteenth of *Adar* and the fourteenth of *Nissan*, should search their rooms for *chametz* and recite the *bitul* declaration before leaving. No blessing is recited.[14]

Pointing to the juxtaposition of the *mitzvah* to destroy *chametz* with the prohibition against eating it (*Shemoth* 12:15), they conclude that anyone included in the prohibition against eating *chametz* is also obligated in its destruction. See also the *Tzlach*'s commentary on Tractate *Pesachim* 4b, and *Sdeh Chemed, Ma'arekheth Chametz U'Matzah*, No. 5:22.

13. *Shulchan Arukh* 434:4 and 436:2. Also see note 8. Although her husband is also required to recite the *bitul* declaration, she should recite it at home in case he forgets.

   The *Shulchan Arukh* 434:2 and the *Mishnah Berurah* 434:9 explain that a person who does not understand the meaning of the *bitul* declaration in Aramaic should recite it in the vernacular.

   If it was recited in Aramaic with a general understanding of the underlying concept of *bitul*, i.e., that *chametz* is declared ownerless, it is not necessary to repeat it. But if a person thought that *bitul* is a type of prayer, the declaration is invalid, and it must be repeated.

14. *Shulchan Arukh* 436:1; *Mishnah Berurah* 436:3–4; *Biur Halakhah* 436, beginning *V'lo yivareikh*. The *Bach* rules that the blessing is recited because a person who leaves home after the fourteenth of *Adar* is *required* to search for *chametz*. But the majority of

If one of the women intends to be in the apartment the night of *bedikath chametz*, her roommates should appoint her their agent, and she should search with a blessing on the night of the fourteenth. If none of them will be there, appointing an agent to search for them is preferable to searching early.[15]

10. A woman who leaves home before the fourteenth of *Adar*, and does not plan on returning until after *Pessach*, is not obligated to search for *chametz* before her departure. On *Erev Pessach* she should recite the *bitul* declaration wherever she is.[16] Some authorities rule that the declaration suffices even when there is definitely *chametz* in her home.[17]

In any case, she should arrange for a competent Rabbi to sell her *chametz* to a non-Jew.[18]

11. Many complex questions arise concerning a woman who lives outside of Israel and travels there for *Pessach*. The best way to avoid problems is for her to transfer title of all her

---

authorities cited by the *Mishnah Berurah* — the *Levush, Magen Avraham, Taz,* and *Eliyahu Rabbah* — rule that the blessing is only recited on the night of the fourteenth of *Nissan*.

According to *Darkey Moshe, Tinyana,* No. 30, all laws connected to the search for *chametz,* including the prohibition against eating or engaging in any work beforehand, also apply to a person who searches early.

15. It is always best to fulfill a *mitzvah* in its prescribed time. See the *Shulchan Arukh HaRav* 433:7.

Even when a third party is appointed to search the apartment, each woman should recite the *bitul* declaration wherever she is. See note 8.

16. *Remah* 436:1.

17. This is the view of the *Levush, Eliyahu Rabbah, Pri Chadash, Mekor Chayim,* and *Magen HaElef,* but according to the *Bach, Magen Avraham,* and Vilna Gaon, known *chametz* should be destroyed before leaving. The latter view is also held by the *Chaye Adam* 119.

18. *Mishnah Berurah* 448:25.

chametz to another Jew who will sell it to a non- Jew. When she returns home after *Pessach*, she should reacquire the *chametz*. The same procedure should be followed by a woman who lives in Israel and will be outside the country for the holiday.[19]

A Guest

12. A guest in a private home is not required to search her room for *chametz*, even if she arrives before the night of *bedikath chametz*.

A woman who checks into a hotel before the night of *bedikath chametz* is required to search her room.[20]

Selling Chametz

13. A woman may arrange for the sale of her husband's *chametz*.[21] If possible, her husband should specifically appoint

---

19. This suggestion is offered by HaGaon Rav Chaim Pinchus Sheinberg. There is a dispute as to whether *chametz* must be sold before *Pessach* begins where the *chametz* is or where the owner is. When a woman who lives in North America travels to Israel, her *chametz* will be sold in North America after *Pessach* has already started in Israel. A woman who lives in Israel and travels to North America for *Pessach* encounters a similar problem. Her *chametz* will be repurchased after *Pessach* in Israel while it is still *Pessach* in North America. Also see the article by HaGaon Rav Betzalel Zolty in *Noam*, Vol. 17.

20. *Shulchan Arukh HaRav* 432:8. Someone who accepts the keys to a hotel room acquires tenant's rights, a form of ownership. Since the room is in her possession at the time of *bedikath chametz*, she is obligated to search. A guest in a private home does not acquire any ownership in her room. She is not obligated to search.

If for some reason her host does not search her room, she should do so. Otherwise, she may come upon some *chametz* during *Pessach* and eat it.

21. *Chaye Adam* 119:7.

her his agent for the sale.[22] This can even be done over the telephone.[23]

Preparing the Home for Pessach

The myriad details in the laws of preparing the home for *Pessach* are extremely complex. A complete and comprehensive list of them is clearly beyond the scope of this book. This section is intended to provide the reader with an initial awareness of *some* common problems and procedures.

14. Metal utensils in which *chametz* was cooked with liquid of any kind may be rendered fit for *Pessach* use by means of a process known as *hag'alah* (purging), whose basic procedure is as follows:

a) Clean the utensil thoroughly so that no food or rust particles remain on it.[24]

b) Fill a large pot of water and bring it to a full boil.

c) Immerse the utensil in the boiling water. It is not

---

22. *Kitzur Shulchan Arukh* 114:5: "A man who leaves home before *Pessach* and wants his wife to sell his *chametz* should grant her specific permission to rent the room [that contains the *chametz* to a non-Jew]."

23. Even if a voice over the telephone is not considered the "true" voice of the speaker, it is sufficient for appointing an agent.

24. It is sometimes very difficult to clean utensils made of different parts which are screwed together. They should be brought to a competent authority to determine whether *hag'alah* is feasible.

If part of a utensil cannot be completely cleaned, *libun kal* may be performed on it. This is done by exposing that part directly to fire until it reaches the temperature at which a string placed on it will be severed. *Hag'alah* may then be performed on the other parts of the utensil.

necessary to immerse the whole utensil at once, but the water must boil *while* the utensil is immersed in it.[25]

d) Remove the utensil from the water and immediately immerse it in cold water. (If this is not done, the *hag'alah* is still valid.)

It is most important that neither the utensil which is to be be kashered nor the large pot which is to hold the boiling water be used during the twenty-four hours preceding *hag'alah.*[26]

15. A utensil in which *chametz* was cooked without liquid, e.g. a frying pan or a grill, is kashered through *libun*. This is done by directly exposing the utensil to fire until it reaches an extremely high temperature. *Libun* is a difficult process which should only be performed by an expert. In fact, it is recommended that a person well-versed in the laws of *hag'alah* be present to supervise that procedure as well. A

---

25. If the utensil cools the water to below boiling, it should be left in the water until the water begins to boil again.

26. When a *chametz* utensil is kashered through immersion in boiling water, the flavors which have been absorbed by it are exuded into the water. If the utensil absorbed *chametz* within the previous twenty-four hours, the *chametz* flavor enters the water to be reabsorbed by the utensil and renders the *hag'alah* futile.

If more than twenty-four hours have passed, the absorbed *chametz* becomes *pagum* (stale), and therefore not forbidden by Torah Law. Rabbinic Law still requires the utensil to be kashered, but the Rabbis permit immersing the utensil in boiling water. They are not concerned with the reabsorption of a Rabbinically prohibited flavor.

If waiting twenty-four hours is difficult, disinfectant or bleach may be added to the large pot of boiling water to render any flavors exuded into it inedible. The utensil may then be kashered. Another suggestion is to add a solution of bleach and water to the utensil that needs to be kashered and bring it to a boil. All the absorbed flavors in the utensil will become *pagum* and it may then be kashered normally. See *Siddur Pessach KeHilkhethah*, Vol. 1, Chapter 7:2.

woman who is well-versed in its laws may be relied on to perform *hag'alah*.[27]

16. Below is a partial list of general procedures and tips to keep in mind when preparing the home for *Pessach*:

a) Kitchen counters. A stone counter is made fit for *Pessach* use by heating a piece of metal or stone to a red-hot temperature, placing it on the dry counter, and immediately pouring water over it so that it will flow onto the counter while boiling. This should be done for each small section of the counter. Each section should be dry before the water is poured on.[28]

After kashering the counter, it is customary to cover it with wood, P.V.C., or some other material.

A formica or wood counter cannot be kashered. It may only be used during *Pessach* if it is covered.

b) Sinks. An enamel sink cannot be kashered. It should be cleaned out well and used only when a mat or tub is placed in it to prevent utensils from coming in contact with it.

A stainless steel sink is kashered the same way a stone counter is.

Even if the sink is covered, it is advisable to pour a solution of hot water and disinfectant into the drain. It renders any *chametz* in the drain inedible. If this is not done, an aroma may be emitted by the *chametz* when hot water is poured down the drain during *Pessach*, and the aroma may be absorbed by the utensil.[29]

---

27. See the *Sdeh Chemed, Ma'arekheth Chametz U'Matzah* 5:16.
28. An alternative method is to boil water in an electric coffee pot and pour it over the counter while still boiling. If neither method is used, the counter should be thoroughly cleaned and covered.
29. For this reason, some authorities advise that the utensil from which hot water is poured into the sink not be used for *Pessach*; it may have absorbed an aroma from *chametz* in the drain. See the *Shulchan Arukh HaRav* 433:59.

c) Gas stoves. Grates should be exposed to fire until they reach a temperature at which a string placed on them would be severed. If possible, a second set of grates should be purchased for *Pessach*.

Burners should be cleaned out well, especially the holes. They should then be burned out for about an hour to destroy any remaining *chametz* particles.

If possible, the area around and under the burners should be kashered through *hag'alah*. At a minimum, boiling water should be poured over them. It is customary to cover them. Ideally, a second set of parts for this area of the stove should be purchased for *Pessach*.

d) The oven. Kashering an oven involves many questions which depend on the type of oven to be kashered. A reliable halakhic authority should be consulted.

e) The *Shabbath blech*. After a thorough cleaning on both sides, it should be placed on the fire for about two hours. Boiling water should then be poured over it. It is also advisable to cover it with aluminum foil.

f) The refrigerator. It should be thoroughly cleaned, especially the holes and grooves. The rubber door gasket should be carefully inspected, and the cracks between it and the door cleaned with a brush. It is customary not to place *Pessach* food on the same shelves on which *chametz* was placed during the year unless they are covered.

g) Tips. When cleaning the doorways, care should be taken not to pour water over the *mezuzoth*, as it may seep into them and invalidate them.

An easy way to clean small children's toys, such as Legos, is to put them in a pillow case with a little bit of laundry soap and run it through the washing machine.

It is a good idea to unscrew the mouthpiece cover of the

telephone and clean it just before *Pessach*.

The vacuum cleaner should be cleaned as one of the last steps.

People often change brooms and mop heads, because many particles of *chametz* are often stuck in them.

Benchers, cookbooks, and prayer books which are normally used at the table near food should be put away with the *chametz* dishes.

Baby carriages and school bags should be thoroughly cleaned out. A baby's pacifier should be replaced for *Pessach*, but if necessary, the one used during the year can be thoroughly cleaned and used on *Pessach*.

17. Kneading utensils and others things that come in regular contact with flour and dough should not be kashered for *Pessach*. Some authorities rule that a ring which a woman wears while kneading dough should be sold with the *chametz* because it is very difficult to clean properly.[30]

Baking Matzoth

18. A God-fearing woman may bake *matzah* under the supervision of someone competent in all the relevant laws of baking it.[31]

A minor may not participate in baking the *matzoth* which are to be used at the *Seder*.[32]

---

30. *Remah* 451:17–18. A metal bread box may be kashered for *Pessach*. Only utensils which are used for raw dough should not be used.
31. *Mishnah Berurah* 460:6; *Chok Yaacov* 460:4.
32. *Shulchan Arukh* 460:1, and *Mishnah Berurah*. *Matzah* for the *Seder* must be kneaded and baked *lishmah* (for the sake of the *mitzvah*). In *halakhah*, minors are deemed incapable of peforming an act *lishmah*.

The Fast of the First-Born

,19. It is customary for first-born males to fast on *Erev Pessach* in commemoration of their exclusion from the plague of the first-born. The fast is waived for a first-born male who participates in a *se'udath mitzvah*, such as the meal held at the conclusion of the study of a Tractate of Talmud.[33] Although some authorities require first-born females to fast,[34] this is not the accepted practice.[35] In some places it is customary to bring them food from the *se'udath mitzvah*.[36]

The *Mishnah Berurah* states, "In the multitude of our sins, many people allow children to mix the water with the flour. This is contrary to the law, for many authorities include this in the kneading process. (See the *Shulchan Arukh* 324:3.) One cannot fulfill the *mitzvah* with these *matzoth*."

33. *Shulchan Arukh* 470:1; *Mishnah Berurah* 470:10.

34. *Shulchan Arukh, Ibid.* The *Tur* reports that the German custom is for women to observe the Fast of the First-born. This custom is based on the *Midrash P'sikta Rabathi, Parshah* 17, which relates how Pharaoh's daughter Batya was spared from the plague because she saved Moshe Rabbenu.

35. *Remah* 470:1, citing the *Maharil; Chida*, in *Simchath HaRegel*, p. 42; *Ben Ish Chai, Shanah Rishonah, Parshath Tzav* 25; *Kaf HaChayim* 470:16–17. The Vilna Gaon explains that nowhere does the Torah confer first-born status on females. The *Shulchan Arukh HaRav* adds that all the warnings concerning this plague and its actual execution are in the masculine gender.

The *Midrash, Shemoth Rabbah, Parshah* 15:12, implies that only first-born males were killed. It explains that the *Pessach* sacrifice must be from a *male* sheep "because He smote the first-born Egyptians and had mercy on the first-born Israelites."

36. *Zekhor LeAvraham*, Vol. 2, No. 406; *Yabia Omer*, Vol. 4, *Orach Chayim*, No. 42. To gain an exemption from fasting, a man must actually attend the *se'udath mitzvah*, but since a woman's obligation to fast is questionable, it is sufficient if food from the meal is brought to her. *Ye'chaveh Da'ath*, Vol. 3, No. 25, concludes, "If attending the *se'udath mitzvah* does not entail hardship, it is fitting and proper for her to do so."

20. Some authorities rule that the wife of a man who is a first-born himself should fast for their first-born son until he grows up.[37] (If the father is not a first-born, he should fast for their first-born son.) Once a woman begins this practice, it becomes a vow, which must be annulled if she wishes to discontinue it.[38] If she suffers any hardship from fasting, or is pregnant, or nursing, or has recently given birth, she need not fast even if there is no father.[39]

Preparing for the Seder

21. All preparations for the *Seder* should be completed before dark.[40] Although some authorities rule a woman should set the *Seder* table while her husband is in the synagogue,[41] others maintain that he himself should set it.[42]

---

37. *Remah* 470:2; *Mishnah Berurah* 470:9–10. The *Mishnah Berurah* points out that a parent needs to fast only for a child who is more than one month old.

38. *Mishnah Berurah, Ibid.* The *Shulchan Arukh HaRav* 470:5 limits this to a case where "it is her intention to continue this practice until her child grows up."

39. *Mishnah Berurah, Ibid.*

40. *Shulchan Arukh* 472:1. One reason to prepare everything in advance is the admonition in Tractate *Pesachim* 109a to begin the *Seder* as soon as possible after dark so the children will not fall asleep. Another is that it is the manner of noblemen and kings to have the table set in advance of their meal; this expresses freedom. Starting the *Seder* as early as possible also enables the participants to eat the *afikomen* before midnight.

41. *Misgereth HaShulchan*, commentary on the *Kitzur Shulchan Arukh* 118:6.

42. *Va'Yaged Moshe* 1:5 reports that many great Torah personalities were particular to prepare the *Seder* table themselves. The *Chida*, writing in *Moreh LeEtzba*, No. 206, and *Chayim LeRosh, Inyaney Arikhath HaShulchan*, par. 4, cites the Zohar as the source for this practice. It can also be inferred from the words of the *Ben Ish Chai*,

22. A God-fearing woman who knows how to check lettuce for insects[43] may be relied on.[44] It is better to rely on a

---

Shanah Sh'niah, Parshath Va'Yeira 17: "When a woman puts the *challah* on the table, she should...place her hands on the table and recite the verse, 'And he spoke to me, this is the table that is before God.' On *Erev Pessach* her husband should stand next to her and recite this verse."

43. The procedure for checking lettuce for insects is: Separate all the leaves from the head, and rinse them under the faucet. Straighten out their folds and ridges, rub them well, and check each of them a few times by sunlight or the light of a fluorescent lamp. Experts advise placing the lettuce in a dilute solution of vinegar or dishwashing detergent for a few moments before rinsing it off. This loosens the insects, which may then be easily rinsed off under the faucet. (The lettuce should not be left in vinegar for more than a few moments, for this will "pickle" it, invalidating it for use as *maror*.) See *Minchath Yitzchak* Vol. 7, No. 31, and *Siddur Pessach KeHilkhethah*, Vol. 2, Chapter 1:5.

44. *Shulchan Arukh, Yoreh De'ah* 84:11; *Shakh* 84:35; *Kaf HaChayim, Orach Chayim* 472:121; *Chokhmath Adam* 38:25.

   The *Orukh HaShulchan* concludes, "Women may be relied on to check legumes, fruits, and vegetables... We have not heard of even the most righteous Torah scholars not relying on their wives to check for insects. Jewish maids may be also relied on if they are God-fearing and conscientious in Torah observance."

   To appreciate the seriousness of checking for insects properly, it is well to note the words of the *Ben Ish Chai, Shanah Sh'niah, Parshath Tzav*: "Women should be very cautious when they check the lettuce and *karpas*. Eating a single insect [is punishable] with five sets of lashes. Since everyone is relying on her, if she takes checking lightly, [all their transgressions] will be hung on her neck [and she will be liable to more sets of] lashes than she has hairs on her head... In our countries, many tiny insects are frequently found on vegetables.

   "Once a wise man entered a courtyard on *Erev Pessach* and found a woman with two large baskets. She was washing lettuce leaves, giving them a perfunctory look, and placing them in the second basket. The wise man asked her, 'How many hairs do you have on your head?' 'I have never counted them,' the woman answered, 'and I don't think it's possible to do so.' He then said to her, 'The hairs on

trustworthy woman than on a man who is busy with other things.[45]

The Seder

23. Women are obligated in all the *mitzvoth* of the *Seder*. Young girls who have reached the age of *chinukh* should be trained to fulfill these *mitzvoth*.[46]

Reclining

24. Ashkenazic authorities report that today it is not customary for women to recline at the *Seder*.[47] Some

---

your head can be counted, but the number of lashes that you will be accountable for cannot be counted.' 'What can I do,' she asked, 'I have so many people in my home.' 'This will not save you on the day of judgement', admonished the wise man, 'Take my advice. Throw away all the leaves, which require time-consuming checking, and only use the [middle] stalks [that do not contain insects]. Check only a small amount of *karpas*, just enough to fulfill the obligation (less than a *kezayith* per person).'"

45. *Kreithi U'Pleithi*, commenting on the *Shulchan Arukh, Yoreh De'ah* 84.

46. *Shulchan Arukh* 472:14.

47. The *Shulchan Arukh* 472:4 states, "A woman is not required to recline unless she is an *ishah chashuvah* (important woman)." The *Remah* adds, "Today, all women are considered *chashuvoth*, yet they are not accustomed to recline. They rely on the view of the *Ravi'ah*, who maintains that today [even men] are not required to recline because it is no longer the manner for kings and noblemen to do so."

HaGaon Rav Shlomo Zalman Auerbach explains why women rely on the *Ravi'ah*, while men continue to recline. The original enactment only required men to recline. Important women voluntarily accepted reclining as a custom. Since reclining no longer expresses

Sephardic authorities maintain that they should recline.[48]
Women should not stand while eating the *matzah* oɪ

---

freedom, women discontinued their custom. Men, however, who are required by Rabbinic Law to recline, continue the practice today. Whenever the Rabbis enact a law for a particular reason, the law remains in force even when the reason appears to become obsolete.

In explaining why *Chazal* excluded women from the original enactment to recline, *She'ilthoth D'Rav Achai, Parshath Tzav*, No. 77, points out, "It is not the way of women to recline". The *Biur HaGra* 472 concludes that no distinction is to be drawn between married and unmarried women according to this view.

The *Rashbam*, Tractate *Pesachim* 108a, offers a different explanation: Women were not required to recline "out of reverence for their husbands." The *Tur* explains that according to this view, an unmarried woman is required to recline. The *Bach* and the *Pri Chadash* rule in favor of the *She'ilthoth*, and his interpretation is the only one cited by the *Mishnah Berurah* 472:11, the *Birkey Yosef*, and the *Shulchan Arukh HaRav* 472:10.

Contrary to the *Remah*, the *Orukh HaShulchan* 472:6 indicates that Ashkenazic women who are *chashuvoth* should recline even today. The journal *HaOhel, Nissan*, 5716, cites the recollection of the *Kethav Sofer* that his mother, the daughter of Rabbi Akiva Eiger and the wife of the *Chatham Sofer*, was accustomed to recline. The *Chatham Sofer* used to prepare a special bench for her to recline on. It is possible that even the *Remah* would concede that such women, known far and wide for their exceptional personalities, should recline. The *Kaf HaChayim* 472:28 concludes, "Blessing shall come on Ashkenazic women who recline."

The *Kesef Mishneh*, commenting on the *Rambam, Hilkhoth Chametz U'Matzah* 7:8, gives three examples of an *ishah chashuvah* in the name of Rabbenu Mano'ach: An unmarried woman who is the "mistress of the home"; a woman whose actions stand out and who is known to be a "woman of valor", such as the daughter of a leader of the generation; a woman who has maids and other servants and does not have to spend time on domestic chores.

48. *Kaf HaChayim* 472:26–28; *Ben Ish Chai, Shanah Sh'niah, Parshath Tzav* 28; *Hagadath Chazon Ovadiah*, Vol. 2, p. 120. The *Beith Yosef* does not indicate that women rely on the view of the *Ravi'ah*. Today, therefore, they should all recline since they are all considered *chashuvoth*.

drinking the four cups of wine, for they must be consumed in a way that expresses freedom.[49]

Telling the Story of the Exodus

25. On the first night of *Pessach*, the Torah requires every Jew to recall the Exodus from Egypt in detail. This *mitzvah* is fulfilled by reading the *Hagadah* at the *Seder*. Some authorities rule that Torah Law obligates women in this *mitzvah*,[50] but most rule that their obligation is Rabbinic. A woman may not, therefore, recite the *Hagadah* for a man.[51]

---

49. Freedom is not expressed by wandering around while drinking. A woman who is busy in the kitchen should be particularly careful about this.

50. *Sefer HaChinukh* 21; *Tosafoth*, Tractate *Sukkah* 38a and Tractate *Megillah* 4a; *Birkey Yosef* 473:15; *Chaye Adam* 130:12; *Ye'chaveh Da'ath*, Vol. 2, No. 65.

   HaGaon Rav David Feinstein, writing in *Hagadath Kol Dodi* 11:2, states, "The *Hagadah* should be explained to women so they will be able to fulfill the *mitzvah*. This is especially true of the section beginning with 'Rabban Gamliel used to say...' My father[HaGaon Rav Moshe Feinstein] was particular that women should recite the *Hagadah* from the beginning of that section to the end of *Magid*...This is indicated by the *Remah* 473:6. I believe that evidence may be found for this in Tractate *Pesachim* 116b, where *Chazal* link the *mitzvah* of *Hagadah* with the *mitzvah* of *Matzah*."

51. *Pri Megadim, Eshel Avraham* 479:2, and *Mishbetzoth Zahav* 484:1.

   The *Shulchan Arukh* 472:14 states, "Women are included in the *mitzvah* to drink four cups of wine and in all other *mitzvoth* of the *Seder*." The Vilna Gaon understands the *Shulchan Arukh* to include women in all the *mitzvoth* of the *Seder* as an extension of their obligation to drink the four cups. Since each of the four cups of wine must be drunk in connection with one of the four *mitzvoth*— *Kiddush, Hagadah, Birkath HaMazon* and *Hallel* — women must perform these *mitzvoth* in order to fulfill the *mitzvah* of drinking the four cups properly.

26. Difficult sections of the *Hagadah* should be explained by the leader of the *Seder*. A woman who understands the content of the *Hagadah* fulfills the *mitzvah* by listening to a

---

The Vilna Gaon's interpretation implies that Torah Law does not obligate women to recite the *Hagadah*. Rather, their obligation to recite it is a corollary of their Rabbinic obligation to drink the four cups. Since it is time-bound, it is easily understood why women should be exempt from the *mitzvah* of *Hagadah*. See the *Chaye Adam* 129:12 and *Hagadath Chazon Ovadiah*, Vol. 1, No. 20.

In fact, the *Sefer HaChinukh* 21 rules that Torah Law does obligate women to recall the story of the Exodus. This amazes the *Minchath Chinukh*: "Why should this time-bound *mitzvah* be incumbent on women? I have not found any reason to obligate women in it." The *Minchath Chinukh* rejects the possibility of women being obligated because of *af hein hayu b'otho ha'nes* (They, too, were included in the miracle.), by citing *Tosafoth*, Tractate *Pesachim* 108b, where this principle is limited to Rabbinic *mitzvoth*, i.e., drinking the four cups, kindling *Chanukah* lights, and the *mitzvoth* of *Purim*. It does not serve to obligate women in a Torah *mitzvah* such as *Hagadah*.

A number of sources explain why women may be obligated by Torah Law to recite the *Hagadah*. *Cheshek Shlomoh* derives an obligation from the verse, "Remember this day that you left Egypt...and you shall not eat *chametz*" (*Shemoth* 13:3). The author submits that everyone who is cautioned against eating *chametz* is also required to "Remember this day".

In *Hagadath Chazon Ovadiah*, HaGaon Rav Ovadiah Yosef cites the *Ritva*, *Kiddushin* 29a, who offers an explanation why the Talmud searches for an explicit Scriptural source exempting women from the *mitzvah* to circumcise their sons. The fact that the *mitzvah* is time-bound (performed on or after the eighth day of the infant's life) is not a reason to exempt them. The *Ritva* postulates that the exemption of women from time-bound *mitzvoth* only applies to those performed on one's own body. Women are not automatically exempt from *Milath HaBen* (circumcising the son), which is performed on someone else. *Hagadah*, argues HaGaon Rav Yosef, is fulfilled by eliciting the child's questions in order to answer them. It is a *mitzvah* performed "on someone else", thus the fact that it is time-bound does not give rise to an exemption.

man recite it, even if she does not know how to read it herself.[52]

27. Women who are busy arranging the table and serving should at a minimum recite or listen to *Kiddush* and the section of the *Hagadah* beginning with "R. Gamliel used to say...", which deals with the symbolic meaning of the *Pessach* sacrifice, *Matzah*, and *Maror*, and ending with the drinking of the second cup of wine. It is also customary to call the women to the table for the reading of the Ten Plagues.[53]

28. A woman who is home alone with her child must tell him the story of the Exodus by reciting and explaining the *Hagadah*.[54]

29. In a family which has only daughters, one of them should ask the "Four Questions". If there are no children, a wife asks her husband the questions.[55]

The Four Cups

30. Women are obligated to drink four cups of wine at the

The *Minchath Chinukh* attempts to explain the *Sefer HaChinukh* by referring to the view of Rav Yosef of Yerushalayim, cited in *Tosafoth*, Tractate *Megillah* 4a. Rav Yosef maintains that *af hein hayu b'otho ha'nes* can obligate women in Torah *mitzvoth* as well as Rabbinic ones. This may be why the *Sefer HaChinukh* obligates women in *Hagadah*. Also see the *Biur Halakhah* 472, beginning *She'lo k'seder.*

52. *Remah* 473:6; *Mishnah Berurah* 473:64.
53. *Mishnah Berurah* 473:64, based on the *Chaye Adam*. Also see the *Shulchan Arukh HaRav* 473:43 and *Ma'asey Rav*, No. 187.
54. *Shulchan Arukh* 473:7; *Orukh HaShulchan* 473:21.
55. *Shulchan Arukh* 472:14, and *Biur Halakhah*, based on Tractate *Pesachim* 108b.

Seder in the order prescribed by Chazal. The first cup is drunk after Kiddush, the second at the conclusion of Magid, the third after Birkath HaMazon, and the fourth at the conclusion of Hallel.[56] Young girls who have reached the age of chinukh should be trained to fulfill this mitzvah. Small children should also be given cups of wine, but they do not have to hold a revi'ith, the minimum size necessary for the mitzvah.[57]

31. Some authorities rule that the preference for men to drink wine instead of grape juice does not apply to women.[58]

---

56. Shulchan Arukh 472:15. Tractate Pesachim 108b states, "Everyone is required to drink four cups of wine — men, women, and children." The Rashbam, commenting on the words, "and children", explains, "For they were also redeemed." His interpretation implies that the requirement that children drink four cups of wine represents more than the general mitzvah of chinukh. Children have a specific obligation to express thanks for their redemption.

The Shulchan Arukh HaRav 472:25 indicates the contrary: "Young girls who have reached the age of chinukh should be trained to drink the four cups." Tosafoth, Tractate Pesachim 99b, beginning V'lo yifchi'thu, also indicates that a child's obligation is based on the general mitzvah of chinukh. See Siddur Pessach KeHilkhethah, Vol. 2, p. 33, note 5.

Although adults should drink a minimum of slightly more than half the cup, the Mishnah Berurah 472:47 rules that a child need only drink a maley lugmav (cheekful) of wine.

The age at which a child should begin fulfilling this mitzvah, estimates the Mishnah Berurah 269:1, is about six or seven, depending on the child's level of understanding. The Shulchan Arukh HaRav 472:25 explains that it is an age at which the child can appreciate the concept of a holy day and comprehend the context of the Hagadah.

57. Chok Yaacov 472:27, citing the Maharil. Seder HaYom states, "It is customary to place a cup before each person, even a small child, so he will inquire [as to the reason for this]. This is a beautiful custom."

58. In Mikra'ey Kodesh, Pessach, Vol. 2, p. 130, HaGaon Rav Tzvi Pessach Frank rules that a man should use wine for the four cups

Matzah

32. Torah Law obligates women to eat a *kezayith* of *matzah* on the night of the fifteenth of *Nissan*.[59] They are also included in the prohibition against eating *matzah* on *Erev Pessach*. A child who is old enough to understand the story of the Exodus should not be served *matzah* on the fourteenth of *Nissan* beginning in the morning.[60]

---

rather than grape juice. He explains that "wine that brings joy" should be used for the *mitzvah*, and the intoxicating effect of wine brings about this joy. In his notes, Rav Yosef Cohen brings evidence from the *Mordekhai* and the *Rashbam* that "wine that brings joy" should be drunk for the sake of *Simchath Yom Tov* (Rejoicing on the Festival). It has no connection to the *mitzvah* of drinking the four cups. The *Rambam, Hilkhoth Yom Tov* 6:17, points out that a woman does not fulfill *Simchath Yom Tov* by drinking wine, but by receiving gifts from her husband in honor of the holiday: "He should buy her clothes and ornaments according to his ability." Consequently, concludes HaRav Cohen, there is no reason for a woman to use "wine that brings joy"; she may use grape juice, if she so desires, without any hesitation.

A man also fulfills the *mitzvah* with grape juice although not in an ideal manner. See *Hagadath Kol Dodi, Hilkhoth Leil Pessach* 3:4, in the name of HaGaon Rav Moshe Feinstein.

59. Tractate *Pesachim* 43b, based on the juxtaposition of the prohibition against eating *chametz* with the commandment to eat *matzah*, in the verse, "You shall not eat *chametz*; seven days you shall eat *matzoth*" (*Devarim* 16:3). All those who are warned against eating *chametz* are also commanded to eat *matzah*.

60. *Remah* 471:2; *Mishnah Berurah* 471:13. The *Magen Avraham* comments on the words of the *Hagadah*: " 'And you shall tell your children...on account of *this*' (*Shemoth* 13:8). 'This', refers to the time that *matzah* and *maror* are placed before you." The *Magen Avraham* explains that if a child has already eaten *matzah* that day, he will find nothing novel in seeing it on the *Seder* table, and the *mitzvah* will not be properly fulfilled.

Hallel and Afikomen

33. Women are obligated to recite *Hallel* at the *Seder*.[61] Some Sephardic authorities also require them to recite the whole *Hallel* with its blessings on the night of *Pessach* before the start of the *Seder*.[62]

34. Women are required to eat the *afikomen*, a *kezayith* of *matzah* eaten at the end of the *Seder* meal. They should be particular to eat it before midnight as men do.[63]

Kitniyoth

35. It is an established custom among Ashkenazic Jews to refrain from eating legumes (*kitniyoth*), such as rice, corn, and beans, during *Pessach*. If an Ashkenazic woman marries a Sephardic man, and he wants her to discontinue her custom, she should annul her vow and adopt his custom. If a

---

The *Magen Avraham* explains further that although it is normally prohibited to feed forbidden food to a young child, on *Erev Pessach* *matzah* may be fed to a child who has not reached the age of *chinukh*. Eating *matzah* on *Erev Pessach* violates a positive commandment, so it is not considered to be "forbidden" food. See the *Terumoth HaDeshen*, No. 125. A detailed analysis of the *Magen Avraham* may be found in *Chanokh LeNa'ar*, p. 54, note 17.

61. The *Biur Halakhah* 422, beginning *Hallel*, cites *Tosafoth*, who obligates women to recite *Hallel* at the *Seder* because it offers thanks to God for the miraculous deliverance from Egyptian bondage, and women were also included in this miracle. Also see the *Birkey Yosef* 473:15. According to *Torath Raphael, Orach Chayim*, No. 75, *Hallel* recited on the morning of the first day of *Pessach* also gives thanks for the miracle, and women are required to recite it.

62. *Ye'chaveh Da'ath*, Vol. 5, No. 34.

63. *Mishnah Berurah* 477:2; *Chaye Adam* 130:12.

Sephardic woman marries an Ashkenazic man, and he wants her to refrain from eating *kitniyoth*, she should do so.[64]

Some authorities rule that an Ashkenazic woman who marries a Sephardic man should not abandon her custom.[65] Others allow her to eat *kitniyoth*, even if she does not annul her vow.[66]

36. A woman who does not eat *kitniyoth* may cook them for her husband if he does eat them. Similarly, a Sephardic woman who marries an Ashkenazic man and no longer eats *kitniyoth* may cook them for her parents in their home. Some authorities forbid her from doing this on *Yom Tov*.[67]

37. Rice and corn cereal may be cooked for an infant who does not eat other food. Similarly, a person who needs to eat

---

64. *Tashbatz*, Vol. 3, No. 179; *Rav Pe'alim*, Vol. 3, No. 30; *Panim Me'iroth*, Vol. 2, No. 161. The custom to refrain from *kitniyoth* only applies if it does not cause undue hardship or friction in the family. See *Sdeh Chemed, Ma'arekheth Chametz U'Matzah* 6:10, and *Divrey Malki'el* 28:17–20.

65. *Ran, responsum* No. 48; *Maharik, Shoresh* 143; *Maharam Alashker*, No. 49.

66. *Iggeroth Moshe, Orach Chayim*, Vol. 1, No. 158, explains that a woman adopts all her husband's customs when she gets married. Also see *Minchath Yitzchak*, Vol. 4, Nos. 43–44. Since opinions vary, a competent halakhic authority should be consulted for practical guidance.

   I queried HaGaon Rav Ben Tzion Abba Shaul concerning a Sephardic returnee to Jewish observance who lives with an Ashkenazic family. Must she accept the decree of *kitniyoth*? His response was that she may follow the custom of her forefathers and eat *kitniyoth* without hesitation.

67. *Yabia Omer*, Vol. 5, *Orach Chayim*, No. 37; *Hagadath Chazon Ovadiah*, Vol. 2, p. 56. Cooking *kitniyoth* on *Yom Tov* is not considered "preparing food" for a person who does not eat them. See the *Remah* 527:20; *Rav Pe'alim*, Vol. 3, No. 30; *Orukh HaShulchan* 453:4.

kitniyoth for health reasons may do so, even when there is no danger to life.[68]

When cooking *kitniyoth* in any of the above situations, it is customary to use separate utensils.[69]

---

68. *Mishnah Berurah* 453:3, citing the *Chatham Sofer, Orach Chayim*, No. 122, and the *Chaye Adam*.

     If rice grains are cooked they should be inspected very carefully three times to be sure there are no particles of flour on them. Some people scald the grains in boiling water before cooking them, which prevents possible particles of flour from fermenting. See the *Chok Yaacov* 464 and *Kaf HaChayim* 453:14.
69. Kaf HaChayim 453:27. If *kitniyoth* are mistakenly cooked in a pot, the pot does not become invalid for *Pessach* use.

CHAPTER 24
Days of Sephirah and Shavuoth

Counting the Omer

1. Counting the *Omer*[1] is a time-bound *mitzvah* from which women are exempt.[2] Some authorities maintain that

---

1. *VaYikra* 23:15: "And you shall count for yourselves on the day after the *Shabbath* [the day after the first day of *Pessach*]...seven complete weeks..."

   In the days of the *Beith HaMikdash* a special sacrifice was offered on the second day of *Pessach*. Known as the *Korban HaOmer*, it consisted of a specific measure of barley which had been harvested on the night following the first day of *Pessach*.

   The Torah commands us to count forty-nine days from the day that the *Omer* is offered and celebrate *Shavuoth* (literally, weeks) on the fiftieth day. The counting of forty-nine days prepares us for the momentous occasion of *kabbalath ha'Torah* (receiving the Torah), which is the focal point of the *Shavuoth* holiday. For a discussion of whether the *mitzvah* of counting the *Omer* is a Torah or Rabbinic requirement in our day, when sacrifices are no longer offered, see note 2.

2. The *Rambam, Hilkhoth T'midin U'Musafin* 7:24, states, "This

women have accepted this *mitzvah* as an obligation.[3]
Sephardic women do not recite the blessing before counting

---

mitzvah is incumbent on every Jewish man, in every place and at all
times. Women and slaves are exempt."

The *Avney Neizir, Orach Chayim,* No. 384, is amazed that the
Ramban, in his novellae on Tractate *Kiddushin* 34a, includes the
mitzvah of *Sephirath HaOmer* in the category of positive *mitzvoth*
that are *not* time-bound.

HaGaon Rav Yerucham Fishel Perlow, cited in *Mikra'ey Kodesh,
Hilkhoth Pessach,* Vol. 2, No. 67:2, explains the *Ramban* by taking
note of the *Turey Evven's* explanation of why women are obligated in
the *mitzvah* of *Bikkurim* (bringing first fruits to Jerusalem) in spite of
the fact that *Bikkurim* may only be brought between *Shavuoth* and
Chanukah. The *Turey Evven* explains that the time factor for
Bikkurim is a function of the growing season, not intrinsic to the
mitzvah. In spite of its time limits, *Bikkurim* is not a time-bound
mitzvah.

By the same token, the *Ramban* maintains that *Sephirath HaOmer*
is not time-bound, but linked to the *Omer* sacrifice: "And you shall
count...from the day that you bring the sacrifice" (*VaYikra, Ibid*).
Bringing the *Omer* is linked to a specific time, but *counting* the *Omer*
is linked to the sacrificial offering.

HaGaon Rav Tzvi Pessach Frank explains the difference between
the *Rambam's* view and that of the *Ramban.* The *Rambam* rules that
the Torah requirement to count the *Omer* applies even in our day,
when there is no *Beith HaMikdash* and no *Omer* sacrifice. His ruling
implies that the *mitzvah* of counting is linked to the time of the year,
and only coincidentally to the sacrificial offering. The *Ramban's*
view, however, is that the requirement to count the *Omer* is Rabbinic
in our days. The Torah obligation to count applies only when the
Beith HaMikdash is standing and the *Omer* is offered. Counting the
Omer is linked to the *Omer* sacrifice; its relationship to the time of
the year is only coincidental. See also *Divrey Malki'eil,* Vol. 3, No. 8.

3. *Magen Avraham* 489:1, cited by the *Shulchan Arukh HaRav* 489:2.

The *Minchath Chinukh* 306 challenges the *Magen Avraham's*
ruling that women become obligated in the *mitzvah* of *Sephirath
HaOmer* by performing it: "This concept requires investigation. It is
a new idea...that I have not found in any place...Some authorities
even prohibit them from reciting the blessing, but all agree that

the *Omer.*[4] An Ashkenazic woman who lives in a community in which women do not generally count is advised not to recite the blessing.[5] If she does wish to recite the blessing, she should be particularly conscientious to count the correct number of days each night.[6]

A woman may not *motzie* a man with her blessing.

[counting the *Omer*] is not obligatory." See also *Minchah Chadashah*, Laws of *Sephirath HaOmer* 489:2, and *Sdeh Chemed, Ma'arekheth Mem*, No. 136.

The opinion of the *Magen Avraham* is best understood when one assumes that once a person performs a *mitzvah* three times, even on a voluntary basis, the practice attains the status of a vow unless it was done on condition that it not become binding. It may not be discontinued unless the vow is annulled. See the *Shulchan Arukh, Yoreh De'ah* 214:1. For a full discussion, see *Machazeh Eliyahu*, No. 21:2.

4. *Kaf HaChayim* 489:9. *Rav Pe'alim*, Vol. 1, *Kuntres Sod Yesharim*, No. 12, quotes the *Ari*: "Women have no connection to the *mitzvah* of counting the *Omer* and they are forbidden to recite the blessing."

HaGaon Rav Ben Zion Abba Shaul rules that a Sephardic woman who began counting with a blessing should discontinue this practice. The *Kaf HaChayim, Ibid.*, suggests that a woman listen to a man recite the blessing.

5. In accord with the *Remah*, who permits women to recite blessings over time-bound *mitzvoth*, the *Shulchan Arukh HaRav* 489:2 permits Ashkenazic women to recite the blessing over *Sephirath HaOmer*. The *Birkey Yosef* 489:24 arrives at a similar conclusion: "It appears to me that if they recite the blessing over the *lulav* and other such *mitzvoth*, they may follow the same practice for *Sephirah*." Nevertheless, the *Mishnah Berurah* 489:3 discourages reciting the blessing: "In our communities, women generally do not count. *Shulchan Shlomoh* writes that [even those who do] should not recite the blessing, since they will inevitably make an error [in counting] one of the days."

6. If she is not careful, she will almost certainly make a mistake in one night's counting. It is usual for women who recite *Ma'ariv* to count, because they are less likely to forget.

2. It is customary for men and women to refrain from work for a short time every day after sunset between *Pessach* and *Shavuoth.*[7] Most authorities maintain that once the *Omer* has been counted, work is permitted.[8]

Weddings and Cutting Hair

3. The days of *Sephirath HaOmer* (Counting the *Omer*) are days of semi-mourning in commemoration of the plague that took the lives of 24,000 of Rabbi Akiva's students at this time of the year.[9] Weddings and cutting hair are forbidden. Women also refrain from cutting their hair unless there is a special need.[10]

---

7. *Shulchan Arukh* 493:4; *Mishnah Berurah* 493:18–19. The *Tur* cites two reasons for this custom: The students of Rabbi Akiva were buried during twilight, and it is written concerning *Sephirath HaOmer*, *sheva shabbathoth* (seven weeks). The word *Shabbath* indicates cessation of work. We refrain from work during the time that the *Omer* is counted.

8. *Mishnah Berurah, Ibid.*; *Kitzur Shulchan Arukh* 120:10. This accords with the second reason cited in note 7, which traces the custom of refraining from work to the *mitzvah* of counting the *Omer*, not to the burial of Rabbi Akiva's students. Also see HaGaon Rav Y.M. Tokitzinsky's *Lu'ach Eretz Yisrael.*

9. There are a number of customs regarding *Sephirah* and semi-mourning. One is to observe mourning restrictions from the beginning of *Sephirah* until the the thirty-third day of the *Omer* (*Lag B'Omer*). Sephardim only permit cutting hair from the thirty-fourth day of the *Omer*. Another is to begin the restrictions on *Rosh Chodesh Iyar* and conclude them three days prior to *Shavuoth*. This is the practice in many Ashkenazic communities. A custom based on the *Kabbalah* is to observe the restrictions from the beginning of *Sephirah* until three days prior to *Shavuoth*. *Chabad* communities observe them the entire *Sephirah*, until *Erev Shavuoth.*

10. *Iggeroth Moshe, Yoreh De'ah*, Vol. 2, No. 137.
   It may be necessary for a woman to cut her hair if it interferes with proper immersion in the *mikvah* or protrudes from her head-covering.

Purchasing New Clothes

4. Most authorities permit purchasing new clothes during *Sephirah* and reciting the blessing *She'he'che'yanu* over them. *She'he'che'yanu* may also be recited over a fruit which is eaten for the first time that season. Some Sephardic authorities advise not wearing garments for the first time during *Sephirah*, except on *Shabbath* or for a *bar mitzvah* or a *brith milah*.[11]

Music and Dancing

5. It is forbidden to listen to music during *Sephirah*, even in private.[12] This restriction applies only to listening to music for pleasure. Someone who earns her livelihood as a music teacher may give lessons.[13]

Similarly, though dancing for enjoyment is forbidden,[14] a teacher may supervise a rehearsal which is accompanied by

---

11. *Kaf HaChayim* 493:4; *She'arim Metzuyanim BeHalakhah* 121:17; *Torath Yekuthiel, Orach Chayim*, No. 48; *Yabia Omer*, Vol. 3, *Orach Chayim*, No. 26; *Ye'chaveh Da'ath*, Vol. 1, No. 24.
12. *Iggeroth Moshe, Yoreh De'ah*, Vol. 2, No. 137 and *Orach Chayim* Vol. 1, No. 166.
13. *Iggeroth Moshe, Orach Chayim*, Vol. 3, No. 87. The purpose of the prohibition against listening to music is to diminish joy during this period. Practicing an instrument does not constitute "playing for pleasure". HaGaon Rav Feinstein rules, "If a person does derive pleasure [from playing], it is forbidden even to practice, for this is included in the *Sephirah* restrictions against joyous activities."
14. *Mishnah Berurah* 493:3. The *Sha'ar HaTziyun* 493:4 raises the possibility that dancing is forbidden the entire *Sephirah*, even before *Rosh Chodesh Iyar* and after *Rosh Chodesh Sivan*, when many people are accustomed to cut their hair. The *Pri Megadim, Mishbetzoth Zahav* 493:2, forbids dancing for pleasure even during *Chol HaMoed Pessach*.

song and dance, providing it is performed in a closed room.[15]

Shavuoth

6. Some authorities rule that women should not recite *Tikkun Leil Shavuoth*, the collection of readings from the Oral and Written Torah customarily recited by men on *Shavuoth* night.[16]

---

15. I have heard this in the name of a number of contemporary authorities. If the singing and dancing is for a specific purpose, not for pleasure, one may be lenient in private.

    A teacher may incorporate a recorded song into a lesson as an instructional aid. But she should emphasize to her students that the custom to refrain from listening to music should not be taken lightly and that she is only playing the recording to further the learning process.

    According to *Tzitz Eliezer*, Vol. 15, No. 33:2, the restriction against listening to music includes singing without instrumental accompaniment and recorded songs.

16. The *Ben Ish Chai, Shanah Rishonah, Parshath VaYishlach* 6, and *Rav Pe'alim*, Vol. 1, *Kuntres Sod Yesharim*, No. 9, explain that the *tikkun* recited on *Shavuoth* night is linked to the *mitzvah* of *Sephirath HaOmer*.

CHAPTER 25
Bein HaM'tzarim

Communal Fast Days

1. Women over the age of twelve are obligated to fast on the seventeenth of *Tamuz*, the third of *Tishrei* (*Tzom Gedalyah*), and the tenth of *Teveth*.[1]

Minors are not required to fast on these days. When they are old enough to appreciate the tragic events commemorated on these days they should be trained to participate in the fasts by eating only what is necessary for their well-being.[2]

2. Pregnant and nursing women customarily observe these fasts, but one who suffers a great deal of discomfort or feels any weakness at all should not fast.[3]

---

1. *Shulchan Arukh* 550:1; *Biur Halakhah* 550, beginning, *HaKol chayavim*; *Chaye Adam* 133:6; *Kaf HaChayim* 550:1; *Ye'chaveh Da'ath*, Vol. 1, No. 35.

2. *Mishnah Berurah* 550:5.

3. *Shulchan Arukh* and *Mishnah Berurah*, *Ibid*. The *Remah* states, "Pregnant and nursing women who suffer a great deal of discomfort

A woman who has given birth within the preceding thirty days should not fast if she feels weak.[4]

Dancing and Music

3. Dancing, or playing or listening to musical instruments is forbidden during the Three Weeks (between the seventeenth of *Tamuz* and *Tishah B'Av*). During this period, known as *Bein Ha'M'Tzarim*, all forms of music are forbidden. This restriction is observed by both Ashkenazic and Sephardic Jews.

An exception is made for people who earn their livelihood by playing professionally for non-Jews; they may continue playing until *Rosh Chodesh Av*.[5]

---

should not fast. They are not *required* to fast even if they do not suffer discomfort, but they are accustomed to be strict and fast." We have therefore stated that it is *customary*, but not required, for pregnant and nursing women to fast.

The *Mishnah Berurah* explains that although Jewish Law generally considers a woman pregnant only after she is recognizably pregnant, at approximately the end of the first trimester, with respect to fasting her pregnancy is recognized as beginning forty days after conception. He then draws a distinction between a woman in early pregnancy who experiences discomfort from fasting and one who experiences weakness: "If less than [forty days have passed since conception], she is considered like all other women unless she suffers a great deal of discomfort. But if she experiences any weakness at all, she should not act stringently [and fast]...Those who must eat should not indulge in meat and wine, but [only eat] what is necessary."

Da'ath Torah explains that a nursing woman who feels able to fast may do so even if her baby subsists exclusively on her milk. Neither pregnant nor nursing women are required to make up a missed fast.

4. *Eshel Avraham* (Butchach) 550.

5. *Mishnah Berurah* 551:16; *Biur Halakhah* 551, beginning, *Mi'ma'a'tim*; *Kaf HaChayim* 551:39–41; *Ben Ish Chai, Shanah Rishonah, Parshath Devarim* 5.

4. Songs without joyous content may be sung with young children who have not reached the age of *chinukh*.[6]

Shabbath Zemiroth may be sung, even on the *Shabbath* preceding *Tishah B'Av*.[7]

She'he'che'yanu

5. In order to avoid reciting the blessing *She'he'che'yanu* during the Three Weeks, one should refrain from wearing an expensive new garment or eating a fruit for the first time that season. On the *Shabbathoth* before *Rosh Chodesh Av* and on *Rosh Chodesh* itself, many authorities permit reciting the blessing.[8] Other authorities, including many Sephardic ones, advise against reciting *She'he'che'yanu* the entire Three Weeks.[9]

According to *Tzitz Eliezer*, Vol. 15, No. 33:2, "listening to music" includes listening to singing without instrumental accompaniment, and listening to recorded music.

HaGaon Rav Moshe Feinstein, writing in *Iggeroth Moshe, Orach Chayim*, Vol. 1, No. 166, rules that children who have reached the age of *chinukh* should be trained to observe these restrictions.

6. *Kaf HaChayim* and *Ben Ish Chai, Ibid.* This view is shared by a number of contemporary authorities.

7. *Iggeroth Moshe, Orach Chayim*, Vol. 4, No. 112:1. This also applies to those who are not accustomed to sing *Zemiroth* every *Shabbath*.

8. *Mishnah Berurah* 551:45 and 551:98.

A person who wears an expensive new garment or eats a fruit for the first time that season recites the blessing *She'he'che'yanu* to thank God for reaching this joyous occasion. *She'he'che'yanu* is thus inappropriate during the Three Weeks, which recalls tragic events.

If a new fruit will be out of season after *Tishah B'Av* or spoil before *Shabbath*, one may eat it during the week and recite *She'he'che'yanu*. See *Kitzur Shulchan Arukh* 122:2.

9. *Birkey Yosef* 551:10; *Kaf HaChayim* 551:205; *Magen Avraham* 551:42; *Misgereth HaShulchan* 122:2. This ruling is cited in the name of the *Ari*, who asked, "How can one say 'that He has kept us alive to this time' during this period of the year?" The *Kaf HaChayim*

A pregnant woman who feels an urge to do so may eat a new fruit but she should not recite *She'he'che'yanu*.[10]

New and Freshly Laundered Clothes

6. Beginning *Rosh Chodesh Av* (the week of *Tishah B'Av* for Sephardim), one should not wear a new garment for the first time, even if it was purchased before the seventeenth of *Tamuz* and *She'he'che'yanu* was recited at that time.[11] Even garments over which *She'he'che'yanu* is not said, i.e., underwear, stockings, and so forth, should not be worn for the first time after *Rosh Chodesh Av*.[12]

551:208 cites *Yosef Ometz*, who rules that one should refrain from reciting *She'he'che'yanu* until the afternoon of the tenth of *Av*.

10. *Mishnah Berurah* 551:99. If a pregnant woman desires to eat a piece of fruit and refrains, she may harm the fetus. The *Sha'arey Teshuvah* 551:38 advises her to eat another new fruit after *Tishah B'Av* with the intention that the *She'he'che'yanu* include the new fruit that was eaten during the Three Weeks.

The *Kaf HaChayim* 551:211 indicates that a pregnant woman who eats a new fruit during the Three Weeks should recite *She'he'che'yanu*.

11. *Mishnah Berurah* 551:45; *Kaf HaChayim* 551:85; *Iggeroth Moshe, Orach Chayim*, Vol. 3, No. 83.

According to the *Mishnah Berurah* 223:17, when a person buys a garment which does not need tailoring, *She'he'che'yanu* is recited at the time of purchase. If it needs tailoring, the blessing is postponed until the finished garment is worn for the first time. The garment should then not be worn the entire Three Weeks in order to avoid *She'he'che'yanu*. See paragraph 5. Purchasing a finished garment is also forbidden during the entire Three Weeks.

The *Kaf HaChayim* 225:30 rules that *She'he'che'yanu* is always recited when a garment is worn for the first time, not when it is purchased. According to this view, one should not wear a new garment for the first time during the Three Weeks, but a completed garment may be purchased until *Rosh Chodesh Av*.

12. *Mishnah Berurah, Ibid.*, and 551:47. The *Kaf HaChayim* 551:96 remarks that it is praiseworthy for a person who purchases new

7. Beginning *Rosh Chodesh Av* (the week of *Tishah B'Av* for Sephardim), new garments should not be purchased, even if they will not be worn until after *Tishah B'Av*.[13]

8. Beginning *Rosh Chodesh Av* (the week of *Tishah B'Av* for Sephardim), freshly-laundered clothes may not be worn.[14] If the weather is hot, and requires frequent changes of clothing, one should "try on" a number of clothes and wear each of them for a short time before *Rosh Chodesh*. These are no longer considered "freshly-laundered", and they may be worn during the Nine Days.[15]

9. Someone who forgets to prepare changes of clothing before *Rosh Chodesh* may follow this procedure: Before *Shabbath*, put on a fresh change of clothing. On *Shabbath* morning, change to a second fresh set of clothes, which are worn for the rest of *Shabbath*. Both sets of clothing may now be worn during the week.[16]

---

shoes for *Tishah B'Av* before *Rosh Chodesh* to wear them once before *Tishah B'Av*. But according to the law, they may be worn for the first time on *Tishah B'Av* because they are being worn for the sake of a *mitzvah*, not for pleasure.

13. *Shulchan Arukh* and *Remah* 551:7, and *Mishnah Berurah*.
14. *Mishnah Berurah* 551:25. *Salmath Chayim*, Vol. 4, No. 4, permits freshly laundered socks and underwear.
15. *Kaf HaChayim* 551:91; *Ben Ish Chai, Shanah Rishonah, Parshath Devarim* 6. HaGaon Rav Yosef Sholom Eliashiv rules that wearing the clothes for ten or fifteen minutes is sufficient.

When there is not time to put on changes of clothing, some people throw their garments on the ground so they will no longer be fresh. This option is not cited by any of the authorities.
16. *Ibid.* If she would constantly change clothes during *Shabbath*, it would be obvious that she is preparing for the week, which is forbidden. Since it is normal for a person to wear a fresh set of clothing *Shabbath* morning, she does not appear to be preparing for the week.

Some authorities advise women to take their clothes off before their *Shabbath* afternoon nap. When they awaken, they may put on a third change of clothing for the rest of *Shabbath*.[17]

10. A woman who serves as *kvaterin*[18] at a *brith milah* during the Nine Days may wear freshly laundered clothes.[19]

Laundering Clothes

11. Beginning *Rosh Chodesh Av* (the week of *Tishah B'Av* for Sephardim), it is forbidden to launder clothes, sheets, and tablecloths, even with the intention to use them after *Tishah B'Av*.[20] This restriction includes underwear and it also applies to *Shabbath* clothes.[21]

Laundering is permitted for the sake of a *mitzvah*. For example, a woman may launder white underwear which is to be worn during the seven clean days following her menstrual period. This may even be done during the week of *Tishah B'Av* itself.[22]

The *Mishnah Berurah* reports that it is common to follow the custom of Vilna, which permits wearing fresh clothes in honor of *Shabbath*, even on the *Shabbath* before *Tishah B'Av*.

17. *Ye'chaveh Da'ath*, Vol. 1, No. 39.
18. The *kvaterin* is the woman who brings the baby to the room where the *brith* will be performed.
19. *Shulchan Arukh* 551:1, and *Mishnah Berurah*.
20. *Shulchan Arukh* and *Remah* 551:3, and *Mishnah Berurah*.
21. *Mishnah Berurah* 551:32, based on the *Magen Avraham* and the *Chaye Adam*. The *Mishnah Berurah* rules that a person who owns only one garment may launder it until the week of *Tishah B'Av*. This also applies to a person who does not have a white shirt for *Shabbath*.
22. *Shulchan Arukh* 551:3; *Mishnah Berurah* 551:30–31.

12. Although the restriction against laundering clothes also applies to children's clothes, it is customary to launder clothes of infants and toddlers.[23] Large piles of laundry should not be done at one time and they should only be done in private.[24]

Sewing, Weaving and Mending

13. Beginning *Rosh Chodesh Av* (the week of *Tishah B'Av* for Sephardim), sewing and mending garments are forbidden.[25] This restriction includes weaving, knitting, and embroidering. Repairing a tear, sewing on a button, and patching an old garment are permitted.[26]

A professional seamstress may work until the week of *Tishah B'Av*.[27]

---

23. *Remah* 551:14. Toddlers' clothes should only be washed when there is an urgent need. The *Kaf HaChayim* and *Chaye Adam* limit this to the clothes of children who are less than two or three years old. Some contemporary authorities permit laundering clothes for children up to age four.

24. *Shulchan Arukh* 551:14; *Mishnah Berurah* 551:82–83.

25. *Shulchan Arukh* 551:7, and *Mishnah Berurah*.

   Iggeroth Moshe, Orach Chayim, Vol. 3, No. 79, explains that repairing a garment is only forbidden if new material is added and it is done in a professional way.

   Rivevoth Ephrayim, Vol. 1, No. 373, permits shortening a garment that was completed before *Rosh Chodesh*.

26. *Kaf HaChayim* 551:107, based on the *Ben Ish Chai*. The *Kaf HaChayim* adds that one may not embroider decorations on pieces of material that have not yet been sewn on a garment. Spinning threads to prepare them for weaving is permitted. See the *Mishnah Berurah* 551:54.

27. *Biur Halakhah* 551, beginning, *V'nahagu le'ha'keil*. According to the *Remah* and the *Magen Avraham*, a professional seamstress may work until *Tishah B'Av* itself. The *Biur Halakhah* explains that because there are authorities who rule to the contrary, she should refrain

14. Shoe polish may be applied, but the shoes may not be shined, except on *Erev Shabbath*.[28]

Meat and Wine

15. Beginning *Rosh Chodesh Av*, Ashkenazic custom forbids wine, meat, or any food cooked with meat.[29] (Concerning Sephardic custom, see note 29.) There is no restriction against purchasing meat during these days.[30]

Meat may be served at a *se'udath mitzvah*, for example, a *brith milah*, *pidyon ha'ben*, or *siyum* (a meal which celebrates the conclusion of the study of a Tractate of Talmud).[31] Family members and close acquaintances of the host who

---

from working during the week of *Tishah B'Av*.

28. This is the conclusion of HaGaon Rav Moshe Feinstein in *Iggeroth Moshe, Orach Chayim*, Vol. 3, No. 80, contrary to *Salmath Chayim*, Vol. 4, No. 4. See also the notes to *Mo'adim U'Zmanim*, Vol. 5, No. 335.

29. *Shulchan Arukh* 551:9; *Mishnah Berurah* 551:58. The *Shulchan Arukh* cites three Sephardic customs regarding when this restriction begins: the week of *Tishah B'Av*; from *Rosh Chodesh Av*; from the seventeenth of *Tamuz*. The *Kaf HaChayim* 551:125–126 cites a number of authorities who rule that it begins from the second of *Av*. This is also the view of *Ben Ish Chai, Shanah Rishonah, Parshath Devarim* 15: "It is forbidden by custom to eat meat...during the week of *Tishah B'Av*. Some observe this restriction from *Rosh Chodesh*, some from the seventeenth of *Tamuz*. In our city of Bagdad, we are accustomed to [begin] the restriction from the night of the second of *Av*."

30. *Iggeroth Moshe, Orach Chayim*, Vol. 4, No. 112:3. Since it is normal to purchase food in advance, a person will not be suspected of buying meat for the Nine Days.

31. *Remah* 551:10. HaGaon Rav Chaim Pinchus Sheinberg rules that a person arriving at a meal celebrating the *siyum* after actual study has been completed should not eat meat even though the meal is in progress.

would normally attend are permitted to eat meat.[32]

16. Meat and wine may be consumed on *Shabbath*, but not at a *melaveh malkah*.[33]

17. A *pareve* dish cooked in a *fleishig* utensil may be eaten.[34]

18. Children may be served meat or wine during the Nine Days if it is essential to their health.[35]

---

32. *Biur Halakhah* 555, beginning *VeSiyum*. Anyone whose presence adds to the celebration is permitted to eat meat. The *Mishnah Berurah* 551:75 explains that this includes "anyone, such as a family relation or close friend who would attend the meal at other times of the year. Any women who would normally be invited are also permitted [to eat meat]. The *Chaye Adam* rules that the wife of the person celebrating the *siyum* is permitted [to eat meat] even if she would not have participated at another time. The same is true of the host's children."

33. *Iggeroth Moshe, Orach Chayim*, Vol. 4, No. 21. This is true even if a person normally eats meat at the *melaveh malkah*.

    HaGaon Rav Feinstein adds that children who have reached the age of *chinukh* should not be fed meat on Friday afternoon before *Shabbath*. But if they are usually fed dinner before *Shabbath* during the summer, they may be served at the usual time.

34. *Mishnah Berurah* 551:63; *Kaf HaChayim* 551:142. This is true even if a utensil was used for meat within the last twenty-four hours.

    According to the *Shulchan Arukh, Yoreh De'ah* 95:1, *pareve* food cooked in a meat pot is *pareve* and may be eaten with dairy. This is the accepted Sephardic practice. Ashkenazic practice follows the *Remah, Yoreh De'ah* 95:1: Such food should not be eaten with dairy, but it may be eaten if it was mixed with dairy by mistake. See also the *Shakh, Yoreh De'ah* 95:19, and the *Shulchan Arukh, Yoreh De'ah* 96:1, with the glosses of Rabbi Akiva Eiger.

35. *Mishnah Berurah* 551:70. This also applies to children who have no understanding of the concept of mourning for the *Beith HaMikdash*.

    A child who is weak and needs to eat meat may do so even after reaching the age of *chinukh*.

19. A nursing mother may eat meat if her milk supply will otherwise be affected.[36] Pregnant and nursing women may eat meat if it is essential to their health.

Women who have given birth within the preceding thirty days may eat meat, but they customarily refrain from the seventh of *Av* unless it is essential to health.[37]

Cutting Hair and Fingernails

20. Cutting hair is forbidden during the Three Weeks.[38] Many Sephardic Jews practice this restriction only during the week of *Tishah B'Av*. Others follow the Ashkenazic custom.[39] Children should not be given haircuts during this time.[40] A married woman may trim hair that protrudes from

---

Some authorities permit children to eat meat leftover from *Shabbath*, but this custom is not generally accepted.

The *Remah* 551:10 and *Mishnah Berurah* rule that the *Havdalah* wine should only be given to a child. The child should be old enough to recite blessings but too young to understand the concept of mourning. The *Kaf HaChayim* notes that Sephardic practice follows the view of the *Beith Yosef*, in the *Shulchan Arukh* 551:10, which permits the person making *Havdalah* to drink the wine. If no child is available, many Ashkenazim also follow this practice. Others make *Havdalah* over a social beverage (*chamar medinah*), such as beer.

36. *Mishnah Berurah* 551:64.
37. *Mishnah Berurah* 551:61; *Sha'arey Teshuvah* 551:78. The *Sha'arey Teshuvah* adds that a menstruating woman may eat chicken if she feels that it is necessary for her well-being.
38. *Mishnah Berurah* 551:79; *Kaf HaChayim* 551:47; *Noda BeYehudah, Kama, Yoreh De'ah*, No. 99. The *Mishnah Berurah* 551:32 points out that hair may not be cut even in preparation for *Shabbath*.
39. *Ben Ish Chai, Shanah Rishonah, Parshath Devarim* 5.
40. *Shulchan Arukh* 551:14; *Mishnah Berurah* 551:81–82. The *Chaye Adam* 133:18 includes children who have not reached the age of *chinukh* in this restriction. The *Mishnah Berurah*, however, cites authorities who rule that it is necessary to refrain from cutting small children's hair only during the week of *Tishah B'Av*.

under her head covering.[41] Hair may be combed in the normal manner.[42]

21. There is no halakhic source for prohibiting makeup during the Nine Days. Makeup is only forbidden on *Tishah B'Av* itself, as are all fragrant oils.

22. Although some authorities forbid cutting fingernails during the week of *Tishah B'Av*, they all agree that a woman who attends the *mikvah* may cut them.[43]

Bathing

23. Beginning *Rosh Chodesh Av* (the week of *Tishah B'Av* for Sephardim), it is forbidden to bathe the whole body at one time, even in cold water. A pregnant woman close to term may bathe in warm water if she feels it will be beneficial. A woman who has given birth within the preceding thirty days may also bathe, even during the week of *Tishah B'Av*.[44]

24. Children with head sores may shampoo in the normal manner.[45]

---

41. *Mishnah Berurah* 551:79, based on the *Pri Megadim*. See also *She'arim Metzuyanim BeHalakhah* 122:5.
42. *Mishnah Berurah* 551:20. One need not be concerned that hair is being detached since this is not considered "cutting" hair. The *Ben Ish Chai, Shanah Rishonah, Parshath Devarim* 14, only permits women to comb their hair, not men.
43. *Mishnah Berurah, Ibid.* The restriction against cutting fingernails only applies during the week of *Tishah B'Av*. If the ninth of *Av* occurs on *Shabbath*, all authorities agree that fingernails may be cut on Friday.
44. *Shulchan Arukh* 551:16; *Mishnah Berurah* 551:88; *Sha'ar HaTziyun* 551:94. The *Sha'arey Teshuvah* 551:37 explains that a "woman close to term" refers to one in the ninth month of pregnancy.
45. *Mishnah Berurah* 551:93.

25. Bathing in warm water is permitted for a *mitzvah*. For instance, a woman may bathe in warm water to prepare herself for immersion in the *mikvah*. A woman who will attend the *mikvah* on the night following *Tishah B'Av* may bathe on *Erev Tishah B'Av*. A woman who needs to perform a *hefsek taharah* may wash herself in the normal manner.[46]

26. A person who feels uncomfortably dirty from the lack of bathing may bathe and wash the hair with soap and warm water. This is not considered bathing for pleasure.[47]

Erev Shabbath Chazon

27. The *Shabbath* before *Tishah B'Av* is called *Shabbath Chazon*, referring to the first word of the special *haftorah* read on that *Shabbath*. People who are accustomed not to mop floors after *Rosh Chodesh Av*[48] may mop them on *Erev Shabbath Chazon*.[49]

28. Although authorities have traditionally ruled that one may not bathe the whole body at one time on *Erev Shabbath Chazon*,[50] many contemporary ones permit bathing in the normal manner on that day because in our time people are

---

46. *Remah* 551:16, *Mishnah Berurah* and *Biur Halakhah*.
47. *Salmath Chayim*, Vol. 4, No. 19. This is based on a ruling of the *Chazon Ish*. See also *Halochos of the Three Weeks* (Eider), p. 12.
48. This custom is cited by Rav Moshe Sternbuch in *Mo'adim U'Zmanim*, Vol. 5, No. 338, in the names of HaGaon Rav Shmuel Salant and HaGaon Rav Yosef Chayim Sonnenfeld.
49. *Beith Avi*, Vol. 1, No. 27. This custom cannot be stricter than the restriction against wearing freshly laundered clothes, which is waived for *Shabbath*.
50. *Mishnah Berurah* 551:95. The *Mishnah Berurah* only permits washing parts of the body separately with hot water. Hair may only be rinsed with cold water.

relatively sensitive and they cannot properly accept *Shabbath* without a hot bath or shower.[51]

29. A freshly-laundered tablecloth may be put on the table in honor of *Shabbath*, but bed linens may not be changed[52] except for infants and toddlers.[53]

Tishah B'Av

30. Women are obligated to fast on *Tishah B'Av* and adhere to all its restrictions.[54] A pregnant or nursing woman who finds it difficult to fast on *Tishah B'Av* should consult a competent halakhic authority.[55]

---

51. *Halochos of the Three Weeks* (Eider), p. 13, citing HaGaon Rav Eliyahu Henkin and HaGaon Rav Moshe Feinstein.
52. *Remah* 551:3; *Mishnah Berurah* 551:33.
53. See paragraph 12. One should only change toddlers' bed linens when necessary.
54. *Shulchan Arukh* 550:1; *Biur Halakhah* 550, beginning, *HaKol chayavim.*
55. According to the law, pregnant and nursing women are obligated to fast on *Tishah B'Av* (See the *Chaye Adam* 135:2.). Nevertheless, many authorities rule leniently in this case, especially during the first months of pregnancy. A woman should always consult a competent halakhic authority regarding her particular situation.

    If a *brith milah* is performed on *Tishah B'Av*, and the mother is not fasting, she may drink the wine used for the blessing after the *brith*. See the *Shulchan Arukh* 559:7. The *Mishnah Berurah* 551:4 permits her to put on a fresh change of clothing for the *brith*.

    It is customary to change the normal manner of sleeping on the night of *Tishah B'Av* by sleeping with fewer pillows or none at all, or even using a stone for a pillow. The *Remah* 555:2 indicates that pregnant women do not follow these practices.

The Se'udah HaMafseketh

31. Meat, chicken, fish, radish, or salted foods may not be served at the *se'udah ha'mafseketh* (the last meal before the fast). Only one cooked item may be served,[56] but fresh fruits and vegetables may be eaten without limit.[57]

Work and Food Preparation

32. It is customary to refrain from work until *Tishah B'Av* afternoon. One should prepare food only for a *mitzvah* or for children.[58] Such preparations are permitted even in the morning.

33. Although some authorities rule that on other communal fast days a woman may taste a little of the food she has prepared if she does not swallow it,[59] they forbid it on *Tishah B'Av.*[60]

---

56. *Shulchan Arukh* 552:1–4, and *Mishnah Berurah*. Roasted food is considered "cooked", as is cooked food that could have been eaten raw. If a quantity of food is cooked in two pots, and the contents of one pot have a consistency different from the other, the contents of the pots are considered to contain two separate foods. The *Remah* 552:5 reports that it is customary to serve a hard-boiled egg as the cooked food. Many people are accustomed to dip it in ashes.

57. *Ibid.* As long as the fruits and vegetables are eaten raw, one may eat many different kinds in any amounts. If they are cooked, only one kind may be eaten.

58. *Shulchan Arukh* 559:10, and *Mishnah Berurah*. This is to avoid distractions from mourning.

59. *Shulchan Arukh* 567:1. The *Remah, Ibid.*, also rules stringently with respect to other fast days. The *Mishnah Berurah* 567:6 relies on the lenient opinion if she prepares food for a *se'udath mitzvah.*

60. *Shulchan Arukh, Ibid.*

34. Some women are accustomed to clean and arrange the house on the afternoon of *Tishah B'Av* as a sign of their faith in the coming of *Mashiach*.[61]

Bathing on Tishah B'Av

35. Washing any part of the body in either hot or cold water is forbidden. A woman whose night to attend the *mikvah* occurs on *Tishah B'Av* postpones her immersion until the following evening. She should bathe and shampoo her hair thoroughly on *Erev Tishah B'Av* and once again, superficially, just before her immersion. If she does not shampoo on *Erev Tishah B'Av*, she is required to shampoo thoroughly after the fast.[62]

36. During the first thirty days after marriage, a bride is permitted to wash her face on *Tishah B'Av*.[63]

---

61. *Birkey Yosef* 559:7. There is a tradition that *Mashiach* will be born on *Tishah B'Av* afternoon. Preparing the house for *Mashiach* is an old Italian custom which is still practiced in many Sephardic communities.

62. *Shulchan Arukh* 554:8, and *Mishnah Berurah*. Some women are accustomed to wash their hair on *Tishah B'Av* afternoon in preparation for the coming of *Mashiach*. The *Beith Yosef* 554 objects: "This custom should be suppressed... Whoever wishes to be lenient, man or woman, should be strongly reprimanded not to transgress the words of the Sages [who forbid bathing the entire day of *Tishah B'Av*]."

63. *Mishnah Berurah* 554:29. She may apply fragrant oils to her body so as not to be disagreeable to her husband. The *Mishnah Berurah* 613:26 rules that on *Yom Kippur* a bride should not wash; her husband stays in the synagogue all day, which is not true on *Tishah B'Av*.

37. Washing fruits and vegetables is permitted even if the hands become wet. Washing the hands is only prohibited if it is done for pleasure.[64]

Wearing Shoes

38. Leather shoes may not be worn on *Tishah B'Av*. A woman who has recently given birth may wear leather shoes if she is uncomfortable wearing other kinds.[65]

Studying Torah

39. Torah study is forbidden on *Tishah B'Av*, except for sections of *Tanakh* and Talmud which deal with the destruction of the *Beith HaMikdash*, the Book of *Iyov*, the Laws of Mourning, and the Laws of *Tishah B'Av*. This restriction applies to men and women.[66]

Motzo'ei Tishah B'Av

40. Although many of the restrictions of the Nine Days are customarily extended until the afternoon of the tenth of *Av*, a woman who has recently given birth may eat meat and drink wine immediately after *Tishah B'Av*, even if she observed the fast.[67]

---

64. *Mishnah Berurah* 554:19; *Kaf HaChayim* 554:46. She may wash the fruit in hot or cold water.
65. See Chapter 19, paragraph 44.
66. *Shulchan Arukh* 654:1–2, and *Mishnah Berurah*. See also *Rivevoth Ephrayim*, Vol. 2, No. 155:14.
67. *Shulchan Arukh* 558:1, *Mishnah Berurah* and *Biur Halakhah*. Also see *Sha'arey Teshuvah* 558:2.

41. If *Tishah B'Av* occurs on a Thursday, one may bathe, launder clothes, and cut hair on Friday morning in honor of *Shabbath*.[68] Some authorities permit a hotel or institution that does laundry for numerous people to launder on Thursday night.[69] Others permit private people to do laundry on Thursday night.[70]

42. When the ninth of *Av* occurs on *Shabbath*, the fast is postponed to Sunday. When this happens, meat and wine may be consumed on Monday morning. Hair may be cut on Sunday night.[71] Some authorities also permit laundering and bathing on Sunday night.[72]

Extending the restrictions of the Nine Days to the afternoon of the tenth of *Av* is based on a tradition reported by Rabbi Yochanan in Tractate *Ta'anith* 29a: The Romans set fire to the *Beith HaMikdash* towards evening of the ninth of *Av*, and it continued to burn until the afternoon of the tenth. In fact, Rabbi Yochanan comments, if he had been alive in that generation, he would have been tepmted to establish the fast on the tenth. For this reason, the restrictions were extended throughout the period that the *Beith HaMikdash* was burning.

Pareve food which was cooked with meat may be eaten before noon the next day.

If *Havdalah* is recited on Sunday night because the ninth of *Av* occurs on a Sunday, the wine may be drunk.

Meat may be served at a *se'udath mitzvah* on the night following *Tishah B'Av*, but there should be no music.

Ye'chaveh Da'ath, Vol. 5, No. 41, rules that Sephardic Jews may bathe and cut hair immediately after the fast. It should be noted, however, that according to the *Beith Yosef* in the *Shulchan Arukh*, *Ibid.*, the restriction against eating meat and drinking wine extends throughout the tenth of *Av*, not just until afternoon, as is customary with Ashkenazic Jews.

68. *Mishnah Berurah* 558:2–3.
69. *Be'er Moshe*, Vol. 3, No. 79.
70. *Birur Halakhah*, commenting on the *Shulchan Arukh* 558.
71. *Shulchan Arukh* 558:1, and *Mishnah Berurah*.
72. *Birur Halakhah, Ibid.*

43. When *Tishah B'Av* is observed on Sunday, *Havdalah* is said over wine at the conclusion of the fast on Sunday night. A woman who does not recite the *Ma'ariv Shemoneh Esrey* on Saturday night must say the words *Barukh ha'mavdil bein ha'kodesh u'vein ha'chol* before performing *melakhah*. If she does recite *Ma'ariv*, she should remember to recite the paragraph beginning with the words *atah chonantanu*.[73]

A woman who does not fast on *Tishah B'Av* that falls on Sunday should recite *Havdalah* before eating. The wine should be given to a child.[74]

Commemorating the Destruction of the Beith HaMikdash

44. After the destruction of the *Beith HaMikdash*, the Sages decreed that one who prepares a meal for guests should leave an empty place at the table and serve one course less than is customary.[75] They also decreed that a woman should leave a small part of her gold or silver jewelry missing so that the ornaments are incomplete.[76] They also forbade a bride to wear a silver crown at her wedding.[77] Many of these restrictions are not generally practiced today.[78]

---

73. *Mishnah Berurah* 556:2.
74. *Mishnah Berurah* 559:37; *Sha'arey Teshuvah* 556; *Az Nid'biru*, Vol. 6, No. 53; *Birkey Yosef* 556:3.
75. *Shulchan Arukh* 560:1–2, and *Mishnah Berurah*. This applies even to a *se'udath mitzvah*, but not on *Shabbath* and *Yom Tov*.
76. *Shulchan Arukh Ibid.* The *Mishnah Berurah* adds that a woman should not wear all her jewelry at one time, even on *Shabbath* and *Yom Tov*.
77. *Shulchan Arukh* 560:4, and *Mishnah Berurah*.
78. Although these laws are cited explicitly in the *Shulchan Arukh*, they are not commonly practiced today. The *Biur Halakhah* has commented, "This requires investigation, for many of these rules are not observed." See the *Kaf HaChayim* 660:18 for a possible explanation.

Building the Beith HaMikdash

45. "It is a positive *mitzvah* of the Torah to build a House to God that will be used for the offering of sacrifices. As it is written, 'And they shall make for Me a sanctuary' (*Shemoth* 25:8). Men and women are obligated to participate in this *mitzvah*, with physical labor and with donations of money.''[79]

In many places, it is customary for people to remind themselves of the destruction of the *Beith HaMikdash* by leaving unpainted a square *amah* (approximately two sq. feet) inside their homes, opposite the front door. See the *Mishnah Berurah, Ibid.*

79. *Rambam, Hilkhoth Beith HaBechirah* 1:1 and 1:12. Even though the *Beith HaMikdash* cannot be built at night, or on *Shabbath* or *Yom Tov*, it is not categorized as a time-bound *mitzvah*. See *Responsa of Rabbi Akiva Eiger*, No. 17; *Beith Yitzchak, Orach Chayim*, No. 3; *Minchath Elazar*, Vol. 2, No. 2; *Shoneh Halakhoth*, Vol. 6, No. 326.

Glossary

Afikomen — A portion of *matzah* set aside until the end of the *Seder*, at which time it is eaten in remembrance of the *Pessach* sacrifice

Amah — A measurement of length, approximately the length of a forearm (48 or 57 centimeters)

Aravoth — Willow branches, one of the Four Species used on *Sukkoth*

Arvuth — A principle of mutual responsibility which allows one person to recite a *birkath ha'mitzvah* on behalf of another

Ba'al tokey'ah — A person who blows the *shofar* in the synagogue

Basis le'davar ha'asur — When *muktzeh* is placed on a non-*muktzeh* base, the base assumes the status of *muktzeh*

Bedikath Chametz — The *mitzvah* to search the house for leaven the night before *Pessach*

Beith HaMikdash — The Holy Temple in Jerusalem

Bikkurim — The *mitzvah* to bring the first fruits to the *Beith HaMikdash*

Birkath HaGomel — A blessing recited by those delivered from danger

Birkath HaMazon — Grace after Meals

257

Birkath ha'mitzvah — A blessing recited on performing a *mitzvah*

Birkath ha'ne'henin — A blessing recited before eating

Bitul — To render non-existent

Brith milah — A circumcision

Challah — The *mitzvah* to separate a portion of dough when baking bread

Chamar medinah — A social beverage

Chametz — Leavened flour from the five grains

Chinukh — Religious training

Chol HaMoed — The intermediate days of *Pessach* and *Sukkoth*, during which certain forms of work are prohibited

Chupah — The bridal canopy

Eiruv — An enclosure, usually made from poles connected by a string or wire, rendering the enclosed area a private domain and allowing people to carry within its bounds on *Shabbath*

Eiruv Tavshilin — The *mitzvah* to set aside two food items on *Erev Yom Tov* when *Yom Tov* falls on Friday

Hadassim — Myrtle branches, one of the Four Species used on *Sukkoth*

Hag'alah — A process which renders metal utensils in which *chametz* was cooked with liquids fit for *Pessach* use

Hefsek taharah — The internal examination made by a woman after her menstrual flow has stopped

Ishto k'gufo — Literally, a man's wife is as himself

Kaddish — A prayer which includes the highest form of praise to God

Kaparoth — A ritual performed on *Erev Yom Kippur* whereby a fowl is swung around the head three times. Money is often substituted for the fowl.

Kavod Shabbath — Literally, in honor of *Shabbath*

K'betzah — A dry volume measurement equivalent to the volume of an egg

Kibbud Av V'Eim — The *mitzvah* to honor one's father and mother

Kiddush LeVanah — The blessing over the new moon

Kitniyoth — Legumes, for example, rice, corn and beans, which are not eaten by Ashkenazic Jews during *Pessach*

Kri'ath HaTorah — The reading of the Torah in the synagogue

K'zayith — A dry volume measurement equivalent to the volume of an olive

Lechem Mishneh — The *mitzvah* to recite *HaMotzie* over two loaves of bread at every *Shabbath* meal

Libun — A process which renders utensils in which *chametz* was cooked without liquid fit for *Pessach* use

Lishmah — Literally, for the sake of the *mitzvah*

Lulav — A date palm frond, one of the Four Species used on *Sukkoth*

Ma'ariv — The evening *Shemoneh Esrey*

Ma'aser Ani — A tithe set aside for the poor during the third and sixth years of the seven-year *Shmittah* cycle

Ma'aser Kesafim — Ten percent of a person's income separated for charitable purposes

Ma'aser Rishon — A tithe separated from all produce grown by a Jew in *Eretz Yisrael*, which is given to a Levite

Ma'aser Sheni — A tithe separated in the first, second, fourth and fifth year of the seven-year *Shmittah* cycle, which must be eaten in Jerusalem

Machatzith HaShekel — The *mitzvah* for every adult male to donate a half-shekel to the *Beith HaMikdash* for the purchase of communal sacrifices

Machzor — Holiday prayer book

Maley Lugmav — A measure of liquid that fills a cheek

Maror — Bitter herbs, eaten at the *Seder*

Mechalel Shabbath b'farhesya — A public desecrator of *Shabbath*

Mechitzah — A partition between men and women

Melakhah — Categories of work forbidden on *Shabbath*

Me'machek — Literally, scraping, one of the *melakhoth* forbidden on *Shabbath*

Mikvah — Ritualarium

Milath ha'ben — Circumcising a son

Milchemeth mitzvah — An obligatory war

Minchah — The afternoon *Shemoneh Esrey*

Minhag — Custom

Minyan — A group of ten adult Jewish men

Mitzvah — A commandment of the Torah

Mohel — The person who performs a circumcision

Motzie — The act of fulfilling a religious obligation on behalf of others

Motzo'ei — The evening following

Muktzeh — Literally, set aside, a rabbinical term denoting objects that are forbidden to be handled on *Shabbath* and *Yom Tov*

Niddah — Halakhic status of a woman from the onset of her menstrual period until she purifies herself through immersion in a *mikvah*

Omer — A sheaf offering brought to the *Beith HaMikdash* on the sixteenth of *Nissan*, after which it was permissible to eat from the new harvest

Oneg Shabbath — Literally, enjoyment of *Shabbath*

Pagum — Literally, stale

Pidyon HaBen — Redemption of the first-born son

Pirsumey nissa — Literally, publicizing a miracle

Plag ha'minchah — A time of the day, approximately one and a quarter hours before sunset

Prutah — A monetary value equal to 25 milligrams of pure silver

Revi'ith — A volume measure equal to either eighty-six or one-hundred and fifty cubit centimeters

Rosh Chodesh — The beginning of a lunar month

R'vai — The fruit which grows on a tree in the fourth year after planting

Sandek — The person who holds the baby during a circumcision

Segulah — Remedy

Selichoth — Special penitential prayers

Se'udah ha'mafseketh — The last meal before a fast

Shalmey Simchah — A peace-offering of joy

Shamor — Literally, to guard

Sha'oth zemaniyoth — A method of calculating time where an hour is defined as one-twelfth of the day

Shem and *malkhuth* — Elements of a blessing referring to God's name and the declaration of His kingship

Shmittah — The sabbatical year

Siyum — A meal which celebrates the conclusion of the study of a Tractate of Talmud

Tahor — Ritually pure

Tam'ey — Ritually impure

Tefillah — Prayer

Tekioth d'm'umad — The sounds of the *shofar* blown during the repetition of *Mussaf* on *Rosh HaShanah*

Tekioth d'm'yushav — The thirty sounds of the *shofar* blown before the silent *Mussaf Shemoneh Esrey* on *Rosh HaShanah*

Terumah Gedolah — A portion of produce given to a *cohen*

Terumoth and *ma'asroth* — The separations that must be made from produce grown by a Jew in *Eretz Yisrael* before the produce may be eaten

Tikkun Leil Shavuoth — Selections from the Written and Oral Law customarily recited on *Shavuoth* night

Tosafoth Shabbath — Adding to *Shabbath* at its start and at its conclusion

Tzedakah — The *mitzvah* to donate to charity

Uvdin d'chol — Acts forbidden on *Shabbath* because they have the character of weekday activity

Yirath Av V'Eim — The *mitzvah* to show reverence to one's father and mother

Zakhor — Literally, to remember

Zemiroth — Hymns sung during the *Shabbath* meal

Zimun — The introductory sentences to *Birkath HaMazon* where one person 'invites' the others to recite with him

Index

Numbers before a colon refer to chapters; numbers after a colon, to paragraphs; "n" after a number refers to note. Thus, "15:13, 14n.; 17:5" means: Chapter 15, paragraph 13 and note 14; Chapter 17, paragraph 5.

Index